Alan Hollinghurst

MANCHESTER
1824

Manchester University Press

Alan Hollinghurst

Writing under the influence

Edited by
Michèle Mendelssohn and Denis Flannery

Manchester University Press

Published by Manchester University Press
Altrincham Street, Manchester M1 7JA
www.manchesteruniversitypress.co.uk

British Library Cataloguing-in-Publication Data
A catalogue record for this book is available from the British Library

ISBN 978 0 7190 9717 1   hardback
ISBN 978 1 5261 3428 8   paperback

First published by Manchester University Press in hardback in 2016
This edition first published 2018

Typeset
by JCS Publishing Services Ltd

Contents

Figures

Notes on contributors

Angus Brown is Stipendiary Lecturer in English at St Anne's College, Oxford. He is currently writing a monograph on the style of close reading in the Anglo-American university.

Robert L. Caserio is Professor of English and Comparative Literature at Pennsylvania State University. He is co-editor of *The Cambridge History of the English Novel* (Cambridge University Press, 2012) and editor of *The Cambridge Companion to the Twentieth-Century English Novel* (Cambridge University Press, 2009). He is at work on *The Cambridge Introduction to British Fiction, 1900–1950* (Cambridge University Press).

Denis Flannery is Senior Lecturer in American and English Literature at the University of Leeds. His published writings include his first monograph, *Henry James: A Certain Illusion* (Ashgate, 2000), and *On Sibling Love, Queer Attachment and American Writing* (Ashgate, 2007). Currently he is working on a new study of Henry James's relationship to Ireland, while completing a collaborative memoir begun with his father, Denis Kevin Flannery (1919–2009). He has also begun a major research project on the Dutch theatre company Toneelgroep, Amsterdam.

Geoff Gilbert is Associate Professor of Comparative Literature and English at the American University of Paris. He is the author of *Before Modernism Was: Modern History and the Constituency of Writing* (Palgrave Macmillan, 2005). He is currently working on translation, capital, the semantic, and audible distance in contemporary realist writing.

Hermione Lee has written biographies of Virginia Woolf, Edith Wharton and Penelope Fitzgerald, and is President of Wolfson College, Oxford.

John McLeod is Professor of Postcolonial and Diaspora Literatures at the School of English, University of Leeds. He is the author of *Life Lines: Writing Transcultural Adoption* (Bloomsbury, 2015), *J. G. Farrell* (Northcote House, 2007), *Postcolonial London: Rewriting the Metropolis* (Routledge, 2004) and, as co-editor, *The Revision of Englishness* (Manchester University Press, 2004).

Michèle Mendelssohn is Associate Professor of English Literature at Mansfield College, Oxford, and Deputy Director of the Rothermere American Institute. She is the author of *Henry James, Oscar Wilde and Aesthetic Culture* (Edinburgh University Press, 2007) and a co-editor of *Oxford 21st-Century Approaches to Literature: Late Victorian into Modern, 1880–1920* (with Laura Marcus and Kirsten Shepherd-Barr, Oxford University Press, 2016). She is writing a biography of Oscar Wilde.

Kaye Mitchell is Senior Lecturer in Contemporary Literature at the University of Manchester. She is the author of *A. L. Kennedy: New British Fiction* (Palgrave, 2007), *Intention and Text: Towards an Intentionality of Literary Form* (Continuum, 2008) and the editor of *Sarah Waters: Contemporary Critical Perspectives* (Bloomsbury, 2013). Her current research includes a monograph on shame, gender and contemporary literature and an edited *Companion to Women's Experimental Literature, 1900–Present* (Edinburgh University Press, 2017).

Bernard O'Donoghue was born in Cullen, County Cork in 1945. Since 1965 he has lived in Oxford, where he taught medieval literature at Magdalen and Wadham Colleges. He has published seven volumes of poems, of which the most recent was *Farmers Cross* (Faber and Faber, 2011).

Alan O'Leary is Associate Professor in Italian and Director of Research and Innovation in the School of Languages, Cultures and Societies at the University of Leeds. He has published several books on Italian cinema. He co-founded the annual Film Issue of *The Italianist*. His current projects include *Italian Cinemas/Italian Histories* and two monographs – one on film and history in Italy (for Donzelli), and another on the 1966 film *The Battle of Algiers* (for Mimesis).

Julie Rivkin, Professor of English at Connecticut College, is the author of *False Positions: The Representational Logics of Henry James's Fiction* (Stanford University Press, 1996) and co-editor (with Michael Ryan) of *Literary Theory: An Anthology* (Blackwell, 1998, 2004). She has also written about Henry James and his afterlives, and is editing *What Maisie*

Knew for *The Complete Fiction of Henry James* (Cambridge University Press). Her other current project is on Canadian short-story writer Alice Munro.

Joseph Ronan teaches English Literature at the University of Brighton and the University of Sussex. He received his PhD in Sexual Dissidence in Literature and Culture from the University of Sussex in 2015. His research focuses primarily on bisexuality in contemporary literature, popular culture and queer theory. His current project explores narratives of sexuality, adolescence and futurity in literary representations of punk.

Abbreviations

Full details of works cited are given in each chapter's endnotes. Page citations for the following works by Alan Hollinghurst appear parenthetically. In each case the first UK edition has been used.

CCB *Confidential Chats with Boys* (Oxford: Sycamore, 1982)
FS *The Folding Star* (London: Chatto & Windus, 1994)
LB *The Line of Beauty* (London: Picador, 2004)
S *The Spell* (London: Chatto & Windus, 1998)
SC *The Stranger's Child* (London: Picador, 2011)
SPL *The Swimming-Pool Library* (London: Chatto & Windus, 1988)

Introduction: a dialogue on influence

Michèle Mendelssohn and Denis Flannery

MM: This collection is the result of a serendipitous conversation you and I had many years ago. So, perhaps unusually, we have decided to forgo the traditional editors' introduction and to use dialogue instead.

DJF: That's right. We first thought of this collection while talking by the ocean at a Henry James conference in Newport, Rhode Island.

MM: *Alan Hollinghurst: Writing Under the Influence* explores the way in which Hollinghurst is in conversation with his various influences. It seeks to chronicle these exchanges and observe the intellectual give-and-take in his writings – from his early poetry and scholarship to his novels, translations for the theatre and work as an editor of Housman and Firbank.

There's a formal logic at work in our decision to 'talk out' our introduction: our 'dialogue on influence' echoes the phenomenon our book examines. It also anticipates the concluding chapter, in which Hollinghurst is in dialogue with the biographer Hermione Lee.

DJF: 'Influence' carries a number of different meanings in the context of this book. There is the literal sense of 'flowing in' – the entry of life, literature, ideas. For literary scholars, of course, the word 'influence' has a Freudian sense, as channelled by Harold Bloom in *The Anxiety of Influence*, with its outlining of intergenerational, conflict-laden psycho-dramas between poets young and old, strong and weak. This Bloomian – and homoerotic – sense is certainly around in Hollinghurst. Allan Johnson wrote about this in his 2014 book *Alan Hollinghurst and the Vitality of Influence*.[1]

Yet Hollinghurst's works also have a genial, accommodating sense of acceptance about their influences, one that feels very English to me.

In *The Line of Beauty* the narrator describes how Toby Fedden 'amiably accepted the evidence' that he and Nick Guest are friends (4–5). For me, Hollinghurst seems to accept just as amiably the evidence that Ronald Firbank, Henry James, Alfred Tennyson, Rupert Brooke and Jean Racine are components of his writing life. And, like Toby Fedden, he seems to get a lot out of this.

MM: So, it's as if Hollinghurst were holding out his hand to authors dead and alive, to the past and to the present. Yes, his influences are often English. But he's also something of an armchair cosmopolitan. *The Folding Star* captures both these sensibilities.

One of the pleasures of putting this collection together has been listening in, so to speak, on Hollinghurst's 'amiable' interactions. The collection is centrally interested in exploring how Hollinghurst breaks new ground even as he prowls the precincts of certain well-established literary traditions – from the English novel at its most canonical to early homosexual literature. Like Jane Austen and E. M. Forster, he displays a certain realism – an attention to domestic detail and a wry, well-observed sense of humour. But his work is also daringly eccentric and charmingly iconoclastic. One critic claims that he brought 'within the orbit of serious fiction subjects and acts that other writers, even gay writers, might "tastefully" elide'.[2] I think that's true. And what he covers is an 'A to Z' of cultural practices, legacies and secret histories ranging from AIDS and architecture to bathhouses, bisexuality, camp, decadence, ekphrasis, French theatre ...

DJF: ... postcolonialism, property prices, rimming ... the list goes on.

MM: He holds a paradoxical position as an author who is a pioneer of 'a tradition on the margin of the mainstream'.[3] His works are not those of a young fogey or an R-rated Max Beerbohm. But, in important and substantial ways, they articulate a new–old narrative. They enrich the novel form by playing with its most entrenched practices in formally sophisticated ways.

Writing Under the Influence, as a title, seeks to capture the sense of intoxication that operates in so much of this writing. *The Line of Beauty* registers this literal and metaphorical valence when Wani grabs one of Nick's Henry James monographs and cuts a line of coke on it. Under the crosshatchings Wani makes with his credit card, the young James peers out from his cover photo. He's a 'quick-eyed, tender, brilliant twenty-year-old' (*LB* 254) who seems to be watching Hollinghurst's two twenty-somethings get high. The novel is about intellectual intoxication – the highs Nick gets from 'his passion for Henry James' (*LB* 435) – as well as intoxication from sex, drugs and alcohol.

DJF: Or we might think of Alex in *The Spell*: lost in house music and enjoying his first ecstasy pill, newly able 'to see his own happiness as wave on wave of lustrous darknesss, each with a glimmering fringe of light' (*S* 84). 'Influence' is also related to the drinking metaphor on which our title plays: being under the influence. There's a criminal aspect: DUI, driving under the influence. This kind of 'influence' can be dangerous but also ritualized and structured. Think of drinking games and bar-going habits, as well as drug culture and the rituals of clubbing.

MM: There's a similarly ritualistic, repetitive dynamic in the way Nick lives under James's influence in *The Line of Beauty*. He's drunk on James: he's 'at the height of a youthful affair with his writer' (208). His party piece is to quote bits of James to amuse his philistine chums – what he calls 'prostituting the Master'. He's drunk on the attention he gets when he does this.

DJF: That sense of intoxication is one that many readers feel when they read Hollinghurst. The power and beauty of his writing – its sonorous style and formal deftness – produce moments of somatic, sometimes ecstatic, intoxication. Judith Butler has observed that 'to be ec-static means, literally, to be beside oneself'.[4] She elaborates on this particular state as being a 'porous boundary, given over to others, finding oneself ... taken out of oneself'.[5] These affective states are ones in which Hollinghurst's protagonists often find themselves. This sense of transport and susceptibility is a huge part of reading his works.

MM: Yes, I agree. And his writing can be so humorous. Laughter is another form of transport. So is parody. At times, his works overtly inhabit and appropriate other artistic worlds and styles. That's another way of 'writing under the influence'.

Then there's Hollinghurst's proclivity for pseudo-history and made-up 'facts' about real people, like Nick dancing with Margaret Thatcher or, in *The Stranger's Child*, Cecil Valance's acquaintance with Rupert Brooke. There's something inventive and mischievous about these intrusions. They remind me of the Ordnance Survey's inclusion of made-up streets in its maps, tiny intentional errors intended to foil plagiarists.

DJF: It's interesting that you go to geography, with those Ordnance Survey maps riddled with 'traps for the unwary', as James might have put it. The link between pained, exiled subjectivity and its sometimes comic encounters with new geographies of reality throbs through Hollinghurst's work.

MM: There's also something to be said about the large generic terrain he covers, despite the fact that he is best known for his novels. This collection is the first to encompass the variety of genres in which he has worked.

DJF: That was always one of the book's ambitions: to deliver a historically tessellated exploration of Hollinghurst's breadth. It's easy to forget the multi-generic nature of his archive in the face of the novels' success.

So it's appropriate that our book opens by attending to Hollinghurst, the poet and scholar. Bernard O'Donoghue begins 'Abjuring innocence: Hollinghurst's poetry' by reminding us that poetry was Hollinghurst's first love. Judging by *The Stranger's Child*'s recent focus on a single poem, it's a love that hasn't gone away. Surveying Hollinghurst's poetic career, O'Donoghue reminds us of how beautiful Hollinghurst's poetry is, especially his Housman-inspired, 'highly patterned', 'Nightfall (For an Athlete Dying Young)' with its 'eloquent numbness' and its tantalizing, withholding relationship both to narrative resolution and to the Shakespeare of *Hamlet*. The capacity of Hollinghurst the poet to transport his readers is also, for O'Donoghue, there in 'Alonso', a poem that channels the Shakespeare of *The Tempest* and is distinguished by a remarkable 'imaginative underwater vision'. This poetic capacity is also vividly evident in the powerful prose style of his writings *on* poetry, especially that of Mick Imlah. For O'Donoghue, Hollinghurst the poet vividly anticipates how Hollinghurst the novelist combines a drive towards narrative with a readiness to tell stories that refuse resolution but are none the less substantial.

Angus Brown's chapter traces the trajectory from Hollinghurst the brave – if maybe stolid – postgraduate student, to Hollinghurst the aesthetically inspired critic, to Hollinghurst the groundbreaking novelist of *The Swimming-Pool Library*. For Brown, the early years of Hollinghurst's career, from his 1977 M.Litt. thesis to the publication of his first novel in 1988, constitute the era when a major preoccupation of his work – what Brown terms 'the secret choreography of book and body' – is established. Many of our contributors are attentive to Hollinghurst as someone who writes about sex, as we'll discuss later on, and Brown explores how, in early Hollinghurst, processes of writing and reading are themselves an often-forgotten corporeal and erotic affair of eyes, bodies and, especially, hands.

Your chapter, 'Poetry, parody, porn and prose' outlines the mischievous laughter Hollinghurst elicits as he turns an American doctor's prurient, paranoid and homophobic counsels on sexual morality into chiselled queer verse that, as you point out, lacerates normative ideas about masculinity. That parodic drive is often there in the novels' relationships with literary precursors as well as visual objects – the photography of Robert Mapplethorpe, the homoerotic drawings of Tom of Finland or the religious painting of Holman Hunt. Reading *The Folding Star* is 'like looking at a portfolio of brilliant sketches and elaborations on Tom's work' that reflects on a festive sexual world with a supple melancholy. In your reading, Hollinghurst explores the gap between these erotic carnivals: those weighty, disruptive moments of disappointment, disconnection and grief that give such sombre substance to the aesthetics of his writing.

MM: As editors, we also wanted this collection to reflect on sexuality in Hollinghurst's work. That relationship correlates in fascinating ways to the historical circumstances of its publication.

DJF: That's right. So much of the sexual-political landscape has changed since Hollinghurst first began publishing, yet so much of the neoliberal political culture he depicts (especially in *The Line of Beauty*) is utterly persistent. He's a writer of 'now', yet he's also part of the past. One of my favourite lines in his works acknowledges this implicitly: 'I'm always forgetting how sexy the past must have been', Will says in *The Swimming-Pool Library* (247). It signals not only Hollinghurst's passion for sex as an engine of history but also the very quirky and eroticized historical sensibility of his writing.

Hollinghurst came into my life through history. In 1988 my then boyfriend, Mark Cornwall, gave me a copy of *The Swimming-Pool Library* as a gift. That was a charged year, particularly with regard to sexual politics. These were the days of Clause 28 (the Thatcherite ban on discussing homosexuality in schools) and a time when, in retrospect, death was coming – via HIV/AIDS. Michel Foucault had died in 1984 of this illness and his great friend, the author Guy Hocquenghem, died similarly in 1988. So my earliest memories of reading Hollinghurst are braided around the tragic stories of their deaths. Mark is now a professor of History. For me, *The Swimming-Pool Library* forged a very enlivened sense of the relationship between history and subjectivity.

MM: Over the years, several men have told me similar stories about the personal nature of their relationship to Hollinghurst's works. Some of them have been older, and they can remember the times Hollinghurst chronicles. Others have been young adults – I remember an eighteen-year-old mentioning Hollinghurst in his Oxford admission interview. He tried to be casual and offhand, but he just lit up when he talked about the novels.

DJF: That's just great!

MM: That's not to say that women don't also have stories to tell about their particular connection to his works, of course. We live in a culture that still fetishizes women's bodies, and I've been interested to observe how, in Hollinghurst's novels, men's bodies come under similarly intense scrutiny. To read him is to be confronted with an overwhelmingly male aesthetic tradition. I can understand this intellectually through nineteenth-century decadent and aesthetic cultural traditions in which women are often marginal, idealized or dreaded. Still, it's jolting to read novels partly set in the late twentieth century in which women are, generally, outsiders. His works cover historical periods that have been transformative and liberating for all sorts of other groups, too, but they are not part of his remit, so to speak.

A woman undergraduate told me her mother gave her *The Stranger's Child*, and that the intergenerational aspect was something they both relished. That's symptomatic, I think, of Hollinghurst's changing place in literature. Until the publication of *The Stranger's Child*, in 2011, it was commonplace to consider him a 'gay' writer, but his categorization is one that Kaye Mitchell and Joseph Ronan acknowledge and interrogate.

In '"Who are you? What the fuck are you doing here?"': queer debates and contemporary connections', Mitchell reads Hollinghurst as an author who is not necessarily considered 'queer' despite being 'gay'. One of the problems she observes is that the pessimism and internal criticism that currently preoccupy queer studies and queer theory do not sit comfortably alongside writings so attentive to a pre-Stonewall past. By reading Hollinghurst in conjunction with David Leavitt, Colm Tóibín, and Michael Cunningham, Mitchell reveals that his works are in tune with many of his contemporaries. His fiction 'retains a strong seam of critique' of certain aspects of gay culture – including politics and sociality – yet the ambivalence of Hollinghurst's protagonists, Mitchell argues, reflects how 'the past crucially inflects and affects how he engages with the present', including AIDS and the ephemerality of homosexual communities. Hollinghurst's portrayal of relationships oscillates between ethics, interconnectedness and a certain 'rejection of sociality and futurity' that makes him 'more of his time than we might imagine'.

'We find in Hollinghurst's fiction a fundamental ambivalence about assuming something as definite and concrete as a gay identity', Mitchell observes. Taking this as its point of departure, Joseph Ronan's chapter observes the ostentatiously discreet bisexuality in *The Stranger's Child*. That the word 'bisexual' never appears in the novel is symptomatic, he argues: its loud silencing replicates a broader cultural erasure of bisexuality. The novel makes a virtue of this situation by turning to 'camp excess' to manifest bisexuality as an absent presence in the characters' lives. This approach, Ronan suggests, critiques the socio-cultural dynamics responsible for the erasure in the first place and problematizes the flattening, oversimplifying effect of reading stories as 'gay' at the expense of 'more ambiguous sexual possibilities'. Although Ronan did not known this when he wrote his chapter, in our book's last chapter Hollinghurst discusses Cecil's bisexuality as a 'fact'.

DJF: Hollinghurst's readiness to make literary absent presences manifest is also evident in his most recent work, as Julie Rivkin shows. In '*The Stranger's Child* and *The Aspern Papers*: queering origin stories and questioning the visitable past', the absent presence relates not only to sexual possibility but also to the affectively determining and, in many ways, nation-building, work that narratives of literary influence can be made to carry out. Situating James's 1888 novella *The Aspern Papers* at the centre of the webs of literary influence that constitute *The Stranger's Child*, Rivkin reads a will to 'unmask a triumphalist public narrative and reveal its terrible costs and distortions' as central to Hollinghurst's project – and not only in his novel of 2011. For Rivkin, Hollinghurst is consciously, admiringly, influenced by *The Aspern Papers'* critique of the violent naivety attached to gaining access to the 'reality' of the past. He is also susceptible to what she terms an 'allergic reaction to queer theory'. The presence of Tennyson as another dominant figure of influence in this novel serves, though, to align it with recent theoretical work on queer temporality. Rivkin, then, reads Hollinghurst as an 'active contributor' to the conceptualization of queer temporality that has, in recent years, been carried out by the very academic trend he has been prompt to parody.

MM: His concern with time is matched by a preoccupation with places and spaces, as Geoff Gilbert emphasizes. In 'Some properties of fiction: value and fantasy in Hollinghurst's house of fiction', Gilbert attends to the connection between the affective and economic values of property as observed in *The Line of Beauty*'s sexually explicit scenes. For the reader, these scenes open up erotic internal worlds that stretch beyond the strict geography of the book. The keyholders-only London garden where Nick loses his virginity, the Feddens' French home that frames Toby as an object of Nick's interest: these are the kinds of spaces, Gilbert suggests, where the novel observes the story of private property as it intersects with personal narratives and 'the historical determination of a collectivity'. Thatcherism, Gilbert contends, is a libidinal arrangement that structures the characters' lives and loves. The book operates as more than a class critique, however. He considers the novel's correlation between psychic reality and real-world values by building on Laplanche and Pontalis's psychoanalytic work on the construction of the subject in relation to its place in the world, as well as on Virginia Woolf's vision of autonomy.

DJF: One of the joys of editing this collection has been what its contributors have taught me about Hollinghurst. I've always found *The Folding Star* dense, gloomy and, for a novel about erotic obsession, oddly unsexy. Robert L. Caserio's 'Hollow auguries: eccentric genealogies in *The Folding Star* and *The Spell*' has helped me understand the extent to which those qualities are at work in ways that constitute one of Hollinghurst's richest affective and aesthetic projects. For Caserio, Hollinghurst submits 'his narrative structure, his protagonist and his reader to a surfeit of genealogical explanation in order to provoke a cold reaction, not merely a polite one'. Well, he certainly succeeded with me! Like Rivkin, Caserio is bravely attentive to the temporal complexity and negativity of Hollinghurst's lines of influence here. If, for Rivkin, *The Stranger's Child* explores the weak foundations and agonizing costs of national narratives as and through literary influence, then *The Folding Star* does the same with more enclosed, self-generating narratives of restored objects of desire, historical explanation and fantasies of new love. The result is, for the characters, a wild goose chase that also amounts to something 'moving' that grounds Hollinghurst's subsequent work. Early in his chapter, Caserio refers to A. E. Housman, whom Hollinghurst edited and thought singularly unsuited to narratives of development. Later on, Caserio's discussion of *The Spell* examines the way in which it is in conversation with *The Well-Beloved*, Hardy's novel of stonily compulsive repetition. I wouldn't have linked Alex's dancefloor joys in *The Spell* with Hardy's treatments of intergenerational eros. But now I do.

MM: And where Caserio excavates Hollinghurst's Georgian archae-ologies, you explore his readings and translations of seventeenth-century French theatre. 'Using Racine in 1990; or, translating theatre in time' is also concerned with the particular moment with which Hollinghurst engages. Your chapter proposes a transhistorical approach to his trans-lation of Racine that renders into English the French of one of the most formal writers. But, as you show, the years of his translations (especially 1990 for *Bajazet*), bring Hollinghurst's interpretation of this tight, seventeenth-century formalism into free but indirect dialogue with the late twentieth-century queer theory of Eve Kosofsky Sedgwick, Tony Kushner's adaptation of Corneille, and films such as Derek Jarman's *Edward II* and Denys Arcand's *Jesus of Montreal*.

DJF: What does a Racinian hero or heroine do if not act 'under the influence'? *Phaedra*, which Hollinghurst knows well but has not translated, is the most obvious example, but all of the characters in *Bajazet* are – deeply, claustrophobically – under the influence. So too is Titus in *Berenice*, which Hollinghurst went on to translate in 2012. This is a state of primal susceptibility. Across Hollinghurst's *oeuvre* its usual manifestation has something to do with male homosexual desire. The arc of his career shows that that state of affective, physical and aesthetic susceptibility extends beyond the narrowly, 'identifiably', sexual.

'Race, empire, and *The Swimming-Pool Library*', John McLeod's chapter, documents this, outlining the extent to which the pursuit of pleasure in the metropolis can become a reenactment of the racist violences and attitudes of Empire. For McLeod, these 'dominant attitudes to race are quietly put under pressure, if not called entirely into question,' by the novel. The means through which this pressure is applied have everything to do with the two key words in the title of this book: 'writing' and 'influence'. The retrospective nature of Will's narrative with its resultant production of two Wills – one who is immersed in the heated summer of 1983 and one who narrates that summer's events in an unspecified later time – creates a space for critique around the worst of his privileged assumptions. This scenario does not present an ideologically salvational alternative, however. In McLeod's view, *The Swimming-Pool Library* 'cannot fully uncouple itself from the prejudicial milieu it seeks critically to expose'. But the presence of different figures of influence, explicitly named and thoroughly threaded through the novel, creates interrogative possibilities that facilitate what McLeod, invoking Edward Said, calls the 'complex counterpointing' of culture and imperialism.

Alan O'Leary's 'Cinema in the library' puts visual media into an economy of antagonistic twinning with the 'writing' of our title. In this reading, the queerness of Hollinghurst's novel emerges from its capacity to link cinema, modernist form and middlebrow culture. For O'Leary, cinema resists *The Swimming-Pool Library*'s dominant aesthetic of pattern and finish. Hollinghurst's first novel has a remarkable formal unity yet cinema – whether as pornography, Hollywood epic, or as it appears in Firbank's fiction – resists this aesthetic. It is a disruptive and 'obtuse' force. Cinema's variegated, unassimilable status also twins it with the historical 'reality' of HIV and AIDS, phenomena that, for O'Leary, are 'all too well-known' beyond the novel's 'suspended summer' and therefore receive no explicit representation in the novel.

MM: While this book attends to the influence of cultural forms, historical turning points, theoretical interventions and literary-critical genealogies, its last chapter acknowledges that none of this would be possible without the author's own influence. Although 'being influenced' sounds passive, in order to *be* influenced an author has to *do* something to his source, as the art historian Michael Baxandall has pointed out.[6] For influence to occur, the author must take the dominant, active role in the relationship.

Creative writers, literary critics and biographers all use their sources differently. Critics tend to operate with an inbuilt sense of Barthes's 'death of the author'. Writing about a living figure, however, requires some recalibration. It made me feel quite keenly that reports of the so-called 'death of the author' have been greatly exaggerated. In the case of Hollinghurst, the author is very much alive: he writes e-mails and gives interviews. Biographers have a different relationship to authors' lives and archives. *The Stranger's Child* is, in many respects, an extended meditation on this. In the interview that forms this book's last chapter, the biographer Hermione Lee tells Hollinghurst that the novel made her 'laugh out loud (and laugh as a biographer)' because 'it's a very dubious picture of the biographer at work'.

'What can I say?: secrets in fiction and biography' explores Hollinghurst's long-standing relationship to biography and discusses how his interest in its evolution informed his 2011 novel. He reveals that the novelist he became is indebted to the biographer he didn't become. Lee observes that Lytton Strachey's 1918 *Eminent Victorians* changed biography and that by including Strachey in the novel, Hollinghurst brought together 'what happens to the history of biography and life-writing in Britain in the twentieth century and what happens to homosexual freedom or the increasing enfranchisement of gay people'. This history included the decriminalization of homosexuality in 1967, the year that Strachey's gay life was laid bare in Michael Holroyd's biography. Entering this new era first as a scholar and, later, as a writer, Hollinghurst felt the need to write in a way that made the most of its possibilities, to write freely and openly about times and places in the early twentieth century. The conversation between Lee and Hollinghurst shows that it takes a great deal of insight into human psychology to make a good biography or novel. Both depend 'not only on proper scholarship and research but on the wisdom of the writer'.

DJF: And that's part of Hollinghurst's work, along with its recognitions, formal (if polite) dismissals and occasional invitations to lingering intimacies. As he tells Lee, 'I'm aware, of course, of often crossing a corner of the territory of some great writer in the past and tipping my hat to them but getting on with my own business.'

Acknowledgements

We are grateful to Adam Guy for his outstanding editorial assistance and professionalism. We would like to thank the Faculties of English at the Universities of Leeds and Oxford for research support. Mansfield College, Oxford, also assisted financially. At Manchester University Press, Matthew Frost's flexibility and enthusiasm for the project helped us make a reality of our vision for it. We also thank the anonymous readers for their recommendations. For permission to quote from his unpublished M.Litt. and from correspondence, we and our contributors thank Alan Hollinghurst. The Centre for Life-Writing at Wolfson College, Oxford, generously allowed us to transcribe the Weinrebe Lecture. Finally, our greatest thanks go to our contributors for their dedication and intellectual verve.

Notes

1 Allan Johnson, *Alan Hollinghurst and the Vitality of Influence* (London: Palgrave Macmillan, 2014) 20–30.
2 Daniel Mendelsohn, 'In Gay and Crumbling England', *New York Review of Books*, 10 November 2011, www.nybooks.com/articles/archives/2011/nov/10/gay-and-crumbling-england/ (accessed 19 January 2016).
3 Georges Letissier, 'Queer, Quaint and Camp: Alan Hollinghurst's Own Return to the English Tradition', *Études anglaises* 60.2 (2007) 198–211: 199.
4 Judith Butler, 'Beside Oneself: On the Limits of Sexual Autonomy' in *Undoing Gender* (New York and London: Routledge, 2004) 17–39: 20.
5 Ibid. 25.
6 Michael Baxandall, *Patterns of Intention: On the Historical Explanation of Pictures* (New Haven, CT: Yale University Press, 1985) 58–9.

1

Abjuring innocence: Hollinghurst's poetry

Bernard O'Donoghue

Although Alan Hollinghurst's reputation as a leading novelist of his time is beyond question, it was important to be reminded by Rachel Cooke in her *Observer* interview with him on the occasion of the publication of *The Stranger's Child*, in 2012, that 'he wasn't always going to be a novelist though. Poetry was his first love.' At school, he says in that interview, he was fascinated by poetical forms; for example he wrote three sonnets for a competition on 'the pleasures of life'. He says, 'Being a poet at school had a certain prestige; it was a source of glamour. And if you could write modernistic poems, which no one could understand, then even more so.'[1] This mischievously blimpish view of poetry disguises a taste for the modern (if not exactly the modernist) that Hollinghurst has never shed. For example, his taste in architecture, about which he has written with some authority, marries the classical, on which he is an informed commentator, with a firm commitment to the imaginatively new.

Hollinghurst's initial love for the practice of poetry continued from school to his distinguished career in English, begun in 1972, at Magdalen College, Oxford, where he was undergraduate, graduate and tutor. From his first year he was tutored and befriended by John Fuller, with whom he was a major mover in the running of the college's very successful poetry group, the Florio Society, of which Hollinghurst was secretary (the only executive post) in his second year.[2] In 1974 his poem 'Death of a Poet' (the assigned subject) won the university's prestigious Newdigate Prize for poetry, and throughout his undergraduate career, at the end of which he got a First Class degree, although he worked with distinction on English fiction and drama it was generally thought that his primary bent was for poetry.[3] After taking his BA in 1975, he stayed on at Magdalen College where he wrote an M.Litt. on a group of novelists: Firbank, Forster and Hartley.[4] In the thesis he argued that (as with Proust's Gilberte and

Albertine) these writers featured innamoratas who were ostensibly female but might be based on male attachments, the celebration of which would have been controversial at the time of publication. Of the three writers considered in the thesis, Firbank remained his strongest enthusiasm: Hollinghurst edited three of Firbank's novels for Penguin Classics and wrote essays on him in the *Yale Review* (2001) and in the *Times Literary Supplement* (2006).[5] Firbank's works and life are a prominent theme in *The Swimming-Pool Library*.

Although his academic interests seem to have shifted towards fiction by the time of his M.Litt. in 1980, Hollinghurst's publications remained primarily in poetry for a while longer. John Fuller's Sycamore Press published two early Hollinghurst pieces: 'Isherwood is at Santa Monica' and 'The Well' were published in 1975 as *Sycamore Broadsheet 22*; in 1982 it published *Confidential Chats with Boys*, a pamphlet made up of five numbered sections in unrhyming quatrains of twenty lines each. In between those two publications, Hollinghurst was one of the six writers included in Faber's *Poetry: Introduction 4*.[6] There were ten poems by him in the Faber volume, including the two from the Sycamore broadsheet. But, he tells Rachel Cooke in the *Observer* interview, after *Confidential Chats*, 'the Muse left me'.[7] In 1981 his friend Andrew Motion included Hollinghurst's three-part poem 'Where the Story Ended' in a Christmas supplement for the Poetry Book Society.[8] 'Where the Story Ended', dwelling on 'Miss Monk's front-garden', is already concerned with the evanescence of lives and the buildings they occur in, a prominent theme in his later fiction: the poem ends with

> the places
> deserted by the dead who woke
> and slept here for a century.

Hollinghurst had still been an undergraduate when the 'Isherwood' pamphlet was published in 1975, and he had not yet come out as gay. But there are plenty of hints in the two poems there – more overt in the 'Isherwood' poem than in 'The Well', which is a strange mixture of Freud and Grendel's mere in *Beowulf*. The context of the 'Isherwood' poem tells us everything we need to know: on St Valentine's Day in 1953, at Santa Monica, Christopher Isherwood, who was forty-eight, met the eighteen-year-old Don Bachardy; they were to remain partners until Isherwood's death in 1986. But there were other reasons why that encounter came to mind in 1975 or the years leading up to it. Significant prompts for the poem may have been two films much celebrated at the time: *Cabaret* was a major event in 1972, based on Isherwood's two *Berlin Stories*, published in 1945 but describing events in Germany in 1931–2 as Hitler was coming to power. (Several other stories in the series had been published in the 1930s, including 'Sally Bowles' in 1937, included in *Goodbye to Berlin* (1939); 'Mr Norris Changes Trains' was published in 1935.) An earlier film based on the two 1945 *Berlin Stories* by Isherwood was *I am a Camera* in 1955, which influenced *Cabaret* in a number of ways. Isherwood had gone to Berlin to take advantage of the sexual freedoms associated with the Weimar Republic as its era was coming to an end and speeding into repression. The second major film– even more celebrated in those years –which may have been a less direct influence was Visconti's *Death in Venice*, based on Thomas Mann's short novel about the writer Gustav von Aschenbach, who is obsessed by a beautiful Polish boy Tadzio as the city is invaded by plague. Three of the five stanzas of Hollinghurst's Isherwood poem end with a refrain: 'A gold-haired boy twirls upside-down on rings' (and the fourth is a variation on it). It is a line that for a filmgoer of the time unmistakably recalls Tadzio in Visconti's film, even if the immediate occasion of the line was a television documentary about Isherwood in which a golden-haired young man did indeed twirl upside down on rings at Santa Monica.

The first line of Hollinghurst's second stanza develops the reference to Isherwood: 'Novelist, camera, and three-poem poet'. The poem ends with the poet/novelist able to be frank, 'a happy escapee, / home, with himself and few secrets'.[9] The sea-traveller in that stanza, 'home from a lost sea', is able to engage with one of the most secure homecoming poems in the language, Stevenson's 'Requiem' (more sardonically evoked in Philip Larkin's 'This Be the Verse'). Hollinghurst's poem is a subtle evocation (remarkable for so young a writer) of a flickering black-and-white film, and it sustains its uncertainties to the end with the word 'escapee': Isherwood has escaped the homophobic judgements such as those of the doctor noted in the poem who labelled him 'Infantilismus', into a free Californian world with 'miles of beach and a crazy pier'; but the 'escapee' also recalls the disapproval that greeted Isherwood and Auden's departure to America shortly before the start of the Second World War.

This poem might lead us to expect Hollinghurst to become a socially engaged – even campaigning – poet, very unlike the schoolboy with his interest in poetical forms. But 'The Well', the second poem in the broadsheet, is entirely different. It is hard to avoid a Freudian interpretation – hard even not to suspect a play with such interpretations:

> Its rim is fringed
> with moss and hart's-tongue fern,

a fronded entry, mysterious
and soft as a vulva.[10]

The spirit of the poem is again secrecy – what is 'never talked of' – though
here applied to the world of female sexuality. Hollinghurst's teasing
references to homosexuality are already striking.

Confidential Chats with Boys took its title from a sententious
American book by William Lee Howard, MD, published in 1911 (and
reprinted in 2006 'as a facsimile of the original' because it was 'a scarce
antiquarian book', according to Amazon).[11] The first of the five sections of
Hollinghurst's pamphlet begins in the spirit that its title promises:

> There are things in trousers called men,
> almost too well-mannered, passing
> as gentlemen – human skunks
> hatched from rattlesnakes' eggs. (*CCB* 1)

And it ends in that same spirit:

> Keep your eye on that jug,
> that candlestick, and when he moves,
> hit him to leave him scarred:
> scar the skunk and coward for life. (*CCB* 1)

It is astonishing, and horrifying now, to realize that the violence here
comes straight from Howard's pathological book: 'Sometimes it is
necessary to smash a boy who makes evil suggestions to you. Don't talk to
him, smash him in the face. Smash him good and hard.'[12]

The campaigning spirit of this first section of Hollinghurst's poem is
maintained only stealthily, though: the following four sections are a series
of detailed and wonderfully evocative memories of the poet's childhood
as the only child of a country bank manager. These memories are perhaps
the most impressive pieces of technical lyricism that Hollinghurst has
written: the first sense of a stable poetic voice. The poem as a whole is
a kind of miniature bildungsroman in verse, moving from the isolation
and sickly terror of section 2, with 'the orchid silence' such women as
the long-legged lady in Sickert's 'pink and green *Ennui*' bring with them
(*CCB* 2), to the child's play at 'Banking Business' in section 3 which hid
the 'hard-core innocence' of cuttings from *Geographics* (*CCB* 3).[13] Section
4 makes more explicit the dawn, or pre-dawn, of sexuality when the 'very
young' boy is thrilled by travesty: the femininity of 'pleated summer
skirts / with swirling flower prints' served as 'gowns that swept the floor'

and – with a suddenly sensual turn – 'licked the naked legs' (*CCB* 4). This section catches the undeveloped language of adolescent romanticism, as it may be encountered in opera:

> Dear, I long for your caress.
> Dear one, will you say yes? (*CCB* 4)

The final section concludes this dwelling on the paraphernalia of romanticism, with 'my Russian music' and 'lilies on the suicide's grave', 'Lorelei and the cold river' (*CCB* 5). The poem ends brilliantly by bringing together all the jumbled images that have operated in this uncertain bildungsroman: like liqueur chocolates taken surreptitiously from an open box:

> sweet, unpleasant, but addictive,
> an overdrawn bachelor's gift
> not likely to be missed. (*CCB* 5)

The closing image is a perfect amalgam of guilt and the innocence which is necessary for guilt to be felt at all, like the 'sunlit innocence' at the end of a later Hollinghurst poem, 'Rain' – a kind of secret stealth which is founded on an addiction which is only dimly sensed.

To get a fuller idea of these secrecies and closed-off realities, we might anticipate something Hollinghurst said in the introduction to his selection of Housman published by Faber in 2001. Writing of Housman's echoing of Shakespeare's songs in *A Shropshire Lad*, he says:

> It was the golden lads who more concerned Housman, of course; and it is perhaps the difficulty of that illicit subject which, while lending the book a fascinating tension, makes too for a certain instability of tone, clumsy humour and forced diction sometimes co-existing in a single poem with passages of limpid sensibility. It would be interesting to know to what extent readers over the past century have considered, or even acknowledged, the homosexual foundations of the book. The disguise in the conventional forms and terms of ballad, song and epigram fits so well; even if nowadays we notice, and are perhaps grateful for, its transparency, and feel that Housman was right to enlist the time-honoured dignity of these forms to his less licensed sufferings.[14]

This is a moving and profoundly illuminating observation about Housman, and the 'disguise' here was the subject of Hollinghurst's thesis on the three novelists. But, while the qualities noted do not exactly correspond to the instabilities in Hollinghurst's own poetry (he could never be accused of forced diction, and even less of clumsy humour), the general point about 'less licensed sufferings' fits the circumstances of his early career in the period when most of his poetry was written: before, one might say, the rather insecure Muse left him in the early 1980s and his more confident fictional persona took over.

Before this there had been a more substantial opportunity to weigh Hollinghurst's poetic achievement rather more extensively in the ten poems of the Faber *Poetry: Introduction 4* in 1978. With the benefit of a brief hindsight (from 1981 and 1982), we can see emerging the typical Hollinghurst poem. The first poem, 'Over the Wall', is the same kind of invaded pastoral as 'The Derelict Houses at Great Barrington' as the children 'climb over the wall', and it echoes 'The Well' in its probing of the unknown: 'How far will they go?'[15] In later life an 'unhurried adult' will see the area inside the wall 'as investment or heritage' (again, a hint of *The Stranger's Child*); but the child's transgressive excitement returns to him 'on the edge of sleep' as he 'instinctively breaks and enters' and ends with 'hands rifling silk'.[16] The fourth poem of the *Poetry: Introduction 4* group, 'Christmas Day at Home', echoes the later section of the bildungsroman of *Confidential Chats*, but it also returns by contrast to the transgressively unfamiliar:

> these journeys
> of our own to permanent places
> can keep us fit to talk to.[17]

Even these familiar places have 'unvisited fields' in them; before the resignation of the poem's dutiful end – 'the still afternoon gives us / happiness and humility, as it should' – a more troubling idea has been entertained: an idea that 'makes us children / and says something of being old'.[18] We are again on the margin of an unfamiliar, or unfaced, realm of experience.

Before this, the poem 'Nightfall (For an Athlete Dying Young)' can, by a longer application of hindsight, be connected to Housman's poem XIX in *A Shropshire Lad*, 'To an Athlete Dying Young', included by Hollinghurst in his selections in 2001. Housman's classically Housmanesque poem contrasts the living young athlete being carried on the townspeople's shoulders after winning a race with the same athlete's coffin being carried on the same shoulders when he is 'Townsman of a stiller town'.[19] The imagery is unrelieved: 'silence sounds no worse than cheers / After earth has stopped the ears'.[20] The oddest note comes at the end when the 'strengthless dead' (like the shrouds in Yeats's 'Cuchulain Comforted') flock to gaze on the 'early-laurelled head',

And find unwithered on its curls
The garland briefer than a girl's.[21]

In Renaissance love-poetry rosebuds (and garlands) were archetypally transient; but this athlete's garland, though it is 'briefer than a girl's' (presumably that of a child in a game), remains 'unwithered'. The transparency in Housman, for which, as Hollinghurst said, we are generally grateful, is suspended in the final image here (and indeed in the sporting terminology throughout which betrays the great classical scholar's insecure grasp of that discourse).

Hollinghurst's response poem is very different, beginning in the tones of his personal pastorals: 'we walk a while alone / on the terrace'.[22] This elegy has an eloquent numbness, sustained by the highly patterned three stanzas, set at three moments of the same day, all 'on the terrace': 'After tea', 'before supper', 'At dusk'. But the movement is not towards any resolution; at the end the 'we' of the poem 'go into the house', 'as if to sleep'.[23] The end, in its suggestion of 'perchance to dream', confirms with its emptiness the illusory nature of the afternoon's only imagining of the 'young man running there'.[24] The elegy, one of Hollinghurst's most beautiful poems, surpasses the disengaged generality of Housman's more conventional original.

If the 'we' of 'Nightfall' remain unidentified, two other poems in *Poetry: Introduction 4* invite more personal questions. Framm, the enthusiastic schoolmaster in 'The Drowned Field', is greeted by the returning narrator. The poem is full of the 'half-pedantic' jokes that its narrator prepares us for: 'Tytania' (whose line in *A Midsummer Night's Dream* provides the poem's title) has an arch 'y' rather than 'i' in the first syllable; Framm hurries off to 'invoke' the schoolboys to 'the pastoral sea' (a verb just about possible in the Latin *invocare* but not in English).[25] And this very elegantly constructed and scanned poem – five five-lined stanzas rhyming ABABA – ends with an unmetrical bump as the expected final iamb is undermined by a banal trochee: 'fields. Or was Framm blinded by those arc-lights?'[26] What stays with the reader of this teasing poem is the element of sexual travesty in the actors of the school play: presumably the twelve-year-old Tytania who was 'lewd with all her mother could devise' was a boy, the vision of whom 'must surely mist Framm's eyes' – 'the orange cheeks and pencilled brows of knights'.[27] But what kind of truth are Framm's eyes blinded to by the unscanning arc-lights?

The other poem in the group that offers us a name to contemplate is 'Ben Dancing at Wayland's Smithy', a love-poem to a young man, set in the heart of England but placed in an historical perspective so long that the actions and affections of the poem's individuals seem heartbreakingly ineffectual. This ineffectuality in the face of all the place's 'weather' is a defeat by 'the noise of the wind ... in league with the silence of the land'.[28] The same geophysical inexorability is evident in the imaginative underwater vision of 'Alonso', where the drowned duke of *The Tempest* is condemned to remember in a Dantesque 'tenebrous confessional'. This beautiful poem ends with an extraordinarily imaginative underwater vision (comparable to Seamus Heaney's perspectives in the later *Seeing Things* (1991) – both in the volume's title poem and the celebrated twelve-liner on Clonmacnoise):

> Boats and the blades of oars
> traverse the sky:
> without parachutes
> divers come spiralling down
> to take from my hair
> the pale cold pearls.[29]

Of the remaining two poems in *Poetry: Introduction 4*, 'Survey' is a surreally inclined description of the geography and contours of England and their manageability:

> In France you could travel the length
> of England and only be half-way down;
> in England everyone has seen the sea.[30]

The *Finnegans Wake*-like perspective on England draws on another of the subjects of Hollinghurst's thesis to describe a view of England:

> the skeleton of the great beast
> stretched out, as Forster saw it in
> 'system after system of our island'. [31]

The conclusion is geophysical again, and each mountain

> range seems
> a longing to be water, thousands of tons
> of ocean held for you here to walk on.[32]

'Convalescence in Lower Largo (Birthplace of Alexander Selkirk)' is in Fife, again away from the centre of England and is surreal in a similar way: 'When I sleep the tide rides into the house'.[33]

It is clear that by 1982 (when the Muse left him) Hollinghurst was a decidedly promising and gifted poet, and he was becoming widely acclaimed as such. While the setting of the poems was English pastoral, the application of it (as perhaps always with pastoral) was decidedly complex. In the poems we repeatedly find a setting which seems to require a larger canvas for its development. We rarely find in these very accomplished pieces a conclusion that resolves to the poet's satisfaction the matter raised. Hollinghurst is an outstanding critic, and one of his finest pieces of criticism – his introduction to the posthumous *Selected Poems* of his friend Mick Imlah – gives us an insight into his own narrative poetics. Of Imlah he writes: 'The narrative impulse and interest were central to his poetry from the start. He never wrote a merely descriptive poem ... the little six-line verses on 'The Counties of England' visit playfully surreal histories on their hapless subjects.'[34] Imlah and Hollinghurst are very different writers; but Hollinghurst's appreciation of the brilliant inventiveness of Imlah's 'hinterland of histories, real and imaginary' is not surprising in the context of his own poems.[35] There are other links too: he praises Imlah for 'relishing formal control and syntactic play' and salutes his 'instinct for rhyme, rhythm and shape shown by few of his contemporaries'.[36] Above all he likes Imlah's sheer fictiveness, as in the minutes he wrote as a student for the Florio Society, which became 'ever more extended and involved fantasias on the relatively ordinary things that had actually been said and done'.[37] Imlah never wrote prose fiction; but one word to describe the qualities that Hollinghurst is extolling here is surely 'novelistic'. Until the end of his short and scintillating poetic career, Imlah's writing could never be called confessional or autobiographical. In Hollinghurst's words, it 'was only at the end of his life that he wrote poems undisguisedly about those he loved, his partner and his children, and they too take the form of anecdotes, transfigured by feeling and an exact instinct for how feeling may be expressed'.[38]

Imlah's total fictiveness and what (adapting the words of Hilaire Belloc) might be termed 'a strict disregard for truth' is a great strength in writers who have an impulse towards privacy (like Imlah himself, as Hollinghurst's introduction to the *Selected Poems* makes clear). It would be too great an irony to imply that there is anything evasive about Hollinghurst's own writing career, given the courage of his exploding of sexual – and other – taboos in novels from *The Swimming-Pool Library* onwards. But one of the most attractive things in his best poems – in 'Nightfall' and 'Alonso' and the middle sections of *Confidential Chats with Boys* – is a mixture of reserve and tact that serves as a kind of second theme behind the main subject in novels like *The Line of Beauty* and *The Stranger's Child*.

There have been occasional poetic sorties in the course of Hollinghurst's celebrated novel-writing life. They display the same accomplishment and sureness of imagery, but they now seem more clearly the by-products of the novelist. Another Poetry Book Society anthology in 1989–90 published 'Dry Season Nights', a poem which has a cool and confident exoticism more in tune with the novels:

> Slick, shuffling demons of the carnival,
> the Jab-Jab boys have bodies black with oil;
> they grab you if you do not give them coins.[39]

As well as the two sections of *Confidential Chats with Boys*, in the anthology *Magdalen Poets*, Robert Macfarlane included Hollinghurst's poem 'Brain-Garden', an intriguing poem which has something in common with the exoticism of 'Dry Season Nights' but echoes too the surrealism in some earlier poems like 'Survey'.[40] It displays too an inclination towards the abstract – even allegorical – that is unusual in Hollinghurst.

> I'm making up my own brain-garden there,
> with old brain corals, big as dinner-plates,
> heavy as masonry, grey, lolling, dumb ...
> Each time I come I add a few
> to make it look like more than happenstance:
> a cairn of absent thoughts.[41]

Increasingly this small poetic corpus (we might pause to note that it is larger than the corpus on which T. E. Hulme's reputation is founded, not to mention the works of Hollinghurst's 'three-poem poet' Isherwood) can be linked in striking ways with the celebrated later novels. There are formidable cases in English of novelists who returned in their later writing lives to concentrate on poetry (the most glorious, of course, is Hardy). It is clear that Hollinghurst has the skills to follow this course if he chooses to: both the technique, gift for narrative and the 'exact instinct for how feeling may be expressed' that he saluted in Mick Imlah. But even as it stands, his poetic corpus has a distinctiveness and variety not quite paralleled by any of his contemporaries, moving as it does from an elegant, understated sense of the transgressive to the fearless creation of a world that makes no apologies for its preferences – pastoral, sexual or critical.

The last significant year of poetic publication for Hollinghurst was 1982: as well as *Confidential Chats*, the powerful and mysterious history poem 'Mud' was published in the *London Review of Books*.[42] But just before *Confidential Chats*, one of Hollinghurst's finest pastoral poems appeared in the Sycamore Press *Florilegium for John Florio*: 'The Derelict Houses at Great Barrington' of 1981 is a poem which exemplifies exactly the kind of direction his poems might have been expected to take.[43] It may be seen too as a distant relative of Hollinghurst's 2012 novel *The Stranger's Child* in atmosphere and in a kind of dialogic, Bakhtinian novelistic way. It is particularly reminiscent of the later book in its evocation of the passage of time: the 'dissonant bells at ten past the hour' which 'bore witness to vanished patrons', 'the slow ascendancy of grass' and the 'slow tilt into nullity'.[44] It is tempting too to compare this kind of historical novelism to another major poem of the era, Derek Mahon's 'A Disused Shed in Co. Wexford'; the comparison is worth making to suggest that the kind of elegiac historical-pastoral of Hollinghurst's poem is not limited to an English tradition. The *Florilegium* contains a second poem by Hollinghurst, 'Rain', a poem of unrequited but imagined love – 'Alone in the huge bed' – which ends with a note which we find again both in the poems and Hollinghurst's novels – a wish for a departed 'innocence' which is not in fact so much innocence as a lost golden age: 'the orderly garden, unbeaten roses, / our stupid, sunlit innocence again'.[45] The real drift of the poem is a wish not for innocence but for experience. Once again, this eighteen-line poem has a protractedness that seems (again with the benefit of hindsight) to want the scope of a more extended, fictional form, the form in which Hollinghurst was ultimately to be a supreme practitioner.

Notes

1   Rachel Cooke, 'Alan Hollinghurst: "The Booker Can Drive People Mad"', *Observer*, 20 May 2012, www.theguardian.com/books/2012/may/20/alan-hollinghurst-strangers-child-booker-interview (accessed 19 January 2016).

2   For Hollinghurst's activities with the Florio Society and with Fuller's Sycamore Press, see *John Fuller and the Sycamore Press: A Bibliographic History*, ed. Ryan Roberts (Oxford: Bodleian Library and Oak Knoll Press, 2010). Hollinghurst contributes some brief memories to this volume (see 21–3).

3   John Wain set the subject of 'The Death of a Poet' in his role as Oxford Professor of Poetry and said that he inherited it from Roy Fuller, who may have chosen it because of Auden's recent death. Of Hollinghurst's poem, Wain says, 'His poem is clearly about Auden – a preference invited, of course, by the choice of that title in that particular year' (John Wain, *Professing Poetry* (London: Macmillan, 1977) 126). Hollinghurst says, 'I seem to remember I didn't much care for Auden at that stage of my life … though at some point I came to value him much more' (e-mail to the

author, 26 September 2014). Of course, his tutor John Fuller would have made Auden a major presence at that point.

4   Alan Hollinghurst, 'The Creative Uses of Homosexuality in the Novels of E. M. Forster, Ronald Firbank and L. P. Hartley', M.Litt. thesis, University of Oxford, 1979.

5   See Alan Hollinghurst, 'I Often Laugh When I'm Alone: The Novels of Ronald Firbank', *Yale Review* 89.2 (2001) 1–18; and 'Saved by Art: The Shy, Steely, Original Ronald Firbank', *Times Literary Supplement*, 17 November 2006, 12–15. The *TLS* article was a version of the third of the 2006 Lord Northcliffe Lectures at University College London where Hollinghurst had taught.

6   *Poetry: Introduction 4* (London and Boston MA: Faber, 1978). For Hollinghurst's poems, see 67–78.

7   Cooke, 'Alan Hollinghurst'.

8   *Poetry Supplement Compiled by Andrew Motion for the Poetry Book Society Christmas '81* (London: Poetry Society, 1981).

9   Alan Hollinghurst, 'Isherwood is at Santa Monica' in *Isherwood is at Santa Monica: Sycamore Broadsheet 22* (Oxford: Sycamore Press, 1975) 1.

10   Alan Hollinghurst, 'The Well' in *Isherwood is at Santa Monica* 2–3.

11   In the Roberts book on the Sycamore Press, Hollinghurst says Howard's book was lent to his parents 'by a well-meaning aunt' (*John Fuller and the Sycamore Press*, 23). That edition, from which he 'lifted' the title, was published in 1928, so it wasn't too scarce to be republished within twenty years.

12   William Lee Howard, *Confidential Chats with Boys* (New York: Clode, 1911) 78.

13   The first and third sections are the parts of the poem chosen for *Magdalen Poets*, ed. Robert Macfarlane (Oxford: Magdalen College, 2000) 167–8.

14   Alan Hollinghurst, 'Introduction' in *A. E. Housman: Poems Selected by Alan Hollinghurst* (London: Faber, 2001) vii–xii: ix.

15   Alan Hollinghurst, 'Over the Wall' in *Poetry* 67–8: 67.

16   Ibid. 68.

17   Alan Hollinghurst, 'Christmas Day at Home' in *Poetry* 70–1: 70.

18   Ibid. 71.

19   A. E. Housman, 'To an Athlete Dying Young' in *Poems Selected by Alan Hollinghurst* 16.

20   Ibid.

21   Ibid.

22   Alan Hollinghurst, 'Nightfall (For an Athlete Dying Young)' in *Poetry* 68–9: 68.

23   Ibid. 68–9.

24   Ibid. 68.

25   Alan Hollinghurst, 'The Drowned Field' in *Poetry* 72.

26   Ibid.

27   Ibid.

28   Alan Hollinghurst, 'Ben Dancing at Wayland's Smithy' in *Poetry* 75–6: 76.

29   Alan Hollinghurst, 'Alonso' in *Poetry* 73–4.

30   Alan Hollinghurst, 'Survey' in *Poetry* 69–70: 69.

31   Ibid. See also the opening of chapter 19 of E. M. Forster's *Howards End*, where Forster takes an aerial view of England that influences these poems of Hollinghurst.

32   Ibid. 70.

33   Alan Hollinghurst, 'Convalescence in Lower Largo (Birthplace of Alexander Selkirk)' in *Poetry* 77.

34   Alan Hollinghurst, 'Introduction' in Mick Imlah, *Selected Poems*, ed. Mark Ford (London: Faber, 2010) ix–xxiii: xii.

35   Ibid.

36   Ibid.

37   Ibid. xi.

38   Ibid. xii.

39   Alan Hollinghurst, 'Dry Season Nights' in *The Poetry Book Society Anthology 1989–1990*, ed. Christopher Reid (London: Hutchinson, 1989) 54.

40   Both 'Brain-Garden' and 'Dry Season Nights', as well as 'Sugar Mill', which was published in the *Times Literary Supplement*, were written during a month spent in Carriacou in the Windward Islands in early 1989.

41   Alan Hollinghurst, 'Brain-Garden' in *Magdalen Poets* 169.

42   Alan Hollinghurst, 'Mud', *London Review of Books* 21 October 1982, www.lrb.co.uk/v04/n19/alan-hollinghurst/mud (accessed 19 January 2016).

43   Alan Hollinghurst, 'The Derelict Houses at Great Barrington' in *A Florilegium for John Florio* (Oxford: Sycamore Press, 1981) n.p. Though authorship was not assigned in the pamphlet, it also contained the first published poem by Mick Imlah, 'Quasimodo Says Goodnight to the Beautiful Gipsy Girl he has Rescued from the Stake', and a particularly fine imagist music-poem by John Fuller, 'Concerto for Double Bass'. The poems are attributable with certainty by later publication in authored volumes, and revealed in Roberts, *John Fuller and the Sycamore Press*, 89.

44   Hollinghurst, 'The Derelict Houses at Great Barrington'.

45   Alan Hollinghurst, 'Rain' in *A Florilegium for John Florio* n.p.

2

The touch of reading in Hollinghurst's early prose

Angus Brown

The pleasure of the book

It was the sex in Alan Hollinghurst's fiction that first alerted me to the physicality of reading him. Absorbed in literary eroticism, critical distance shrank in embarrassment and fascination, inhibition and prurience, in swallowed twinges of disavowal and the engrossing insistence of arousal. As I read, I became more aware of the book in my hands, more sensitive to the feel of cover and page. This cutaneous friction left me open to an acute, embodied kind of reading. In the first movements of Hollinghurst's second novel, *The Folding Star*, a friend of Edward Manners pulls up in 'a kind of jeep, metallic blue, with yards of chrome trim' (71). Leaning over the passenger seat, Matt invites Edward for a swim at the town baths and the novel's protagonist finds himself momentarily distracted:

> Matt's right hand lay on the passenger seat still, its veins sexily fat and blue over the delicate bones, the nails shockingly bitten. I imagined it moving up my thigh as I sat beside him and we burned out of town. (*FS* 71)

By a fluke of typesetting this description of Matt's right hand falls at the foot of a recto page in my personal copy of *The Folding Star*: a thick and worn 1998 Vintage paperback edition. This means that while Edward imagines Matt's hand sliding up his thigh, my own right hand is playing across the back of my book, getting ready to turn the page. As my fingers graze the cover, Matt's moving hand momentarily corresponds to my own and the touch of my reading brushes against Edward's fantasy. In movements like this, the novel's plot, the material book, and the act of reading, come into an oblique yet evocative dialogue structured around the perceptual uncertainty and pleasure of touch.

'The sense of touch', writes Eve Kosofsky Sedgwick, 'makes nonsense out of any dualistic understanding of agency and passivity.'[1] In this way, touch gives the reassurance of contact without a reliable codification of meaning. Judith Butler proposes that this hermeneutic quirk serves to bring the subject into the world, situating us within 'an organic and inorganic object field that exceeds the human'.[2] Although bodily contact confirms our place in the world, it does not necessarily make sense of it: 'we do not always know, or cannot always say, who touched whom first, or what was the moment of being touched and what was the moment of touching.'[3] The right kind of touch, then, promises a weightless and uniting moment of uncertainty between subject and object. Here, this uncertainty offers an intuitive means of thinking about reading and the ways in which we are not always in charge of our reading.

At an elementary level, the material structure of the book dictates the feeling of reading. Standing, sitting, or lying down, fingers and thumbs accommodate quarto, folio, and octavo. Eyes adjust to the size of print. Books hold limbs in unusual and specific arrangements, often for hours at a time. A large part of learning to read, however, consists of learning to forget the somatic environments that books make. 'To take in a text', writes Leah Price, 'is to tune out its raw materials.'[4] We learn to work automatically towards comprehension, to prioritize the imaginative over the corporeal, to follow the twist of the plot rather than the turn of the page. Elaine Scarry goes so far as to describe the sensuous attributes of reading as 'antagonistic to the mental images that a poem or novel seeks to produce'.[5] In this scenario, touch disturbs the very workings of literature itself. More generally, a cognitive incompatibility between sense and making sense informs the critical dissonance between theories of reading and the history of the book. For Elizabeth Long 'the ideology of the solitary reader' obscures the social, institutional, and material realities of literacy and yet it is precisely this ideology, this fantasy, that makes reading for pleasure possible.[6] Although the history of reading concerns the social conditions of literary production and dissemination, a great part of reading's appeal lies in the asocial respite that a book can provide. By holding on to the facticity *and* fictitiousness of reading, Hollinghurst's early writing allows the touch of reading, the secret choreography of book and body, to take hold.

The pleasure of the book plays through much of Hollinghurst's fiction. The lines, folds, and libraries in the titles of his first three novels – *The Swimming-Pool Library*, *The Folding Star*, and *The Line of Beauty* – hint at a fascination with the material text at work in his more eye-catching preoccupation with the male form. These seams between the book and the body are at their most raw, and their most legible, in Hollinghurst's early prose. In his graduate thesis and his first novel, an obsession with Ronald Firbank translates from a set of scholarly interests in form and archive into an aesthetic, erotic equivalence between bibliography and anatomy. As such, this chapter will read *The Swimming-Pool Library* by the light of Hollinghurst's early academic work, tracking the route by which a student's sexually and materially sensitive reading practice became the backbone of a novelist's style.

Close reading and keeping secrets

Alan Hollinghurst arrived at Magdalen College, Oxford, in the autumn of 1972. In 1977, still at Magdalen, he completed his M.Litt: a research-based master's degree that required a substantial thesis. For Hollinghurst, this meant writing 'The Creative Uses of Homosexuality in the Novels of E. M. Forster, Ronald Firbank, and L. P. Hartley' under the supervision of John Bayley, who was the Thomas Warton Professor of English and married to Iris Murdoch. In a 2011 interview with Peter Terzian for the *Paris Review*, Hollinghurst speaks fondly, and even a little proudly, of his graduate work:

> It was quite a new subject then. The Sexual Offences Act had been passed in 1967 and changed what could be said about the private lives of gay people. ... A new freedom to talk about these things was very much part of the atmosphere of the seventies. I think, without wishing to blow my own trumpet, that my thesis was quite an original thing to choose to do.[7]

Although new freedoms came in with the Sexual Offences Act in 1967, old discriminations stood, most notably the disparity in the age of consent between homosexual and heterosexual couples. In the same interview Hollinghurst describes coming out in his final term as an undergraduate at Oxford. It would have been around the time of his twenty-first birthday: just before, or just after, he could legally have sex. The criminal secrecy of Hollinghurst's adolescent sexuality is still fresh in his thesis and informs the abiding sympathy with which he follows the literary improvisations of Forster, Hartley, and Firbank in the face of cultural and governmental intolerance.[8] Crucially, Hollinghurst argues that 'homosexuality entails a special *way* of writing', a style that 'only prevails if homosexuality itself is not discussed'.[9]

'The Creative Uses of Homosexuality' is quick to inscribe an affinity between the secrecy of sex and the secrecy of reading. On the first page of his thesis, Hollinghurst describes choosing his authors in order to 'illustrate different approaches to the relationship of author and reader ... when their homosexuality is a quality which has to be concealed'.[10] The ambiguity of 'their homosexuality' entangles both author and reader, knotting a sexual secret into Hollinghurst's reading. Sexuality and reading coil and loop in his thesis, never quite resolving into distinct experiences:

> however forward the erotic impulse may be, our reactions to the text are constantly affected by the subtle and cumulative sense of the quality of the imaginative world, the kinds of opportunities it admits, as well as by the self-definition authors can achieve by means of style.[11]

The 'erotic impulse' this sentence describes unfolds in 'our reactions to the text', the 'opportunities it admits', and the 'self-definition' of an author's style. Again, Hollinghurst's syntax declines to ascribe the queer charge of his reading to reader, text, or writer. This indeterminate eroticism permeates 'The Creative Uses of Homosexuality', falling somewhere between Forster, Firbank, Hartley, and Hollinghurst, mediated by their intersecting imaginative worlds. When we follow the diffusions of Hollinghurst's 'erotic impulse', we can see how these worlds receive and hold the desires of a reader as they contain and disclose a writer's yearning. This is intimate reading, reading that understands the book as a receptacle of desire: a vessel that both stores and gives shape to a shared need.

Hollinghurst takes this complicity seriously. More often than not, the close readings of his thesis do not expose sexual secrecy but identify and almost luxuriate in it: 'when erotic opportunity has to be secretly pursued, the pursuit is given a further quality of excitement, so that the participants enjoy the sense of danger and repression, and sexual experience is given the further piquancy of risk.'[12] These lines describe the shady pleasures of transgressive 'sexual experience', but such excitements are largely missing from Hollinghurst's reading. In fact, the author's somewhat patchy interest in his critical project characterizes large swathes of his thesis. A dutiful opening chapter takes us through all six of Forster's novels. Next comes a distinctly unenthusiastic analysis of Hartley's fiction. The critical prose here is careful, but the freshness and verve that we might expect from Hollinghurst the novelist is missing. Everything changes with the arrival of Ronald Firbank. Stylish turns of phrase arch up, and lines like 'Firbank's deliquescence of direct statement'[13] and 'the destructive weather of reality'[14] start to punctuate the rather weary plot summaries. When he risks a little more, Hollinghurst goes so far as to assert that 'motive in Firbank is transparently, lyrically, simple, and this enables the novels to seem abnormally externalized, and even to have an abundance of warmth and a continuous sexiness.'[15] In short, Firbank allows the style of Hollinghurst's fiction to unfold in his criticism.

The pleasure Hollinghurst takes in Firbank gleams most suggestively from the page when it comes to reading. 'Firbank's self-awareness', writes Hollinghurst,

> leaves merely in the wide margins the implications of emotional experience that the text hints at. Even in this artificial world, though, the reader's natural sensitivity to the unsaid impinges and questions the conditions of the text and its artificiality. This is part of a desire that the reader who feels touched by the novels has to know of Firbank's own inner life, which he also both hid and expressed by means of an artificial manner.[16]

This passage speaks not only to the imaginative avenues of fiction but to the structure of the book. Notice Hollinghurst's sensitivity to the 'wide margins', the 'artificial world', and 'the conditions of the text'. In describing the reader 'who feels touched by the novels' and their 'natural sensitivity to the unsaid', Hollinghurst emphasizes the tactile connectivity of reading. Here, the touch of reading, 'the conditions of the text', the unnoticed physical moorings of the book, press against Hollinghurst's critical prose. Once again, as the earlier ambiguity of 'their homosexuality' split 'erotic impulse' between reader and author, both Firbank and his readers share the 'desire' of the final sentence in the passage above. In the figure of 'the reader who feels touched by the novels', Hollinghurst outlines the workings of an intricate and intuitive process of queer recognition.

Reaching further into Firbank's bibliography, Hollinghurst begins to describe his own practice of close reading in greater detail. The way in which he does so allows for productive ambiguities, not only between the reader and the author but between the book and the body. In broaching Firbank's work, Hollinghurst argues,

> we are to be implicated and active readers, not at all like the audience in Firbank's fantasy of 'a really charming soothing novel. A sort of Moorish massage ...' (one of his manners is to affect this passive languor, but it would make novels far different from Firbank's if it really applied to his own work.)[17]

Here, Hollinghurst compares his fantasy of reading with Firbank's. On the one hand, Firbank imagines a rather slippery eroticism where the novel's page might soothe the reader's muscles, melting tension with touch. On the other, Hollinghurst envisions a bracing but no less suggestive performance where the reader must be 'implicated and active' in order to take up the flexing strain of Firbank's disconcerting style.

Writing twenty years later in his introduction to *Three Novels* (2001), an edited collection of Firbank's final publications, Hollinghurst returned to the author's transfixing difficulty:

> From the start Firbank's novels, so witty in tone and confidently languid in tempo, nonetheless required total concentration from their readers; in the earlier novels in particular there are passages of heady difficulty, and unannounced transitions which require a kind of intuitive alertness to be properly followed.[18]

The 'total concentration', the 'heady difficulty', and 'intuitive alertness' that Firbank demands all speak to a painstaking mode of close reading. The arousal that might accompany this hard work peeks out in a quotation Hollinghurst lifts from the American novelist Carl Van Vechten: 'Almost all of Firbank is quaint reading and enough to make your hair, even pubic hair, stand on end when you understand it.'[19] The knowing slant of this camp dictum captures the indirect eroticism of Hollinghurst's reading. The inguinal innuendo of 'quaint reading' and, of course, those tingling pubic hairs embody the incriminating hilarity of reading Firbank – what Hollinghurst would call, in the title of a 2006 Northcliffe lecture, his 'Delightful Difficulty'. Published in the *Times Literary Supplement* under the earnest heading 'Saved by Art', Hollinghurst's lecture cites the same Van Vechten quotation and goes on to describe Firbank's fragmentary, compositional practice in some detail.

Nearly thirty years after finishing his graduate work, the excitement of being physically near to Firbank's work still animates Hollinghurst's reading. Shuttling back to the less assured prose of his thesis, we get our first glimpse of Hollinghurst in Firbank's archive:

> By the time of his most explicitly personal, most explicitly homosexual novel *Concerning the Eccentricities of Cardinal Pirelli* (1926) Firbank was able to close his preparatory notebook with Montaigne's: 'I have no other end in writing but to discover myself' – [*sic*] allowing us of course the charged double meaning of *discover*. Firbank's notebooks themselves consist of compilations of sometimes tiny fragments, and clearly it is partly this technique of construction which gives Firbank's novels a peculiar concentration, whilst still moving, when clearly seen, in large curves, just as say Pope's poetry is paragraphed into great

baroque emphases constructed out of the essentially self-enclosing units of the couplets.[20]

Hollinghurst's style of close reading is immersed, accretive, and yet somehow unforthcoming. It is as if he wants to learn and keep the secrets of his subject rather than tell them. As a result, his thesis tends to appraise and compile, accumulating sources rather than digging into the texture of their language. When he notes the 'charged double meaning of *discover*' in Firbank's quotation from Montaigne we must rely on our own 'sensitivity to the unsaid' to link this verb to Firbank's identification as homosexual. Similarly, Hollinghurst glances over the minutiae of Firbank's notebooks, but rather than unpack their fractured 'compilations' he works more broadly, comparing their busy form to the fastidious and varied elegance of Pope's poetry. In places like this, 'The Creative Uses of Homosexuality' reads more like a notebook than a thesis.

Holding hands

The most arresting moments of Hollinghurst's graduate work come when we catch sight of the author learning how to write fiction rather than criticism. In a seemingly incidental comment on Firbank's 1916 novel, *Inclinations*, Hollinghurst writes: 'like many of Firbank's protagonists, Geraldine shares the author's long, beautiful hands'.[21] It is a slight enough observation, lightly authoritative and perfectly true, but it reaches through to Hollinghurst's fiction where, time and again, his eye comes to rest on a character's hands. On the opening page of *The Swimming-Pool Library* the novel's protagonist and narrator, William Beckwith, sees a gang of night workers – transport maintenance men – on the train home. As he imagines the 'lonely, invisible work' of their 'inverted lives', he notices one of the men in particular 'looking at his loosely cupped hands'. Later, 'he turned his hands over and I saw the pale gold band of his wedding-ring' (*SPL* 1). This series of ironic inversions has Firbank's fingerprints all over it. Indeed, this subtle play of hands is bound to a reading of Firbank; the facing page holds an epigraph from his novel *The Flower Beneath the Foot* (1923):

'She reads at such a pace,' she complained, 'and when I asked her *where* she had learnt to read so quickly, she replied 'On the screens at Cinemas.'

Before we get to the first word of Hollinghurst's writing, we find Hollinghurst reading. Firbank's lines cut sharply into the matter of how to read, demonstrating the vulnerability that comes with reading out loud to others and silhouetting the comparatively anonymous comfort that comes with reading in private.

Early on in the novel, Will saves the life of an elderly peer, Lord Charles Nantwich, in a public toilet. The pair strike up a friendship and Nantwich soon asks Will to write his biography. Will is reluctant but Nantwich is convinced and soon hands over files of photographs, documents, and diaries. Over a cup of tea one morning, Will reads an extract in which Nantwich describes his beautiful and beloved young servant Taha: 'He has the most lyrical hands, and as he reaches out & takes my glass to refill it the action of his long graceful fingers suggests to my woozy fancy the playing of a harp' (SPL 206). Where Van Vechten locates Firbank's erotic influence in the absurd prickling of pubic hair, Hollinghurst holds it in his hands. In one diary entry, Nantwich describes meeting Firbank in a London bar. He recalls the author's 'long ivory hands' and his 'curious & characteristic action of sliding his hands down his legs' (SPL 153). As the party catches a cab 'to go and hear a negro band at the Savoy', Firbank slumps into the seat beside Nantwich (SPL 154). In spite of this deliciously queer manual cameo, the most compelling pair of hands in Hollinghurst's novel belong to Nantwich himself. Early in their acquaintance, the peer takes Will on a tour of his house. Moving from room to room, Will supports his host by the arm and, as Nantwich struggles to find his feet, their hands clasp and unclasp:

> In the hall he hesitated. His suited forearm lay along my bare brown one, and his hand gripped mine, half-interlocked with it. It was a broad, mottled, strong hand, the knuckles slightly swollen by arthritis, the fingertips broad and flattened, with well-shaped yellow nails. My hand looked effete and inexperienced in its grasp. (SPL 75)

With the touch of reading we can use this passage to make a link between fiction and literary history. Somewhere between their introduction in the bar and later on, pressed together in a cab, we can assume that Nantwich's monumental hand has touched the ivory of Firbank's, and, as his fingers twine with Will's, our own hands hold onto them all. In the introduction to his thesis, Hollinghurst uses a bibliographic figure to assert, 'it is in the margin between naturalism and fantasy – between responsibility to observed life and to the imagination – that the subversive and unstable element of homosexual concealment flourishes'.[22] Hollinghurst recognizes this tension between realism and fantasy in Firbank's modernism and he carries it confidently into the more solid architecture of his own fiction. In Taha and Matt's hands, in Nantwich and Will's, fantasy infiltrates the acutely observed realism of *The Swimming-Pool Library*. Although sex between men is out in the open in Hollinghurst's work, the tension, the need, and the secrecy of the style his thesis documents is still present in his writing, still activated and implicated by our touch.

Queer bibliography

The textual care that Hollinghurst's thesis takes turns into a more explicit preoccupation with the book in his first novel. This attention to materiality sharpens the erotics of reading that gather in 'The Creative Uses of Homosexuality'. For Will, reading often comes after sex. The first time Will picks up Nantwich's papers, he has just closed the door behind Colin, a 'good but rather professional and chilly trick' he picked up on the tube. He attends immediately to their bibliographic particulars: 'the main part of the archive was a set of quarto notebooks, bound in brown boards, rubbed and worn at the edges – most of them with a clear ink inscription on the front cover' (*SPL* 95). In a similar fashion, the first time Will reads a Firbank novel he has just been to the Brutus Cinema in Soho, not 'so much to see a film,' he tells us, 'as to sit in a dark, anonymous place and do dark, anonymous things' (*SPL* 47).

On the train home from the cinema, Will opens Firbank's *Valmouth* (1919) and, again, the look and feel of his reading material is thickly conspicuous:

> It was an old grey and white Penguin Classic that James had lent me, the pages stiff and foxed with a faint smell of lost time. Wet-bottomed wine glasses had left mauve rings over the sketch of the author by Augustus John and the price, 3/6, which appeared in a red square on the cover. (*SPL* 54)

Firbank's difficulty is immediately evident. The novel is 'tough as nails' and Will knows he will not 'begin to grasp it fully until a second or third reading' (*SPL* 54). The manual physicality of this reading inheres in the book's stiffness, its musk, and its stains. Although only a paperback copy, he must take 'especial care' of James's beloved book (*SPL* 54). For Georges Letissier, this passage 'underscores a bibliomaniac, fetishistic attachment'. But something more than a slavish attention to the book is at work here and, indeed, throughout the novel.[23] The sentimental significance of the book shapes *The Swimming-Pool Library* and reaches out towards its readers, the 'faint smell of lost time' and those foxed pages remind us of the object in our own hands.

This permeability between fictional and material worlds opens up as Will comes across an unusually elongated onomatopoeia in *Valmouth*:

'S-s-s-s-s-s-s-s-s-s-s-s-s-s-s-s-s-s-s-s-s-s-s-s-s-sh!' It was such a long 'Sh!' that I found myself quietly vocalizing it to see what its effect would be. 'Quiet Damian,' the woman opposite me said to her little boy. 'Gentleman's trying to read.' (*SPL* 55)

The woman opposite Will assumes that he is attempting to concentrate on his reading. Instead, Firbank's difficulty externalizes Will's reading within a public setting. In his vocalization, we can hear the tricky and embodied work of reading and re-reading that Firbank demands; in the woman's response we can see how the more frivolous pleasures of reading can be misunderstood or simply missed. Rather than looking for meaning in this chain of letters, Will's collusive, queer public reading experiments with Firbank's formal eccentricity to 'see what its effect would be'. His vocalization, in turn, invites us to purse our own lips and see what happens.

This somatic and material sensitivity contours Hollinghurst's long-standing relation to the older author and manifests most strongly in his bibliographic attention to Firbank's writing. Hollinghurst's Northcliffe lecture lingers over the first editions of Firbank's novels, the layout, spelling, and punctuation, 'the mannered typographical emphasis', and 'off-white jackets', of a 'little coordinated library'.[24] For Hollinghurst, 'Firbank's difficult, inconsequential manner' amounts to 'what is in many ways a homosexualization of the novel'.[25] Alongside a stylistic departure in the history of the novel, Firbank's camp frivolity offers a form of affective protection in its manicured practice of encoded non-disclosure. Most importantly, what Hollinghurst allows us to recognize in Firbank is the queer significance of bibliographic sites that can generate an experimental and anonymous pleasure in which didactic meaning fails to organize and structure lived experience.

Out of touch

In 1988, the first thing that readers of *The Swimming-Pool Library* would have seen was a cover that touched on the literary and material textures of fiction. In certain lights, at certain angles, the pale blue dust jacket of the Chatto & Windus first edition appears to show the disturbed and dappled waters of a swimming pool. Most of the time, it looks more like a sheet of paper, crushed up and then smoothed out. There is a wide tear in the centre from which the contents of the novel appear to spill out in a pulpy collage made up of a bare torso, the curve of a cello, and a sheaf of architectural documents. The fluidity that plays out on the cover between the physical strokes of swimming and the more gentle touch of reading recur throughout the body of the text. Almost exactly at the centre of *The Swimming-Pool Library*, at the beginning of the seventh chapter, the meaning of Hollinghurst's title finally becomes clear. In the heart of this novel, the contiguities between the book and the body in Hollinghurst's early prose take on some of the adrenalin, some of the intimacy, of anonymous sex.

At Will's prep school, the prefects were called librarians: 'there were the Chapel Librarian, the Hall Librarian, the Garden Librarian and even, more charmingly, the Running and the Cricket Librarians' (*SPL* 140). In his final term, Will was appointed Swimming-Pool Librarian:

> My parents were evidently relieved that I was not entirely lost (urged absurdly to read Trollope I had stuck fast on Rider Haggard) and my father, in a letter to me, made one of his rare witticisms: 'Delighted to hear that you're to be Swimming-Pool Librarian. You must tell me what sort of books they have in the Swimming-Pool Library.' (*SPL* 140)

One response to his father's request is obvious: the sort of books they have in the Swimming-Pool Library are boys. Thinking back to that final term, Will sets reading against a more illicit kind of learning, edging Hollinghurst's prose into an aching, almost elegiac register:

> On high summer nights when it was light enough at midnight to read outside, three or four of us would slip away from the dorms and go with an exaggerated refinement of stealth to the pool. In the changing-room serious, hot No 6 were smoked, and soap, lathered in the cold, starlit water, eased the violence of cocks up young bums. Fox-eyed, silent but for our breathing and the thrilling, gross little rhythms of sex – which made us gulp and grope for more – we learnt our stuff. (*SPL* 140)

To adjust our eyes to the dusk of Will's recollection, Hollinghurst asks us to imagine reading by starlight and in doing so draws us into the night to watch the boys steal down to the pool. Sensitized to the touch of reading, we can almost feel the heat of their cigarettes and the visceral sting of cold lather. At the end of this passage, the languages of sex and study fuse in that final clause: 'we learnt our stuff'. At this moment the urgent quiet of the changing-room takes on the silence of the library and, if we prick up our ears, we might hear the sounds of Will's under-age fucking as we read: in the whisper of pages at night, in the quiet clearing of a throat, in the steady drawing of our breath.

On the following page, we discover that this changing-room is, in fact, the Swimming-Pool Library itself:

> I still dream, once a month or so, of that changing-room, its slatted floor and benches. In our retrogressive slang it was known as the Swimming-Pool Library and then simply as the library, a notion fitting to the double lives we led. 'I shall be in the library,' I would announce, a prodigy of study. Sometimes I think that shadowy doorless little shelter – which is all it was really, an empty, empty place – is where at heart I want to be. Beyond it was a wire fence and then a sloping, moonlit field of grass – 'the Wilderness' – that whispered and sighed in the night breeze. Nipping into that library of uncatalogued pleasure was to step into the dark and halt. Then held breath was released, a cigarette glowed, its smoke was smelled, the substantial blackness moved, glimmered and touched. Friendly hands felt for the flies. There was never, or rarely, any kissing – no cloying, adult impurity in the lubricious innocence of what we did. (*SPL* 141)

Schoolboy slang turns the changing-room into the Swimming-Pool Library and Will begins to describe where the touch of reading takes us: 'an empty, empty place', a 'doorless little shelter' for whoever can take it there. In this 'library of uncatalogued pleasure' any identity gets lost in the wilderness, and the night itself seems to move, glimmer, and grasp. Valerie Rohy has observed that 'one function of the queer scene of reading is to enable the reader's entrance into a counter-public sphere, whether that means a sexual liaison, the ability to recognize others, or an introduction to gay and lesbian communities'.[26] In Rohy's view, 'the border of a gay world is always closer than it seems, for reading, like sexuality, marks the precarious boundary between public and private'. Whereas Rohy ties the scene of reading to sexuality, Hollinghurst's early prose ties reading to sex. In that emphasis on exteriority, identity and agency lose a little of their proficiency in making sense of the world. If reading represents a border, or a threshold, between worlds – the public and the private, the fictive and the physical – it also constitutes a wilder world unto itself, not easily or entirely open to the 'adult impurity' of interpretation. These passages are as much about need as they are belonging, as much about comfort as discovery, and as much about anonymity as identity. For Will, reading and sex are never quite separate from one another and, as they touch, they offer the solace of physical contact without the punitive and exclusionary consequences of making identity.

The kind of touch that this chapter explores culminates when a skinhead gang savagely beats Will and destroys his first-edition copy of *The Flower Beneath the Foot*. This attack gives stark outline to the limitations of an affinity to the book while reiterating the force of such attachments. Will is in East London looking for Arthur Hope, a young black man whom he took home a few weeks earlier. On the tube, Will starts reading his Firbank, an impromptu gift from Nantwich: 'the book was beautifully designed, refined but without pretension, with restfully little of the brilliant text on each thick, wide-margined page. It was a treasure, and I could not decide whether to keep it for myself or to give it to James' (*SPL* 168). Arthur is not at home and, as Will heads back to the station, the skinheads stop him near a block of high-rise flats.

Almost immediately they realize that Will is rich, gay, and involved with 'one of our little coloured brothers'. In the words of one skinhead, a 'Fuckin' nigger-fucker' (*SPL* 173). As the skinheads close in, the boundaries of class, race, and sexuality become critically legible. Waving a broken bottle in Will's face, they push him to the ground, spilling rubbish on top of him. Helpless, Will's narration slows and clogs:

> I saw two things: my beautiful new copy of *The Flower Beneath the Foot* had been jerked from my pocket in the scuffle. It was just in front of my eyes, standing on end its pages fanned open. There was a peculiar silence of several seconds, in which I thought they might be calling it off. I read the words 'perhaps I might find Harold ...' two or three times. That must have been enough to show how I cared for it. A boot slammed down on it, buckling the binding, and then again and again, grinding the pages into the warm-smelling spilt rubbish, scuffing to pulp the lachrymose saint on the wrapper. The second thing, as my head was jerked back by the hair, my cheek squashed and grazed on the ground, was a boot drawn back, very large and hard, then slamming towards my face. (*SPL* 174)

Will finds himself implicated and exposed, first by his presence near Arthur's flat and then by a desperate act of reading 'that must have been enough' to show his feeling for the book and to ensure its destruction. In the above passage, Will formulates an urgent reciprocity between his own body and the body of his book through a scrap of text: 'perhaps I might find Harold ...'. In Firbank's novel, this phrase comes from 'the Hon. Mrs Chilleywater, the "literary" wife of the first attaché'.[27] She is looking for her husband. On the pavement, her words get twisted into Will's search for Arthur. This gruesome account of book destruction, the description of an object we ourselves are holding, gives Hollinghurst's fiction an extraordinary solidity as both Will and Firbank are trampled underfoot. Here, the intimacy we associate with the touch of reading renders the violence of this episode more invasive. We feel the grinding of the pages more keenly when we can feel the grain of the page beneath our fingers. We feel the fragility of the book's binding more certainly when we can feel the binding between our hands. As Will frantically reads and re-reads 'perhaps I might find Harold', so do we and, as we imagine these words on the page of *The Flower Beneath the Foot*, we see them on the page in front of us. 'Perhaps I might find Harold' pulls us into Will's terror and pins us to the floor next to him. As the boots stamp down, we almost pull our fingers away. The touch of reading gives out.

The Swimming-Pool Library is a novel about the dispossession and humiliation of gay men across the twentieth century narrated by a young aristocrat who is apparently oblivious to this history. Will's introduction to Arthur's appalling quotidian does not bring him any closer to his erstwhile lover. Instead of seeking him out again, Will retreats back to the safety of West London. Indeed, the following chapter opens with Will lamenting the fate, not of Arthur, but of his ruined first edition. Will's sense of touch feeds an aesthetic detachment, a habitual hunger for physical beauty that sees him beaten, humiliated, and obstinately unwilling to think about why. Unlike the young man who wrote 'The Creative Uses of Homosexuality', Will does not do his homework. Although he delights in the bibliographic details of Nantwich's archive, he fails to do that 'basic research' into his life that would spare him from the humiliation he suffers at the hands of the peer (*SPL* 96). Transported by the delicate structure of *The Flower Beneath the Foot*, he does not recognize the possible dangers of travelling to Arthur's end of town. The racist and homophobic savagery of Will's beating leaves little room for the ambiguous agency of touch: it is all too clear just who is touching whom. At the same time, Will's frantic reading – and the way in which it addresses our own – demonstrates the difficult hold of literary attachment on *The Swimming-Pool Library*. In the end, the touch of reading in Hollinghurst's early prose is not about political mobilization but about personal survival: a contingency against reality; an empty space where comfort can be sought, found, and felt.

Notes

1   Eve Kosofsky Sedgwick, *Touching Feeling: Affect, Pedagogy, Performativity* (London: Duke University Press, 2003) 14.
2   Judith Butler, *Senses of the Subject* (New York: Fordham University Press, 2015) 7.

3   Ibid.
4   Leah Price, *How to Do Things with Books in Victorian Britain* (Oxford: Princeton University Press, 2012) 5.
5   Elaine Scarry, *Dreaming by the Book* (Oxford: Princeton University Press, 2001) 5.
6   Elizabeth Long, *Book Clubs: Women and the Uses of Reading in Everyday Life* (London: Chicago University Press, 2003) 11.
7   Alan Hollinghurst, 'The Art of Fiction No. 214', *Paris Review* 199 (2011), www.theparisreview.org/interviews/6116/the-art-of-fiction-no-214-alan-hollinghurst (accessed 19 January 2016).
8   Hollinghurst's concern with the legality of homosexuality is equally important to *The Swimming-Pool Library*. Virtually all of the sexual encounters the novel describes are illegal according to the 1967 Sexual Offences Act, which prohibited gay sex with men under the age of twenty-one, gay sex in public places, and gay sex with more than one partner. The first legal sexual exchange in the book is with a policeman who later entraps one of the narrator's friends into an act of public indecency.
9   Alan Hollinghurst, 'The Creative Uses of Homosexuality in the Novels of E. M. Forster, Ronald Firbank and L. P. Hartley', M.Litt thesis, University of Oxford, 1979, 47.
10 Ibid. 1.
11 Ibid.
12 Ibid. 5.
13 Ibid. 7.
14 Ibid. 137.
15 Ibid. 117.
16 Ibid. 117–18.
17 Ibid. 116–17.
18 Alan Hollinghurst, 'Introduction' in Ronald Firbank, *Three Novels* (London: Penguin, 2000) vii–xxiv: ix.
19 Ibid. xix.
20 Hollinghurst, 'The Creative Uses of Homosexuality' 127.
21 Ibid. 133.
22 Ibid. 9.
23 Georges Letissier, 'Alan Hollinghurst/Ronald Firbank: Camp Filiation as an Aesthetic of the Outrageous', *Études britanniques contemporaines* 45 (2013), http://ebc.revues.org/742 (accessed 19 January 2016).
24 Alan Hollinghurst, 'Saved by Art: The Shy, Steely, Original Ronald Firbank', *Times Literary Supplement* 17 November 2006, 12–15: 15.
25 Ibid. 15.
26 Valerie Rohy, *Lost Causes: Narrative, Etiology, and Queer Theory* (New York: Oxford University Press, 2015) 116.
27 Ronald Firbank, *The Flower Beneath the Foot* (London: Richards, 1923) 103.

3

Poetry, parody, porn and prose

Michèle Mendelssohn

In 1982, Alan Hollinghurst published a collection of poems he called *Confidential Chats with Boys*. He introduced the topic of his lyric conversation matter-of-factly:

> There are things in trousers called men,
> almost too well-mannered, passing
> as gentlemen – human skunks
> hatched from rattlesnakes' eggs.

> You meet them in fashionable hotels
> where families stay, playing croquet
> and the gallant, sought after for charades;
> their impersonations are famous. (*CCB* 1)

When he wrote this, aged twenty-eight, Hollinghurst was not yet known for his literary impostures and impressions. That was still to come. But that mischievous last line performs a masquerade of its own. Lift its mask and the poem's impersonation reveals itself: the first lines are cribbed from a little-known early twentieth-century sexual hygiene guide. This borrowing has usually gone unnoticed, but Hollinghurst's skilful literary performances have not. They have made him as famous as the gallants and gentlemen in his poem. This chapter explores the playful parodies and erotic charades that pervade Hollinghurst's work, from the poems he published in the 1970s to novels from the 1980s to early 2000s, including *The Swimming-Pool Library*, *The Folding Star* and *The Line of Beauty*. How does Hollinghurst use literary and visual allusions? And how do these allusions renegotiate the parameters of camp? His dirty-looking stories prompt double-takes and repay a second, closer examination with insights into the human condition that go beyond the frisson induced by the first wink.

Looking again at *Confidential Chats with Boys*, we can see that those lines are not the only ones he borrowed. In fact, the title of Hollinghurst's collection is taken from Dr William Lee Howard's 1911 manual, *Confidential Chats with Boys*. In this book on the birds and bees, the avuncular fifty-three-year-old author presented himself as the friendly face of sexual hygiene although his instructions veered towards the bizarre. Howard explained the facts of life but illustrated them with detailed scenarios intended to teach his young readers to be vigilant of the 'perverts' who might be in their midst:

> There are things in trousers called men, so vile that they wait in hiding for the innocent boy. These things are generally well dressed, well mannered – too well mannered in fact – and pass as gentlemen; but they are really human skunks hatched from rattlesnakes' eggs. They hang around fashionable summer hotels, city boarding houses and hotels where families live. They fool your mothers and sisters; ... Look out for these vermin, be suspicious of any man in trousers who avoids real men, who never enters or takes interest in manly sports, who tries to see you alone and prefers to go in bathing with boys instead of men. Don't go to drive or walk with these things, for all the time they are only waiting to teach boys to help them in self-abuse or something far nastier.[1]

Howard was part of a cohort of American physicians who promoted the hypothesis that homosexuality resulted from sinful behaviour, rather than from the manifestation of a biological inheritance.[2] Homosexuality was perverse but 'a vice rather than a disease', according to one of Howard's medical associates.[3] 'Never trust yourself in bed with a boy or man', Howard cautioned: 'Go without sleeping rather than have that "first time" happen to you.'[4] 'Many boys will be tempted to talk and play with each other' and thousands, he claimed, had begun to practise 'self-abuse' by sleeping together.

If we scratch beneath the surface prejudice, his comments reveal expertise on late nineteenth- and early twentieth-century gay cruising. Howard probably acquired most of this connoisseurship at his Baltimore clinic, where he specialized in the treatment of neurotic diseases. Born in Hartford, Connecticut in 1860, Howard was privately tutored in England and France, before studying at European universities including Oxford, Bonn and Göttingen. He served on a whaling ship, travelled from Africa to Iceland and covered the Sudan and Siberia for the *New*

York Herald. It is possible that his acquaintance with sexual perversion predated his career as a physician. After taking his medical degree at the University of Vermont in 1890, he remained something of a maverick, venturing into controversial areas of medicine and promoting then-unorthodox treatments, including hypnotism and mental stimulation through laughter (he said Mark Twain had proven this to him).[5] He crusaded for sex education in American high schools and pronounced on topics ranging from perversion, to dipsomania, marriage, race and sexual problems. He found the time to write a novel called *The Perverts,* as well as books promising *Plain Facts on Sex Hygiene* and *Sex Problems Solved,* articles offering 'Some Subjective Hints of the Morphine Habit' and advice on 'How to make Yourself Germ-Proof'.[6] Advocating 'right sex living', as he called it, became his life's mission.[7]

In the words of his publisher, Howard believed that 'sex knowledge judiciously imparted is the greatest insurance towards development of sterling manhood and womanhood'.[8] Howard claimed that 'the highest aim of the medical profession is to prevent physical and moral disease by teaching people the laws of health'.[9] These laws included the avoidance of same-sex and mixed-race relationships. In *Confidential Chats with Boys,* Howard condemned the goody-goody and the sissy as 'two specimens of half-boys [that] are detestable to all real men and women'.[10] Mixed-race relationships, like same-sex desire, were a sin against nature. 'We have too many lion and tiger marriages in our own society',[11] he wrote in *Confidential Chats with Boys,* as if mixed-race relationships were comparable to Noah loading mismatched animals into his ark. He claimed Nature had good reasons for making it impossible for a mule (a cross between a donkey and a horse) to reproduce. Howard encouraged his young readers to bear this fact in mind when they thought about their own relationships. He directed the same message to his medical colleagues. In one scientific article, he claimed that those 'who would have the African brought into social relations with the white woman' overlooked that 'the negro ..., untrammelled and free from control, is rapidly showing atavistic [health and behavioural] tendencies'.[12] Howard died in 1918. The medical establishment memorialized him as 'an eccentric, irresponsible character'.[13]

When Alan Hollinghurst was thirteen, in 1967, homosexuality was decriminalized in England. When he was fourteen, he discovered Howard's *Confidential Chats with Boys* in a cupboard amid a jumble of old books. Howard's book had entered the Hollinghurst family home when an aunt gave it to his parents, who never mentioned it. Hollinghurst was exactly the age of Howard's ideal boy-reader, but he was far from impressionable. 'I read it rather furtively', he says, 'but also in a mood of astonished hilarity.'[14] He shrugged off Howard's homophobia. By 1982, the year Hollinghurst published his *Confidential Chats with Boys*, homosexuality had been decriminalized in Northern Ireland and Scotland. A year later, his friend Alexander Nairne, then the director of the Institute of Contemporary Arts, sent him to the United States to interview the legendary gay photographer Robert Mapplethorpe. This was Hollinghurst's first visit to the United States. 'I knew nothing more about photography than any vaguely artistic or literary person did, at that age', Hollinghurst has said in interview: 'It was a rather extraordinary introduction to New York for this shy, nervous, literary Englishman!'[15] The chats with boys Hollinghurst had in the 1980s were nothing like those Howard had imagined in his book. The times were changing fast and for the better, but Howard's 'title was irresistible', Hollinghurst says.[16] By choosing to give his poems Howard's title, Hollinghurst allied parody and pleasure, as well as covertly taking aim at the ideas behind the original. It was an opportune decision that invited his readers to share his astonished hilarity. That merriment was short-lived: during the summer of 1982, Terrence Higgins, one of the first victims of an AIDS-related illness in the UK, passed away.

The ideological implications of parody that emerged in the 1980s and 1990s enabled marginalized groups such as feminists, African-Americans and gays to rethink intertextuality in politicized ways, as Linda Hutcheon has pointed out.[17] 'Parody is clearly a formal phenomenon – a bitextual synthesis or dialogic relation between texts', she explains, but 'without the consciousness (and then interpretation) of that discursive doubling by the perceiver, how could parody actually be said to exist, much less "work"?'[18] Divided into five numbered sections, Hollinghurst's *Confidential Chats with Boys* contains several excerpts from Howard's book. The poem's parody works by meeting prejudice face on – and meting out poetic justice. Because his quotations are unattributed, however, they present a set of traps rigged to catch any reader who reads them literally. This is particularly the case with the first stanza, with which this chapter opens. In the absence of the conventional acknowledgement apparatus, the poem risks being read as homage. Yet also reduces this risk by dropping enough hints for readers to infer that it is asking to be read obliquely – not straight. Take, for example, the advice Hollinghurst's mock agony uncle shares in the first section's final quatrain:

> Keep your eye on that jug,
> that candlestick, and when he moves,
> hit him to leave him scarred:
> scar the skunk and coward for life. (*CCB* 1)

Read literally, his incitement to homophobic violence sounds like advice from a well-meaning protector of moral and sexual purity. In a sense, that's what it is: Hollinghurst's quatrain is a direct distillation of Howard's recommendations. But that is not how it comes across.

While Howard advises that 'sometimes it is necessary to smash a boy who makes evil suggestions to you,' Hollinghurst's poem questions the recommendation.[19] 'If you should be so situated that you find yourself in bed with a man,' Howard continues, 'keep awake with your eyes on something you can hit him with. At the slightest word or act out of the way, HIT him; hit him so hard that he will carry the scar for life. Don't be afraid, these skunks are all cowards.'[20] The poem parrots these lines like a patient mocking a quack diagnosis. The false-authority of the man of science in the first section of Hollinghurst's *Confidential Chats with Boys* shares with Robert Browning's dramatic monologues an affection for elaborate irony that turns against the poems' speakers (think of 'My Last Duchess', 'Count Gismond', 'Johannes Agricola in Meditation'). Hollinghurst, like Browning, favours a serpentine, inward-turning structure.

Hollinghurst's parodic poetry turns the sexologist's violence against him through tactical excision and compression. The possible end rhyme between 'coward' and 'Howard' suggests an *ad hominem* attack. 'Keep your eye on that jug' is about using crockery for self-defence as well as about watching out for fools (a 'juggins' or 'jughead' is someone who is easily taken in). The line is a coded statement to the reader: keep your eye on that homophobic fool. Don't be a bad reader of literature or of human behaviour. Hollinghurst himself was no jug, especially when it came to Howard's opinions on homosexuality. 'I was wise enough to know that they were archaic rubbish,' he says, 'even if not quite so archaic as to mean that certain people might not still agree with them.'[21] His ironic, tiny but transformative edits and additions enable the poem to carry out a bait-and-switch: the homophobe is put in the place of those he called 'cowards'. With its intricate allusions to be unlocked, the poem performs an ambiguous double-writing that demands double-reading. This is not clear signalling but, rather, queer signalling: ironizing that parodies the teachings of sexological science.

Where Howard played the authority, Hollinghurst winks at the reader as his own queer double, his *hypocrite lecteur, mon semblable, mon frère*. His poem demands a queer reading, which is to say one that plays on coterie knowledge exclusive to those versed in sexological matters. He puckishly transforms Howard's sociological diagnostic ('They hang around fashionable summer hotels') into a pick-up tip ('You meet them in fashionable hotels'). There are a number of other clues to the poem's mischief-making. In other sections, the speakers implicitly mock the prudish idea of children's innocence with eyebrow-raising accounts of their own less-than-innocent childhoods and impure thoughts. In the third section, the speaker (a bank manager's son, like Hollinghurst and Browning) makes covert erotic speculations by hiding in a drawer marked 'Banking Business' a 'rich investment' of clippings 'that matured their hard-core innocence' (*CCB* 3). In the fourth section, he confesses:

> When I was very young
> my thrill was travesty:
> my tiny aunt's stilettos
> were smuggled to school in a bag (*CCB* 4)

The passage thrills with violence and sexual potential. Is it travesty, transvestism or tragedy? Or all three? The aunt's stilettos may be shoes, but they are also daggers that lacerate normative ideas of masculinity with the faux-innocent question they generate:

> Was virility the first
> sortie, to *Fledermaus*,
> craning at the rail to see
> the wonderful soprano prince? (*CCB* 4)

In the fifth section, the speaker reminisces about the pleasure he found in a box of liqueur chocolates. 'Crushing the little barrels between my molars' (*CCB* 5) in a childish paroxysm of violent delight, he repeats in miniature the first section's violence against the coward.

Confidential Chats with Boys was not Hollinghurst's first foray into lyrical evocations of homosexual history. In 'Isherwood is at Santa Monica', a smirking 1978 poem, he described the gay novelist being diagnosed:

> The doctor in Berlin classed him
> as 'Infantilismus' – he tells us
> with the grin of a baby[22]

But *Confidential Chats with Boys* marked a change from this knowing, early evocation. It pointed to some of the questions that Hollinghurst would confront more explicitly in his novels, including the limitations of style, the place of trauma and the work of coterie parodies and allusions. Although he eventually turned away from poetry, Hollinghurst retained this parodic literary strategy. In *The Swimming-Pool Library* and *The*

Line of Beauty it became one of the distinctive features of his prose. When a group of skinheads accosts Will Beckwith in an alleyway in *The Swimming-Pool Library*, one of them says, 'Fucking poof!' Will thinks about what to do: 'It was an old problem: what to say, what was the snappy putdown? Clever, but not too clever. I acted out a weary sigh, and said, tight-lipped: "Actually, poof is not a word I would use."' Afterwards, Will reflects that 'to them it must have sounded a parody voice' (*SPL* 172). Will's overt rhetorical strategy clashes with the discreet tactics of Hollinghurst's Howard-appropriating lyric speaker. The consequences are tragic: soon enough, the skinheads are smacking Will's head against the concrete and tipping rubbish over him. 'It was actually happening to me', Will thinks, acknowledging the fulfilment of his expectation that he will be subject to homophobic violence, that he will inevitably be beaten because he is gay (*SPL* 174). The scene also enacts Howard's homophobic advice in *Confidential Chats with Boys*. Hollinghurst refrains from gore or sentimentality and meets the banality of such evil with a disruptive humour. Will's assault is counterbalanced by a surprising choreography: Hollinghurst manoeuvres a double scene of reading into this scene of violence. While Will is being kicked by a skinhead (becoming, in another brutal sense, a 'pansy' under his foot), he is also reading a page from Firbank's *The Flower Beneath the Foot*. At that junction in Firbank's novel, a portable altar collapses; in Hollinghurst's novel, a boot slams down on Will's book and then on his face. The book, like the fine-looking Will, was, until then, in mint condition.

But does Hollinghurst's parody-as-critique always work? Does it challenge (or at least problematize) the corrosive forces it thematizes? James Wood, for one, doesn't think so. He sees the conclusion of *The Line of Beauty* – Nick's eviction and the possibility of a positive result on his HIV test – as 'delivering itself of a critique only about the potential uses and abuses of aestheticism' that comes at the cost of

> a narrative unravelling so extreme that the book also ends up holding to a somewhat trite and anachronistic vision of the homosexual as a figure always doomed to be unhoused and exiled from happiness, solitary and lonely, without family or friends, always nostalgic for a bosom that has always, if only secretly, rejected him.[23]

True, the novel's conclusion seems to punish Nick. True, the novel is sceptical of hedonism (as others, such as Jenny Davidson, have also noted).[24] And, yes, the penultimate chapter hinges on castigatory, verbal violence against Nick – 'the little pansy' in Barry Groom's words (*LB* 476). As if paraphrasing Howard, Groom says, 'I never trusted him ... I know the type. ... They can't breed themselves, they're parasites on generous fools who can. ... A typical homo trick, of course' (*LB* 477). Soon enough Gerald Fedden, who had once welcomed Nick into his home, is repeating Groom's bilious diagnosis. 'Didn't it strike you as rather odd, a bit queer, attaching yourself to a family like this?' he asks Nick. 'It's the sort of thing you read about, it's an old homo trick. You can't have a real family, so you attach yourself to someone else's' (*LB* 481). Here the novel parodies itself while refusing to give the Barry Grooms (and William Lee Howards) of the world the last word.

At the end of *The Line of Beauty*, Nick stands on a street corner and faces the future with 'a love of the world that was shockingly unconditional. ... It wasn't just this street corner but the fact of a street corner at all that seemed, in the light of the moment, so beautiful' (501). Wood underestimates the aesthetic and metaphysical counterweight provided by this scene. The world around Nick is 'changed ... revealed. It was like a drug sensation, but without the awareness of play' (*LB* 500). Both the diction ('the fact of a street corner') and its emotional content echo Adrienne Rich's 1974 poem, 'The Fact of a Doorframe', which reflects on a cognate cultural world. Rich identified herself as a 'white, Jewish, anti-Semite, racist, anti-racist, once-married, lesbian' who used poetry to refine the relationship between internal states of being and external circumstances that she described as not 'something "out there" but something "in here" and of the essence of my condition'.[25] In Rich's poem, the speaker establishes a new relationship to the world beyond the suffering she has endured:

> Now, again, poetry,
> violent, arcane, common,
> hewn of the commonest living substance
> into archway, portal, frame
> I grasp for you, your bloodstained splinters,
> ancient and stubborn poise
> – as the earth trembles –
> burning out from the grain[26]

The doorframe, like the street corner, 'represents something concrete and material to the one who crosses over the threshold: that the doorframe exists means that one has a sure grip on reality when one ventures outside convention or tradition'.[27] Simon During calls Nick's street-corner epiphany an exploration 'across a range of registers [of] how spiritual longing and consolation may survive in, and be reconciled to, the mundane social order'.[28] 'Today', During concludes, 'spiritual gravity may inhere in the self-emptying contingencies through which we are concretely placed in history, nature, and place, and for that reason needs no other home than the immediate and the mundane.[29] Nick's experience is not necessarily optimistic, but it nevertheless acts as a historically apposite counterweight to the novel's critique of 1980s capitalism and homophobia.

Erotic ekphrasis

So far, I have analysed the ways in which Hollinghurst uses parody to playfully explore and exploit his writing's ambivalent relationship to literary precursors, including Howard, Browning, Firbank and Rich. In what follows, I examine what happens when his precursors are not literary, but visual, erotic or even pornographic. To put it another way: how are Hollinghurst's aesthetics modified when one of his lines of influence is, to use Wood's phrase, 'the line of beauty that is a boy's ass'?[30] What hidden realities do Hollinghurst's erotic allusions reveal? In his 2006 Lord Northcliffe Lecture, Hollinghurst noted that E. M. Forster abandoned the novel form because he could not homosexualize it. 'The impossibility of writing about the one thing which most determined his view of life' caused a crisis because, as Hollinghurst put it, quoting Forster, 'a forthright novel on homosexual themes was a legal impossibility, something that couldn't happen "until my death and England's".'[31] One critic has described Hollinghurst's writing as an iteration of the novel of manners, 'a sort of "reader I fucked him" rather than "reader I married him".'[32] By bringing explicit gay allusions into his novels, Hollinghurst has done more than Forster dreamed of. He has not only homosexualized the novel; he has rehumanized it.

In the 1983 essay Hollinghurst wrote for the Institute of Contemporary Art's Robert Mapplethorpe retrospective, he praised the controversial photographer of flowers and sex scenes whose studio he had visited earlier that year. Mapplethorpe 'created some of the most formally exquisite photographs of the last decade', he wrote.[33] Defending the racialized, fetishistic nature of some of Mapplethorpe's photographs, Hollinghurst insisted that if people found the pictures' 'sexuality a bit strong' or thought Mapplethorpe's 'use of loaded and stereotypical imagery insufficiently ironic', then his 'consistently witty ... handling of sexual imagery' had not been sufficiently appreciated. For Hollinghurst, the high aesthetic quality of Mapplethorpe's work trumped the question of morality. 'It is not that Mapplethorpe is unaware of the political implications of a white man shooting physically magnificent black men', Hollinghurst explained, but 'the stereotypes are transcended by a potent mood of celebration and sex.'[34]

It was as if, by describing Mapplethorpe, Hollinghurst – the shy poet who was not yet a novelist – had also sketched the blueprint on which he would later build his house of fiction. Already the house's foundations had been established by Hollinghurst's scholarship and its emphasis on late nineteenth- and early twentieth-century authors familiar with art for art's sake. Rationalizing Mapplethorpe was like building a contemporary frame of reference for himself. It was a means of examining the mechanics of a working model of the decadent cultural temperament. Yet Hollinghurst departed from Mapplethorpe in significant ways. He admired the playfulness and range of visual allusions that gave Mapplethorpe's images 'a period whiff' that had a 'naughtiness about it'. Where Mapplethorpe 'adduced second-hand imagery to express the excitements of a world which it could not directly present', Hollinghurst's fiction does the opposite: it uses second-hand pornographic imagery to present directly an erotic world ordinarily excluded from the literary and artistic canon.

The debts to gay pornography in Hollinghurst's novels have been hiding in plain sight and, to my knowledge, they have never been analysed. Tom of Finland is one of the most important sources for his erotic ekphrasis. Tom's hypermasculine men – lumberjacks, farmhands, roughnecks, shower boys, workers, bikers, leathered men and, beginning in the mid-1980s, blacks and punks – have been credited with transforming cruising culture as well as enabling generations of gay men to embrace and explore their sexuality. In his debut novel, *The Swimming-Pool Library*, Hollinghurst decorated Lord Charles Nantwich's home with 'Romans with great big willies, Tom of Finland *avant la lettre*' (*SPL* 85). In his next novel, *The Folding Star*, he dressed Matt, a freelance pornographer with a film subscription business, in denim and a Tom of Finland t-shirt (*FS* 51).

The Finnish pornographer known as Tom of Finland was born Touko Laaksonen in 1920. He moved to Helsinki in 1939 to attend art school. That year, the Finnish-German pact to repel the Russian invasion increased the German military presence in the city, and, in 1941, Finland became Germany's ally. In the 1950s, Tom became a contributor to *Physique Pictorial*, a beefcake magazine published out of Los Angeles. From his modest beginnings, Tom evolved a cult following. According to the art historian Micha Ramakers, Tom was 'one of the gay underground's cultural icons in the heady days of 70s gay lib in New York and San Francisco'.[35] 'All my early sexual experiences were with German soldiers', Tom said in a documentary filmed in 1991, the year of his death.[36] 'Their uniforms looked great!'[37] His biographers are quick to point out that his interest was 'entirely apolitical'.[38] Yet his images unabashedly exploit the uniform's erotic charge, as can be seen from the drawing chosen by the Finnish postal service for a 2014 commemorative stamp (Figure 1). 'They're not great art but they're very good' at doing what they do, the painter David Hockney has said.[39]

Tom's drawings have been labelled 'macho camp'.[40] His hypermasculinity is hyper-inclusive: in Tom's world, no one escapes penetration. According

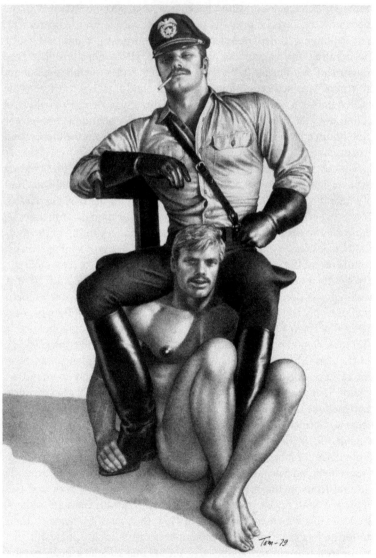

1 Tom of Finland (Touko Laaksonen), *Untitled*, 1979, graphite on paper.

to Hollinghurst, Tom created 'a world of elemental virility' in which masculine types copulate 'in a mood of almost infantile gratification, sanctioned by unwavering opportunity'.[41] For Camille Paglia, the masculinity of Tom's men 'broke, for good or ill, with the cultural legacy of the brilliant Oscar Wilde, who promoted and flamboyantly embodied the androgynous aesthete'.[42] Tom frees his characters from 'entrenched prerogatives' by the 'consistently shifting balances of power' between them, Ramakers observes.[43] 'By eroticizing the symbols of heterosexual masculinity and making them rebound onto themselves, Tom challenged the qualities read into them by straight society.'

In the summer of 2015, New York's Artists Space mounted the first comprehensive American exhibition of Tom's work. *The New Yorker's* art critic warned 'a little of Tom goes a long way: his obsession with power, youth, and beauty may not be yours'.[44] It is certainly Edward Manners's. *The Folding Star* opens with Edward's arrival in Belgium, a photo-booth snapshot in hand. This is a picture of seventeen-year-old Luc, who will become his pupil. Yet Edward is already intimate with an *ur*-version of Luc: one culled from gay pornography of the Tom of Finland variety. He is obsessed by a conflation of these two Lucs – the real photo and the fantasy porno. 'I recalled distantly having taught him already in dreams' (*FS* 8), Edward reflects before meeting the boy, as if remembering a prehistoric teacher–pupil fantasy.

Hollinghurst has described Tom's work as obsessive, exaggeratedly sexual and repetitive. The genius and the weakness of Tom's drawings, Hollinghurst observes, is that they have 'a fantasist's monomaniacal similarity. He created a whole type of men, square-jawed, thick-lipped, with powerfully muscular bodies, packed jutting asses and huge cocks'[45] (Figure 2). *The Folding Star* revels in repeating and transforming such erotic visions. When Edward finally sees Luc in the flesh, the boy is uncannily familiar: his long nose, high cheekbones, puckering lips and narrow eyes give him the appearance of a Tom of Finland blonde Aztec, 'lean and broad-shouldered ... [with a] big flattish backside' (*FS* 28). 'To me of course he wasn't quite new', Edward admits (*FS* 28). Luc 'was a slightly kitsch piece of work from an artist who carved in alabaster like flushed hard honey' (*FS* 58). He is Edward's erotic dream come true.

Reading *The Folding Star* can be like looking at a portfolio of vivid sketches inspired by Tom. The similarities are remarkable: Edward's desires seem culled from Tom's bar scenes (in the illustration accompanying Hollinghurst's Mapplethorpe essay, two men share a young blond Luc-alike).[46] *The Folding Star's* Hermitage evokes Tom's erotic woodland encounters (Figure 3). There are oblique visual allusions to Tom when Edward and Dawn go camping, as well as in the novel's

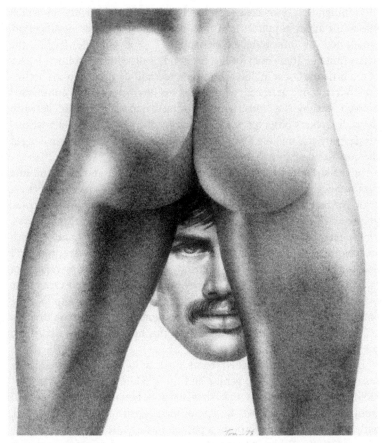

2 Tom of Finland (Touko Laaksonen), *Untitled*, 1978, graphite on paper.

shower scenes (such as when Edward is distracted by two boys – one dark, one blond – who perform a 'sort of improvised act … like someone simulating pleasure in a film' (*FS* 80)). In chapter 8, when Edward and Matt follow Luc and his friends to the beach, the men's fantasies seem to follow on from Tom's 1970s 'Beach Boys' series. Under Edward's infatuated gaze, Luc becomes 'a golden dream made solid flesh' (*FS* 106). 'Well, he's okay,' Matt, the straight-talking pornographer, says, but 'the other kid … has got a *whopper*. A total fucking monster between his legs.'

'Tom of Finland extemporized, in simple and explicit line-drawings, a fantasy-world of uncomplicated and exaggerated male sexuality,'[47] Hollinghurst explains. His own approach has been rather more subtle. His erotics elude the repetitiveness and predictability that are the

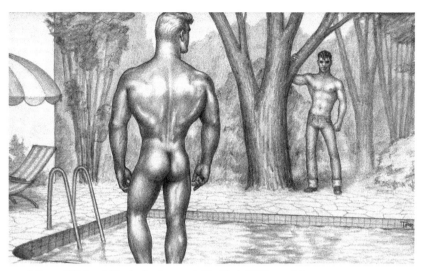

3 Tom of Finland (Touko Laaksonen), *Untitled*, 1958, graphite on paper.

pornographer's trademark. When he rewrote Tom's visual alphabet, Hollinghurst also spelled out what Tom had left out: the consequences of ostensibly simple sexual encounters. In *The Folding Star*, the art-obsessed Paul Echevin, Edward's employer at the Orst Museum, reveals his wartime love affair with Willem, a burly local militiaman whom Paul later discovers is a German collaborator. 'My guilt was suddenly ten times deeper', he confesses, '[because] it was in uniform. But at the same time there was a defiant thrill, as if I was a kind of double agent myself' (*FS* 410). Like Tom of Finland, Paul despises Nazi politics (384), yet he romanticizes his Nazi lover as 'a woodlander' (*FS* 408) while also fantasizing about being swept away by 'huge, blond, actually rather Aryan-looking Americans' (*FS* 410).

Just as Tom's illustrations muse on the attractions of uniformed men who happen to have appalling political allegiances, in *The Swimming-Pool Library*, Will Beckwith reflects on how magnetically attractive skinheads are. 'Cretinously simplified to booted feet, bum and bullet head, they [skinheads] had some, if not all, of the things one was looking for' (*SPL* 172). Hollinghurst's confrontation pits wit against terse brutality and queers both. Before his assault, Will remembers a weekend spent with a skinhead he picked up in Camden Town. Then, focusing on the men menacing him, he notices that one of them, 'braces hoisting his jeans up around a fat ass and a fat dick, was very good. I looked at him for only a second; a phrase from the Firbank I had just been reading came back to me: "Très gutter, ma'am'" (*SPL* 170). This exemplifies Hollinghurst's version of camp: a teetering fairy-butch sensibility that relies on simultaneously exploiting and exploding the conventions it mines.

Camp and carnival

The novels' erotic ekphrasis is not slavishly mimetic of Tom, Mapplethorpe or erotic gay magazines such as *Physique Pictorial*, though it undoubtedly references the protocols and stereotypes of gay art and pornography. In *The Folding Star*, when Edward masturbates to a mental image of Luc, their intimacy feels real because 'I knew his body better than he did himself' (*FS* 118). Likewise, Hollinghurst knows his characters' bodies better than Tom's or anyone else's. His erotic carnivalesques enact a Bakhtinian mode that uses humour and chaos to subvert traditional conventions. The novels lampoon old-fashioned structures through bodily excess; they commingle high literature with low visual culture.

There are continuities between Hollinghurst's linguistically and sexually obsessed characters and the stylized hyper-aesthetic of the novels they inhabit. Hollinghurst's literary and visual quotations harness a recharged version of camp – a mode originally associated with a counter-cultural impulse but one that has mainstream viability today. In recent years, critics have challenged Susan Sontag's well-known definition of camp as 'a vision of the world in terms of style ... a mode of seduction ... which employs flamboyant mannerisms susceptible of the double inter-pretation.'[48] Some have objected to her depoliticization of camp, arguing instead that it 'embodies a specifically queer cultural critique.'[49] Despite these debates over who owns camp, Hollinghurst's novels succeed in having it both ways: they go beyond the boundaries of a politicized, identity-specific mode in service of a humanism that includes, but is not limited to, homosexuality.

Unlike Tom's art, Hollinghurst's novels depict what happens in between the carnivals. Though Hollinghurst's world retains elements of this playful abundance, it also catalogues the emotional and existential famines between the sexual and intellectual feasts. The allusions that bind the characters to rich literary and visual worlds often leave them alone with their thoughts and unable to connect with others. Edward initiates connection through literary codes that often remain undeciphered, because not understood, by the men he loves. While trying to pick up a man in a bar, Edward says, 'Books are a load of crap.' His ironic quotation from Philip Larkin's 'A Study of Reading Habits' goes unrecognized. The man walks away. All Edward gets, he reflects, is 'the private and lonely satisfaction of my quotation' (*FS* 9). Hollinghurst does not supply the reference to this ironic poem on the quasi-masturbatory pleasures of reading. Instead, he makes the sterile fancies of Larkin's bookish speaker ('the women I clubbed with sex!')[50] doubly ironic by dealing Edward the same sexless fate. 'I was always spoiling things with my quotations', Edward thinks, after a reference to Milton is lost on another lover (*FS* 247). His intellectual and literary isolation overshadows the ecstasy of any sexual consummation he achieves. After shepherding his beloved pupil, Luc, into bed, he thinks, 'it felt both a comfort and a sadness to live so much more than him in the world of metaphors and puns' (*FS* 339). Sex cannot make up for everything else: a moment of connection does not soften a fundamental disconnect.

One of Hollinghurst's leitmotifs is the way in which allusions occlude and exclude. *The Folding Star*'s 'characters observe each other from their own private worlds, but find it very hard to communicate', Hollinghurst has said in interview, and he takes a serious interest in chronicling his characters' failures to connect.[51] One of the narrative strategies he employs is to highlight (not remedy) these broken bonds through camp. *The Line of Beauty* exemplifies this method. At Leo's modest family flat in Willesden, Nick turns up his nose at Mrs Charles's religious knick-knacks and tracts. 'I see you been looking at my picture there, of the Lord Jesus in the carpenter's shop', Leo's mother offers, gesturing to her reproduction of Holman Hunt's 1870–3 painting, *The Shadow of Death* (*LB* 160). Nick reacts with donnish hubris to her overture because 'he felt he owned, all ironically and art-historically, more than her, a mere credulous Christian' (*LB* 161). While chronicling this drama of disconnection, the passage is electrified by the intrusion of camp. Nick has not only been looking at the Holman Hunt. The narrator notes that Nick has also been 'taking an almost paedophilic interest' in the childhood portraits of Leo, and that he is imagining 'a vivid image' of Leo ejaculating on the ginger leather of his mother's three-piece suite (*LB* 154–5). The scene balances tragedy against ridiculousness by combining realist mimesis and pornographic fantasy into a sublimely carnivalesque and camp concoction. Meanwhile, Leo, seated below the painting, offers himself as a diversion by stretching his body out in imitation of Christ's muscular, bare-chested contraposto (*LB* 162). Leo redirects the strained conversation, saving Nick from further embarrassment. 'It was the kind of camp you see sometimes in observant children', the narrator notes (*LB* 163). Leo's shadow looms on the wall behind him (an ekphrasis of Jesus's shadow in Hunt's painting) and augurs his death later in the novel. The scene anxiously paints a domestic miniature of 1980s Britain that brings together eros and AIDS, aesthetics and politics, intellectual snobbery and layman's literalism, existential uncertainties and the consolations of belief. There are parallels between Hollinghurst's concerns and Hunt's. According to the art historian Carol Jacobi, *The Shadow of Death* 'is typical of the striking focus on the domestic in Pre-Raphaelite art ... Hunt's preoccupation with subjectivity and its exploration through the family drama reflects a renegotiation of relationships that paralleled broader social changes', including wavering faith, the democratization of art, and high infant mortality.[52]

Grief is the opposite of pornography: it has different modes of attention and demands different forms of engagement. Where pornography enables the viewer to put himself into the scenario – to create an immediate and physical connection with others' pleasures – grief highlights the unbridgeable gaps between people. If pornography is a playground for the ego, grief is a testing ground for the self.

Erotic, literary and visual allusions measure the distance between Hollinghurst's characters. This is more than a postmodern pose. Turning from poetry to prose fiction enabled him to expand his use of allusion, camp and parody into pathos, eros, humour and verbal subterfuge. His works offer no solutions, but they relentlessly seek connection, even as it eludes them and they remain suspicious of it. In doing so, they redirect the narratives beyond their immediate allusions, towards darker truths about the human condition.

At the end of *The Line of Beauty*, camp Leo becomes a secular saint for the 1980s. After his death from AIDS, his ashes live above his mother's gas fire, alongside figures of Jesus and the Virgin Mary. When he is told about his lover's death, Nick remembers how Leo had called for him 'one morning, unannounced, and changed his life' (*LB* 398). Nick's reflections rehearse the idiom of religious awakening and a secular language of love and loss. He worries that 'his own forms of truth could look like insincerity to others' (*LB* 411), yet there is no cynicism to the scene. No camp, no parody, no narrow identity politics. Only a human truth. Hollinghurst portrays nothing more (or less) than the stark reality of grief in all its existential awfulness.

Acknowledgements

I would like to thank Laura Ashe, Alexandra Harris, Erica McAlpine, Kathryn Murphy and Maria del Pilar Blanco for their invaluable comments on drafts of this chapter.

Notes

1   William Lee Howard, *Confidential Chats with Boys* (London: Richards, 1913) 103.
2   Jay Hatheway, *The Gilded Age Construction of Modern American Homophobia* (Basingstoke: Palgrave Macmillan, 2003) 147.
3   Quoted in ibid. 147.
4   Howard, *Confidential Chats with Boys* 102.
5   William Lee Howard, *Breathe and Be Well* (New York: Clode, 1916) 18.
6   William Lee Howard, 'Some Subjective Hints of the Morphine Habit', *Medical News* 16 January 1904: 113; Howard, 'How to Make Yourself Germ-Proof', *Munsey's Magazine* September 1911: 771–5.
7   Howard, *Breathe and Be Well* n. p.
8   Ibid.
9   William Lee Howard, 'The Feminization of the High-School', *The Arena* 35.199 (1906) 593.
10 Howard, *Confidential Chats with Boys* 99.
11 Ibid. 63
12 William Lee Howard, 'The Negro as a Distinct Ethnic Factor in Civilization', *Medical News* 84.19 (1903) 905.
13 Howard A. Kelly and Walter L. Burrage, *American Medical Biographies* (Baltimore: Norman Remington, 1920) 567–8 quoted in *The American New Woman Revisited: A Reader, 1894–1930*, ed. Martha H. Patterson (London: Rutgers University Press, 2008) 279.
14 Alan Hollinghurst, e-mail to the author, 30 December 2014.
15 Julian Gewirtz, 'Interview', *Prac Crit* June 2015, www.praccrit.com/interviews/from-confidential-chats-with-boys-interview-by-julian-gewirtz/ (accessed 19 January 2016).
16 Alan Hollinghurst, e-mail to the author, 30 December 2014.
17 Linda Hutcheon, *A Theory of Parody: The Teaching of 20th Century Art Forms* (Urbana: University of Illinois Press, 2000) xiii.
18 Ibid.
19 Howard, *Confidential Chats with Boys* 78.
20 Ibid. 103–4.
21 Alan Hollinghurst, e-mail to the author, 6 January 2015.
22 Alan Hollinghurst, 'Isherwood is at Santa Monica', *Poetry: Introduction 4* (London: Faber, 1978) 74.
23 James Wood, 'The Ogee Curve' [Review of *The Line of Beauty*], *The New Republic* 9 December 2004, 47–9.
24 Jenny Davidson, *Reading Style: A Life in Sentences* (New York: Columbia University Press, 2014) 162.
25 Rich quoted in Victor Luftig, 'Something Will Happen to You who Read', *Irish University Review* 23.1 (Spring–Summer 1993) 57–66: 62.
26 Adrienne Rich, 'The Fact of a Doorframe', *Adrienne Rich's Poetry and Prose*, eds Albert Gelpi and Barbara Charlesworth Gelpi (New York: Norton, 1993) 62–3.

27   Cheri Colby Langdell, *Adrienne Rich: The Moment of Change* (Westport CT: Greenwood, 2004) 159.

28   Simon During, 'Completing Secularism: The Mundane in the Neoliberal Era', *Varieties of Secularism in a Secular Age*, eds Craig J. Calhoun, Jonathan VanAntwerpen and Michael Warner (Cambridge MA: Harvard University Press, 2010) 105–25: 123.

29   Ibid. 125.

30   Wood, 'The Ogee Curve'.

31   Alan Hollinghurst, 'Saved by Art, the Shy, Steely, Original Firbank', *Times Literary Supplement* 17 November 2006, 12–15: 15. The essay is an edited version of the third of the 2006 Lord Northcliffe Lectures given at University College London.

32   Pat Wheeler, 'Alan Hollinghurst' in *Contemporary British and Irish Fiction: An Introduction through Interviews*, eds Sharon Monteith, Jenny Newman and Pat Wheeler (London: Arnold, 2004) 71–86: 82.

33   Alan Hollinghurst, 'Robert Mapplethorpe' in *Robert Mapplethorpe: 1970–1983* (London: Institute of Contemporary Arts, 1983) 8–17: 9.

34   Hollinghurst, 'Robert Mapplethorpe' 9.

35   *Tom of Finland: The Art of Pleasure*, ed. Micha Ramakers (Cologne: Taschen, 2002) 11.

36   Quoted in Dian Hanson, *TOM: The Comics* (Cologne: Taschen, 2011) 6.

37   Quoted in Micha Ramakers, *Dirty Pictures: Tom of Finland, Masculinity, and Homosexuality* (New York: Macmillan, 2001) 162.

38   Hanson, *TOM* 7.

39   Quoted in Ramakers, *Dirty Pictures* 17.

40   Quoted in ibid. 118.

41   Hollinghurst, 'Robert Mapplethorpe' 11.

42   Camille Paglia, 'Sex Quest' in *Tom of Finland: XXL*, ed. Dian Hanson (Cologne: Taschen, 2009) 82.

43   Ramakers, *Tom of Finland: The Art of Pleasure* 28.

44   'Tom of Finland: The Pleasure of Play', *The New Yorker* 26 June 2015, www. newyorker.com/goings-on-about-town/art/tom-of-finland-the-pleasure-of-play (accessed 19 January 2016).

45   Hollinghurst, 'Robert Mapplethorpe' 11.

46   Ibid.

47   Ibid.

48   Susan Sontag, 'Notes on "Camp"' in *Against Interpretation* (New York: Farrar, Straus & Giroux, 1966) 275–92: 287.

49   Moe Meyer, *The Politics and Poetics of Camp* (London: Routledge, 1994) 1, 18. Meyer argues that camp is 'the only process by which the queer is able to enter representation and to produce social visibility' in the dominant culture. Proponents of this interpretation contend that camp stems from a gay subculture that negotiates, opposes, challenges and transgresses heterosexual monopoly.

50   Philip Larkin, 'A Study of Reading Habits' in *Collected Poems*, ed. Anthony Thwaite (London: Farrar, Straus and Giroux, 1988) 131.

51   Quoted in Wheeler, 'Alan Hollinghurst' 79.

52   Carol Jacobi, 'William Holman Hunt, 1827–1910' in *The Cambridge Companion to the Pre-Raphaelites*, ed. Elizabeth Prettejohn (Cambridge: Cambridge University Press) 116–32: 130.

4

Race, empire and
The Swimming-Pool Library

John McLeod

In 'Saved by Art', Alan Hollinghurst shapes a compelling and considered appreciation of the novels of Ronald Firbank. He juxtaposes their baroque, attenuated plots, treasured inconsequentiality and exquisite *bon mots* with the expansive and forensic writing of Marcel Proust and Henry James. 'Firbank achieved his highly complex originality', Hollinghurst writes, 'not by expansion but by a drastic compression: instead of putting more and more in, he left almost everything out.'[1] William Beckwith, the narrator of *The Swimming-Pool Library*, would undoubtedly share such enthusiasm. As he sits on a London Underground train reading a copy of Firbank's *Valmouth* (1919) lent to him by his best friend James, he confesses to expecting Firbank to be 'a supremely frivolous and silly author. I was surprised to find how difficult, witty and relentless he was' (*SPL* 54). From the convoluted plot of *Valmouth*, both knotted and loose, Will chooses to relate a moment from Chapter V, when the elderly Lady Parvula de Panzoust requisitions a black masseuse, Mrs Yajñavalkya, to help her meet a farm boy, David Tooke, whom she fancies. Will delights in the characterization of Mrs Yaj (as she is known), who 'spoke in a wonderful black pidgin, prinked out with more exotic turns of phrase' (*SPL* 54). Unconcerned that there is no such thing as 'black pidgin' in any meaningful sense, Will does not seem perturbed that Mrs Yajñavalkya's characterization might make for uncomfortable reading at the end of the twentieth century. In addition to her broken English – 'Creator ob de universe has cast us all in de same mould; and dat's vot I alvays say'[2] – which rhetorically stylizes her otherness, Firbank persistently emphasizes her blackness by referring to her, variously, as 'the negress' or 'the Oriental masseuse', or as possessing 'a glinting, sooty face' (effectively puncturing her aspiration to exist beyond the prejudices of race).[3] Her cultural provenance is deliberately withheld so that she and her family come to stand for a kaleidoscopic and undifferentiated exotic otherness. She uses the Arabic word for God, 'Allah', but speaks of love as attaining Nirvana, which has both Buddhist and Hindu associations. One brother, Djali, lives in 'Ujiji Land' (presumably in sub-Saharan Africa) while another, Boujaja, is in Polynesian 'Taihaiti'.[4] When Mrs Yaj speaks to her niece Niri-Esther, Lady Parvula hears a 'twitter of negro voices'.[5] If *Valmouth* leaves 'almost everything out', it nevertheless carries with it problematic ways of constructing otherness that are common in the early twentieth century and reveals them in frivolous yet consequential stylistic markings of race.

As he reads, Will realizes that under Firbank's dazzling 'highly inflected nonsense' there may be 'covert meaning' (*SPL* 54) at work, but he does not elaborate upon what it might be, choosing instead to delight here in the confection of exotica. Hollinghurst, however, is very much interested in such 'covert meaning', and especially the points of contact between the colonialist confections of the early century and the contemporary conditions of the 1980s. *The Swimming-Pool Library* both indicates and ironizes the culpability of gay cultural life in the neocolonialism that marks and mars the postcolonial metropolis. Hollinghurst fashions a Firbankian narrator whose tale both exemplifies that complicity but carries within it 'covert' critical traction. The novel thoughtfully attends to the ongoing vexed relations between gay marginality and political and institutional conformity and thinks about the contradictions created when those who pursued what were once criminalized sexual lives are also found at the heart of the political, colonial and judicial establishment that has often pursued a politics of race.[6] Rather than offer, in his first novel, an image of gay victimization and marginality, Hollinghurst writes a novel of complicities and repetitions that are hard to break. This is a world where the collusion of gay establishment figures such as Lord Charles Nantwich in the judicial operations of colonial administration overseas are replicated in the bohemian philandering of Will, an Oxford graduate who pursues a sexual obsession with exoticized black men as he traverses the multiracial demography of postcolonial London in the early 1980s.[7]

Throughout his career, Hollinghurst has been fascinated by lines of descent – cultural, national, artistic, familial. He frequently focuses on the repetitions and remains that conjoin the present to the allegedly foreign country of the past. As proposed by the form and title of his 2011 novel *The Stranger's Child*, life may be much more intimately, umbilically related to that which can appear distant or unfamiliar, historically remote. Such concerns are clearly established in *The Swimming-Pool Library* and in *The Folding Star*. In the latter, Hollinghurst ruminates on lineages of artistic and historical connection as well as the intimacies between generations (conjured memorably in Edward Manners's thirtysomething obsession with the divinely adolescent Luc). Hollinghurst's early work, too, is notable for its use of flawed, habitually narcissistic narrators whose attitudes and ways of seeing are often deployed for the purposes of sensitive and critical authorial inquiry. In *The Swimming Pool Library*, the loquacious, self-regarding and intellectually capable figure of Will is made to think again about his sexual and racial predilections as indebted to a distinctly colonial inheritance. It is an inheritance which, prior to the novel's memorable summer of loving, he has rarely considered in any kind of depth. As his close friend James remarks,

> Isn't there a kind of blind spot ... for that period just before one was born? One knows about the Second World War, one knows about Suez, I suppose, but what people were actually getting up to in those years ... There's an empty, motiveless space until one appears on the scene. (*SPL* 279)

Yet a cognizance of historical legacies does not immediately lead to a change in attitude. Will's initially carefree engagement with the wisdom discovered through research indexes an irresolvable disquiet at the novel's heart concerning its representation of race after Empire. Hollinghurst probes the extent to which Will's social milieu is able to view race differently, beyond the lenses of colonial exotica and erotica derived from Empire's designs. Re-reading the past may not readily deliver the means to prepare a different future where the constraints of yesteryear give way to new relations that do not uphold the inequities of old. Can the novel's characters regard race beyond the protocols of racism, or does their vision remain overdetermined by the discursive mechanics of another age? And if they do recognize their complicity in race thinking, does anything necessarily change?

The plot of *The Swimming-Pool Library* has as its fulcrum the tasks of reading and writing. Will agrees, somewhat half-heartedly, to write the life-story of Charles Nantwich, a former colonial officer who had been stationed in Africa. Charles shares Will's educational and sexual provenance. They meet, quite by chance it seems, when Charles collapses in a public lavatory which Will had entered in the hope of discovering some sexual enjoyment. To aid his task, Will is given access to Charles's journals that record the comings and goings of life chiefly in Oxford, Sudan, Egypt and inter-war London. These frequently mention Charles's erotic fascination with the black men he encounters in both metropolitan and colonial spaces. Will eventually learns that Charles's arrest after the war and imprisonment for cottaging was connected to Will's distinguished grandfather and benefactor, Sir Denis Beckwith, who spent part of his career seeking to reform the Sexual Offences Act as part of his 'crusade to eradicate male vice' (*SPL* 260 – italics in original). In Brenda Cooper's words, Charles's colonial history and later incarceration 'contextualises Will's own attraction to black men, along with his desire for working-class boys' and enables Will to recover 'the history of the criminalisa-tion of homosexuality'[8] – although, as we shall see, Will is already rather more knowing of Empire's legacies than Cooper assumes. If Will is in one respect the descendant of a form of gay subcultural life located firmly at the heart of the British establishment, he is also the nonchalant inheritor of the imperious designs of the British elite whose exoticizing predilections during colonial service find their repetition in London of the 1980s. Late in the novel, Charles admits to 'this absolute adoration of black people ... . I've always had to be among them, you know, negroes, and I've always gone straight for them' (*SPL* 242). When Will tells his friend James that the journals describe Charles's sexual obsession with the native Sudanese – 'He has only to see the back of a black hand or the curl of a black lip and he's off' – James's retort is as sharp as a paper cut: 'I thought you were rather the same' (*SPL* 178).

The intercalation of Will's narrative with Charles's journals emphasizes the novel's formal mirroring of these characters' lives more than their distinctiveness. This narrative strategy challenges the assumption that contemporary London is a more permissive or liberal environment than in the days before the decriminalization of homosexuality in 1967. No surprise, then, that Will tells us early in the novel that his star sign is Gemini, the twins: 'a child of the ambiguous early summer, tugged between two versions of myself, one of them hedonist and the other – a little in the background these days – an almost scholarly figure with a faintly puritanical set to mouth' (*SPL* 4). Will's characterization depends upon a careful act of doubling on Hollinghurst's part that pervades the novel as a whole. His life is clearly twinned with that of Charles, who comes to seem his fitting if not-quite-perfect double: each has been educated at Winchester and later Oxford and has more than a passing interest in photographic and cinematic representations of gay eroticism. Both frequent the Corinthian Club (or 'Corry') in Great Russell Street, which Will describes as 'a gloomy and functional underworld full of life, purpose and sexuality' (*SPL* 9).

In the first diary extract that Will reads, Charles records the intensity of his arousal for the black men he meets while at Winchester, including Webster, a mixed-race 'little fellow, smooth & brown, with luxuriant curly hair' (*SPL* 113) with whom he occasionally swims, and an unnamed

African-American soldier whom Charles encounters in a pub toilet masturbating provocatively, to his shock and delight. It is instructive that Charles eroticizes Webster's racial distinctiveness in terms of art – 'His colour, among the trees, the green water & the faded grass struck me like a Gauguin' (*SPL* 113) – and so sets him apart as an idealized and aestheticized human figure: 'I formed the impression that I was in the presence of a superior kind of person' (*SPL* 114).

This emblematization of black male bodies is a recurrent theme throughout *The Swimming-Pool Library* that circumscribes the viewpoints of both Will and Charles. It is signalled in the design that appears on the Corry's façade (Will is interested in architecture, we may recall). The Corry's broken-pedimented doorway is 'surmounted by two finely developed figures – one pensively Negroid, the other inspiredly Caucasian – who hold between them a banner with the device "Men Of All Nations"' (*SPL* 9). On the walls of Charles's study, Will spies a portrait of the eighteenth-century black boxer Bill Richmond: 'From its mandorla of gilded oak leaves a livery-clad negro turned towards us. A sky of darkening blue was sketched behind him, and the shadowy form of a palm-tree could just about be made out' (*SPL* 78).[9] Such aestheticizing representations of black nobility might suggest a sympathetic representation of black subjects, but such gestures of ennoblement and pan-racial equivalence only sustain racial objectification and exotic containment, the 'benign' face of modern racism that masks the complicity of desire with derision.[10] And while the banner 'Men Of All Nations' promises welcome without prejudice, the pensive 'Negroid' and 'inspired' Caucasian who frame the Corry's entrance hint at the unequal relations between perceived races which such confections of liberal brotherhood almost always mask and which extend across both Charles's and Will's generations.

As befitting a figure positioned to be seen as Charles's descendant or double, Will's behaviour seems to do little to dislodge neocolonial attitudes to race in the novel's postcolonial present. His unabashed negrophilia exposes the more pernicious side to Charles's aestheticization of colonial subjects and suggests a line of connection between the painterly stylization of the black body and its exploitative instrumentalization in pornographic books and films of the 1980s, some of which we glimpse at the Corry and in James's possession. Crucially, however, the one aspect of his characterization that marks him out from Charles is his readiness to admit to the markings of power that inflect but do not dampen his sexual enthusiasm. This self-consciousness opens an important but complicated opportunity in the novel where Will's blatant negrophilia might be critically assessed.

As the novel opens, Will is seated on a train opposite two London transport maintenance men, one of whom is black and who prompts Will's 'taste for black names, West Indian names' (*SPL* 1). When describing his black lover, Arthur, Will dwells upon his raced physiology, blending Keatsian elation with Firbankian obsessiveness: 'Oh the ever-open softness of black lips; and the strange dryness of the knots of his pigtails, which crackled as I rolled them between my fingers, and seemed both dead and erect' (*SPL* 3). Although Will sleeps with white as well as black partners, black men are everywhere in his narrative. In Hyde Park he follows a 'lone Arab boy' (*SPL* 6) who leads him to the lavatories where he initially encounters Charles; at a London boxing club he watches a bout featuring 'a black boy' (*SPL* 137); he attends with Charles the filming of a pornographic scene featuring the 'very black' waiter from the Corry, Abdul; he recalls leaving the Shaft nightclub in a taxi with 'a black kid, drunk, chilled in his sweat' (*SPL* 192). On another such visit he flirts with Stan, a 'colossal Guyanan [*sic*] bodybuilder' (*SPL* 198). He explores with relish James's collection of erotic magazines that 'specialised in blacks with more or less enormous cocks, and in leaden titles like *Black Velvet*, *Black Rod* or even *Black Male*' (*SPL* 215). Indeed, when these examples are combined with the black figures that appear in Charles's journals, it is fair to say that there seem at least as many black as there are white figures in *The Swimming-Pool Library* – an extraordinarily rare situation in any post-war British-based novel written by a white writer since Colin MacInnes's *City of Spades* (1957).

While Charles's journals enable Hollinghurst to expose the neocolonial designs which animate Will's eroticism, Will's sexual obsession with black lovers exposes the potentially insidious and racist character of Charles's self-declared cross-racial benevolence and penchant for aestheticization. This is in spite of the fact that Charles makes it clear that he wishes firmly to differentiate himself from the violent racism of post-war London which the novel soberly registers in the fate of Taha al-Azhari, a Sudanese whom Charles brought to the UK as his servant, and whose murder he learns of while languishing in prison.

Charles's claims of companionship and camaraderie with colonial peoples fail fully to convince. 'All my true friends were black' (*SPL* 242), he insists, when telling Will of his younger days, as if an enthusiasm for black life is enough to transcend or cancel the malign forms of racism at large on the streets of postcolonial London. He is unmoved by Will's gentle attempts to make him confront his complicity in racialogical thinking, which Charles rightly regards as Britain's 'despairing shame' (*SPL* 244). One such effort concerns Charles's encouragement of Abdul (a waiter at the Corry whom we learn eventually is Taha's son) to participate in the pornographic film recently made by his acquaintance Staines at which Will was present:

> I said I found it hard to reconcile his views on race with the film that Staines had made and he himself – according to Aldo – had paid for. But I did it with as much cheek and charm as possible. [Charles] was bemused.
> 'I don't think *race* comes into it, does it? I mean, Abdul is black and the others aren't ... but I don't want any rot about that. Abdul loves doing that sort of thing – and he's actually jolly good at it. He's a pure exhibitionist at heart.' (*SPL* 245)

Leaving aside the fact that Abdul's view of matters is never recorded, Charles's denial that race mints Abdul's pornographic currency is profoundly disingenuous. Its wilful dishonesty is exposed by comparing it to Will's unashamed representation of his desire for Arthur, which freely admits the markings of an imperial legacy:

> our affair had started as a crazy fling with all the beauty for me of his youngness and blackness. Now it became a murky business, a coupling in which we both exploited each other, my role as protector mined by the morbid emotion of protectiveness. I saw him becoming more and more my slave and my toy, in a barely conscious abasement which excited me even as it pulled me down. (*SPL* 31)

The fusion of beauty with murk, passion with morbidity, arousal with abasement shamelessly foregrounds the exploitative dynamics which characterize Will's racialized relations with his latest lover. Such dynamics remain problematic, but their admission possesses a degree of candour that Charles refuses to present.

Yet Will's frankness also begs an important question. Which is worse: Charles's denial of the culpably racist aspects of his predilection of black lovers, or Will's knowing indulgence in the dubious domain of race and his clear-eyed admission of the excitements derived from toying with slavery's image? As David Dabydeen put it in an influential essay published at almost exactly the same time as *The Swimming-Pool Library*, Empire 'was as much a pornographic as an economic project' and demanded 'a language capable of describing both a lyrical and corrosive sexuality'.[11] The erudition of Will's narrative style, with its touches of Firbankian louche and its baroque descriptiveness, captures redolently the blend of erotic lyricism and corrosive racism which characterizes Will's dealings with black figures in the novel – as in his previous description of his congress with Arthur, and clinched in his admission that he had made Arthur 'half kneel, half lie over the corner of the bed and given him several strokes of my old webbing corps-belt from school' (*SPL* 65), which calls to mind the 'fantasy of domination, bondage and sado-masochism' that Dabydeen characterized as Empire's 'perverse eroticism'.[12] Read in these terms, Hollinghurst soberly presents the London of *The Swimming-Pool Library* as a place where the prejudices, problems and colonial legacies of racially inflected desire are openly admitted yet happily indulged. The pornography of Empire remains prevalent in Staines's movie-making, in James's dirty books and Will's narrative voice. Possessing an understanding of the collusion between race, colonialism and arousal – and Hollinghurst's characters are well-educated men, let us remember – changes little, partly because for much of the novel Will cannot begin to understand what it feels like to be in another position in a racial hierarchy. Indeed, given Will's penchant for enjoying 'murky business' with Arthur as both slave and toy, knowledge stimulates rather than stymies the titillations of power. As we shall see, this is one reason why *literary* culture assumes such an important role in the novel, because it is only here that any kind of critical traction as regards the unfinished matter of race might be made available to Will.

That said, Dabydeen's sense of the 'pornography of empire' does not entirely define the pornographic comings and goings of *The Swimming-Pool Library*. Another conception of pornography animates such scenes in the novel, inflected by the more politically radical rendering of pornography's contribution to how, in the late twentieth century, gay sexual life might be prized. I have in mind here the dissident queering of pornography: where an often heteronormative aesthetic complicit with sexism and misogyny is recast in subversive terms for gay personhood as the means of recognizing an ontologically enabling hedonism and of empowering participation through our bearing witness (watching, reading). In an essay which engages with the work of Robert Mapplethorpe (published one year after Dabydeen's essay), Judith Butler warns against the presumption of anti-pornography campaigners that 'no interpretative possibilities could be opened up by the pornographic text … no interpretative distance could be taken from its ostensibly injurious effects'.[13] While the corrosive racial aspects of Will's erotic life lead him down one avenue, the lyrical elements of his accounts of sexual pleasure may point in another direction, towards a confirmation of queer being. Will's erotic accounts lyrically glimpse an alternative ontology in which the articulation of same-sex intercourse serves the wider political purpose of making visible the particulars of gay personhood. Pornography may offer a route towards an empowering queer hedonism, lyrically rendered in the novel at times, even if that route cannot ever be entirely free from more corrosive complicities. In her support of Mapplethorpe's art, Butler nonetheless notes how the 'naked Black men characterized by Mapplethorpe engage a certain racist romanticism of Black men's excessive physicality and sexual readiness, their photographic currency as a sexual sign'.[14] The representation of black men in Hollinghurst's novel is especially complex because such figures slip ambivalently between often-contending pornographies: reactionary, radical; injurious, inspiring; colonial, queer.

Will's narration of Arthur, as we have seen, is distinctly ambivalent. In addition to his racialization, Arthur appears as a shady and semi-threatening figure whose links to London's underworld supplement his edgy appeal. His proximity to criminality is emphasized in the novel and renders his characterization vulnerable to the weaknesses of cliché, especially in the context of the 1980s, when the connectedness of black Britons to criminal activity was widely assumed. Writing in 1987, Paul Gilroy powerfully demonstrated that across a wealth of popular media the primary threat to national and social cohesion repeatedly identified at the time was 'black criminality',[15] to the extent that black culture and criminality were presumed to be indistinguishable. Arthur first appears in *The Swimming-Pool Library* slumped in Will's doorway, the victim of a violent assault by his brother Harold, and soon confesses that he 'killed my brother's mate' (*SPL* 22) in the dramatic end to the novel's first chapter. After disappearing from Will's flat at the end of Chapter 3, Arthur remains a spectral figure on the edge of Will's consciousness and the novel's action. Like Will's nephew Rupert, we are ever on the alert for Arthur's mysterious movements. He returns only briefly later in the novel when Will sees him by chance at the Shaft club in Soho. Their swift sexual contact is attenuated by Arthur's fear of his brother, whom Will later sees outside:

> a yellow Cortina [appeared], with tinted windows and the wheel-arches flared out over gigantic customised tyres. It came almost to a stop at the entrance to the Club and as I walked up quite fast a thick-set black man stepped out from the pink glow of the doorway, the car's rear door was flung open for him as a voice inside said 'Come on, Harold'. (*SPL* 204)

Such set-pieces of black vernacular culture – customized cars with tinted windows carrying local hoods in the back seats – do little to dislodge predominant paradigms of racialized representation. There is not much else to discover of black life in *The Swimming-Pool Library* other than these popular images of the black subcultural underworld that Will struggles to see past, just as Charles fails to establish an envisioning of black life under colonial patronage beyond the appropriative agency of emblematization and eroticization.

As author, Hollinghurst occupies a precarious position. On the one hand, neither he nor his narrator appears ready to portray the experience of 1980s London from the point of view of its black citizens, and wisely no such pretence is chanced. The novel resists claiming an understanding of black life and instead stays within the horizon of vision which marks the insights and limits of its predominant narratorial standpoint. But on the other hand, in incorporating black Londoners as less visible figures, rarely in view, Hollinghurst runs the risk of minoritizing his minor characters, so that they seem trapped within clichéd renderings of perceived racial or cultural otherness which are not sufficiently put on the move.

In his response to Daniel Mendelsohn's review of *The Stranger's Child* (2012) in the *New York Review of Books*, Hollinghurst opposed Mendelsohn's charge that his work generally conformed to an English literary tradition of anti-Semitic representation by making a distinction between modes of major and minor characterization. He defended *The Line of Beauty* as

> a tragicomic social novel, in which minor characters are inevitably treated more summarily than the principals, and often for comic effect. It may be worth pointing out that Sharon Flintshire is glimpsed only once across a room – she is otherwise an offstage figure, referred to half a dozen times in five hundred pages, and a wholly insubstantial support for any theory of Jewish-sponsored moral decay in the book.[16]

Hollinghurst and his work do not subscribe to a hostile or prejudicial racial politics, in my view. But the politics of representation in his fiction are endangered by the strategy of characterization he speaks of here. The substance of the problem is the very insubstantiality of those figures who bear the markings of race, the fashioning of which exposes Hollinghurst to the charge of stereotypical rather than shrewd characterization.

The Swimming-Pool Library cannot be fully detached from this problem in its black characterizations, but its racial politics are not fully defined by it too. In exposing the racial element of Will's lust, Hollinghurst does not shirk from asking critical questions about the machinations and exploitative relations (of class as well as race, of course) that both configure and disfigure the decade's gay social and cultural life. As Will's reading of *Valmouth* while travelling by train wittily hints, the attitudes of yesteryear are still in motion to script the actions of the novel's present moment. But Hollinghurst is keen to put these attitudes critically on the move too. Tacitly if not overtly, he looks for a critical rendering of relations between races, sexual or otherwise, that pushes outside of Will's less deceived but cheerfully libidinous hunger for erotic contact with black men.

This is a good moment to recall Hollinghurst's essay on the photography of Robert Mapplethorpe. Hollinghurst acknowledges the 'political implications of a white man shooting physically magnificent black men' but moves quickly to defend the integrity of Mapplethorpe's vision by reminding us of the witty formal nature of those photographs that play consciously with the images they frame. While not ignoring the 'time-honoured dodge whereby formal considerations are promoted over controversial content', Hollinghurst clearly prizes Mapplethorpe's innovations with photographic style that can be both wry and profound. It engenders a 'potent mood of celebration' when photographing black subjects that rises above the political minefield of racializing representation.[17] Through Mapplethorpe's 'mastery of technique', he claims, the bored visual rhetoric of pornographic discourse gave way to something 'artistically beautiful'.[18] In *The Swimming-Pool Library*, Hollinghurst engenders a similar procedure of setting, style and substance in dialogue with each other.

As narrator, Will's Jamesian narrowness of vision endangers the novel, and Hollinghurst knows it.[19] While Hollinghurst is unable to imagine what such relations might look like or be, he nonetheless attempts to ironize Will's racializing perspective in terms of form, and in two related ways. The first concerns the ambiguous moment of Will's narration which is not exactly coincident with the story he tells of himself in 1983 and which might enable Firbankian 'covert meaning' to enter Will's tale. In his perspicacious reading of *The Swimming-Pool Library*, Allan Johnson notes Will's comment at the novel's beginning concerning 'that summer, the last summer of its kind there ever was to be' (*SPL* 3). This remark, never repeated, makes Will's ensuing narrative effectively retrospective, although the present moment of its telling is not revealed. 'Indeed', writes Johnson,

> rarely does Will's narration acknowledge any sense of a present moment as clearly as here. The reader joins him in some unspecified time after the summer of 1983, but there are few deictic clues that indicate the location of the present.[20]

This temporal discrepancy between Will as narrator and the Will who appears in his narrative opens up a highly important critical distance between the narratorial present and the recent past and allows Will an opportunity to indulge, assess, admit and ironize the standpoint of his younger self. Appropriately for a Gemini, Will doubles for himself in the novel: both a figure interacting with London life in 1983 and one who narrates those happenings from a different vantage. The perspectives of these two Wills do not entirely align. If 1983's Will knows that he is involved in 'murky business' in his relations with black men, then the Will who narrates these affairs 'in some unspecified time' attempts subtly to connect this self-consciousness to a more critical conscience. He does so, suitably enough, by turning back to writing.

Given the retrospective character of Will's narrative, his reference to gay literary forerunners takes on a strategic purpose. By making mention of figures such as Firbank and E. M. Forster, Will adumbrates a line of writing by gay authors in which dominant attitudes to race are quietly put under pressure, if not called entirely into question. His narrative is deliberately positioned in relation to this genealogy, to beckon others' covert and often contradictory critique of race relations into his contemporary tale. When Will recounts a visit to the opera with his grandfather and James, an 'extremely interesting' (*SPL* 121) conversation occurs concerning Forster's attendance at the opening night of Benjamin Britten's *Billy Budd* (1951), at which Will's grandfather Lord Beckwith was also present. Beckwith noted that Forster, who had written the libretto, was unhappy with Britten's composition:

> there was something distinctly contrary about [Forster]. I was quite surprised when he openly criticised some of the music. Claggart's monologue in particular he thought was wrong. He wanted it to be much more ... open, and sexy, as Willy puts it. I think *soggy* was the word he used to describe Britten's music for it. (*SPL* 121)

The conversation beckons a distinctly critical Forster, contrary and dissatisfied, in pursuit of the 'open' and sensuous. The scene nudges the reader to think of Forster as an interrogative rather than canonical figure, the author of *A Passage to India* (1924) who sought to displace colonialist attitudes and behaviour even if he could not fully escape the constraints of that novel's historical moment. One might think of Firbank too in this regard: legible today as labouring under the axiomatics of a racialogical and colonial imaginary, but working at the time to bring into English letters rounded characters wrought from Firbank's extensive experience of travel, and given more than insubstantial or inconsequential parts. *The Swimming-Pool Library* is keen to nod to this inheritance of gay counter-hegemonic aesthetics – a style of thought and of writing – voiced within the headquarters of high culture, as it provides a literary ancestry towards which is oriented Will's retrospective attempts to ironize his behaviour in 'that summer' of 1983. In these terms, we might consider too how the novel's more progressive political possibilities may be found precisely in its style, housed in Hollinghurst's crafting of Will's self-delightedly Firbankian baroque.

To get the measure of Will's attempt to displace full complicity in racial thinking with recourse to doublings and literary relations, consider the account of his assault by a group of skinheads when he attempts unsuccessfully to track down Arthur at a block of flats in East London. The block is one of several on the estate named after the fiction of Thomas Hardy, thematizing the scene in terms of the literary, but written over with racist graffiti as at 'the turn of each flight "NF" had been scrawled, with a pendant saying "Kill All Niggers" or "Wogs Out"' (*SPL* 171). In the ensuing violence Will is attacked for his identification with perceived racial and sexual deviance, and his assault underscores the complicity between racism and homophobia in the starkest fashion. Will's subsequent medical treatment by his friend James also recalls the aftermath of Arthur's injuries to which James attended. In a novel that makes much of doubling, here Will seems almost to substitute for the absent Arthur in this encounter with London's insalubrious and threatening side, subjecting *him* to the kind of violent experience of London's racism that claimed Taha's life in the immediate post-war years. Previously, when Will imagined himself as racially different, his thinking and vocabulary bore no trace of political conscience. Looking at his suntanned body in the mirror, he is pleased to note that 'I was already as dark as some of the half-caste boys I showered with at the Corry' (*SPL* 71). The attack is an important moment of semi-awakening as it presents Will for the first time with a small taste of black life in London for many of its citizens by putting him momentarily in their place.

Note, too, that Will is carrying a pristine copy of Firbank's *The Flower Beneath the Foot* (1923). Will's possession of this book and its ironic fate trampled beneath a racist foot – an act of physical graffiti, if you will – mark a disjunction between the violent racism of the skinheads and a different relation to racialization – complicit but not corroborative – that is made available to Will and James through their enthusiasm for Firbank, should they want to prize it. By placing the volume of Firbank on the receiving end of a violent assault, Hollinghurst detaches Firbankian narration from mindless racism and suggests, in a distinctly Saidian vein, that the conjunction between culture and imperialism may be one of complex counterpointing rather than simply vulgar compliance.[21] The destruction of the Firbank volume invites us provocatively to ponder the complex ligatures that connect literary culture to prejudicial acts – where the former, however much complicit in the latter, still might open a limited critical space beyond more virulent racism to contest racism's legitimacy. If that space is shut down and trampled underfoot, the novel moots, then racism will certainly have won the day. Through Will's literate and literary narrative self-consciousness, Hollinghurst attempts to keep it open.

In these terms, the louche and baroque style which Will reworks from Firbank maintains the capacity to ironize and weaken full establishment of those racialized ways of seeing which the skinheads enact in their assault on Will and his copy of *The Flower Beneath the Foot*. The critical credentials of *The Swimming-Pool Library* lie in this attempt retrospectively to open an ironic consciousness of race-thinking with recourse to literary examples. This attempt makes the novel more complex than is sometimes perceived in postcolonial readings which, in Johnson's words, 'routinely expose a dangerous core of exploitation and vague corruption in both Charles and Will', even if such critiques are perhaps more scrupulous than Johnson allows.[22]

Hollinghurst is under no illusions, of course, about the limited transfigurative agency of an ironic rendering of race relations with recourse to literary antecedents. Change seems hard to encounter in Will's account of 'that summer'. Immediately after discovering the revelations of his grandfather's complicity in Charles's incarceration, Will has sex with Abdul in an encounter that suggests that the grievances of the past remain and animate the scene of the present. Abdul 'ill-temperedly' undresses Will, administers several 'hard slaps' to his buttocks, enters him with 'thrilling leisured vehemence' and dismisses him with the words 'Fuck off out of here, man' (*SPL* 262). It is hard not to regard this encounter as bound by lines of historical lineage, where the son of a victim of a racial hate-crime penetrates the grandson of the man who was responsible for incarcerating Taha's employer (and adding to Taha's vulnerability in a racist city). The sexual contact they share is shadowed by old grievances that enflame tempers as much as libido and are sounded in the slaps that Abdul vehemently delivers. In terms of the novel's narrative structure, the revelation of Lord Beckwith's complicity in Charles's incarceration makes Taha's actions appear as a quest to settle an old score, so that the divisions, attitudes and sentiments of the past drive the sexual actions of the present in a newly refreshed pornography of Empire. But it is also something of a moment of awakening for Will, who understands at last the serious ways in which sexuality is animated by the injustices of colonialism, and it seeds the beginnings of a different way of thinking about race. The retrospective narrative of *The Swimming-Pool Library* is crafted in the wake of this climactic experience. Will knowingly leads us from his early naive carefree attitudes concerning race towards an understanding, Forsterian in tenor, that his colonial-inspired couplings have sustained his frequent failure to connect with others on equitable terms and that he must count the cost of instrumentalizing them in terms of race.

In his last conversation with Charles, Will famously relinquishes his commission to write up his memoirs: "'All I could write now,' I said, "would be a book about why I couldn't write the book.' I shrugged. "I suppose there are enough unwritten books of that kind to make that of some interest"' (*SPL* 281). This book, of course, is exactly what he *has* written in that unspecified future beyond 1983. The exposure of London's neocolonial conditions is ironized through the novel's metafictional self-consciousness: the many references to Firbank, Charles's memoir which Will half-heartedly reads rather than writes up, the unwritten book about the book which Will could not write. Those representations which *are* successfully scripted in the novel appear problematic and morally bankrupt due to their racism, such as Staines's film of Abdul in which he appears partially unclothed yet fully constrained by colonialist vision: 'With his scarred black skin inside the thick black fur [coat] he struck me, who adored him for a moment, like some exquisite game animal, partly skinned and then thrown aside still breathing' (*SPL* 188). Unsettled, Will excuses himself from the filming of this scene, which is witnessed by Charles. This temporary gesture of departure is ultimately willed by the narrative. The gesture also underlines how permanently leaving behind the prejudices of the past might be a complex operation.

As Will's retrospective narrative, then, *The Swimming-Pool Library* cannot fully uncouple itself from the prejudicial milieu it seeks critically to expose. But it shares the compulsion also found in MacInnes's *City of Spades* and Firbank's *Valmouth* and *Sorrow in Sunlight* (1924; republished as *Prancing Nigger*, 1925) to try to deal a little differently with the attitudes in which it traffics. Since *The Swimming-Pool Library* appeared, Hollinghurst's work has remained intent on exposing the contradictions and tensions that attend the relations between race and sexuality, and the hypocrisies at large within the political class and establishment. Sarah Brophy's skilled and generous reading of *The Line of Beauty* searches hopefully for examples of new forms of queer cosmopolitanism forged across and beyond race and sexuality, and finds in the characters' same-sex erotic bonding 'the nascent, but politically thwarted, potential for a multi-racial, sexually diverse future for Englishness'.[23] But even in this novel, the highly problematic function of race remains to trouble the plot: Denis Flannery has pointed out that the novel's articulation of futurity pivots on 'the sacrifice of a black man'.[24]

In *The Swimming-Pool Library*, then, Hollinghurst begins a much longer, anxious and unfinished task of exposing forms of neocolonial perspective and representation that first need to be brought to an end before any kind of queer cosmopolitanism can be scripted. Will does not announce or engender that task during the 1980s, when nascent forms of cosmopolitan relations are distinctly absent. His embrace of black partners cannot deliver new transpersonal relations, as he acknowledges in the novel's final chapter. 'It was a strange conviction I had', he muses, 'that I could somehow make these boys' lives better, as by a kind of patronage – especially as it never worked out that way' (*SPL* 284). As Hollinghurst has admitted in an interview, his characters usually 'don't follow through the socio-political implications of being gay in any radical fashion'.[25] The novel's central reflex, ironic and self-conscious, is critically to expose the complicity of gay life in neocolonial relations with productive melancholy. Hollinghurst refuses to denigrate the enabling genealogy of gay literary culture while simultaneously marking the collusion of gay life in colonial-derived practices of racialization. This manoeuvre enables us not to lose sight of the significance and value of re-reading gay writers from previous moments while acknowledging the problems which shadow but do not fully terminate their texts' vitality and productivity.

Ultimately, *The Swimming-Pool Library*'s depiction of Firbank captures the contradictions I have discussed in this chapter. If *The Line of Beauty* is Hollinghurst's Jamesian novel, then *The Swimming-Pool Library* is indebted to Firbank. *The Swimming-Pool Library* closes in a distinctly valedictory mode with a screening of a newly discovered film of Firbank at Lago di Nemi, just prior to his death in Rome in 1926. As Alan O'Leary's chapter on cinema discusses, the screening emphasizes Firbank's untimely demise at the age of forty by depicting him clearly struggling during his last days, but also brings him back to life, reanimating him on celluloid. Staines has found the film amongst some home movies he bought at Christie's to inspire ideas for new pornographic films, which feature 'gay young things arsing around with no shame' (*SPL* 284). Firbank appears, looking unwell and uncomfortable, walking the streets of Genzano pursued by children to whom he throws a few coins. Will thinks he possesses 'a sweetly arcadian character' and is 'a bona fide queen' (*SPL* 285), and he dwells upon the mood of the film prompted by the sight of Firbank surrounded by the crowding children:

This marionette of a man, on his last legs, had been picked on by the crowd, yet as they mobbed him they seemed somehow to be celebrating him. ... The children's expressions showed that profoundly true, unthinking mixture of cruelty and affection. (*SPL* 286–7)

In general, we might note that Firbank's position between gay-cultural creativity and colonialist complicity renders him similarly celebrated and threatened, both patron and 'picked on', whose legacy captures precisely the wider legacies of Empire as conjured in Charles's journals as a mixture of cruelty and affection, both corrosive and lyrical. Firbank is the imperfect double for both Charles and Will, and his significance to the novel's ironizing investigation of the legacies of Empire is decisive, as the climactic screening suggests. His achievements as a writer – prized by James, Charles, Will, Staines, and Hollinghurst too – remind us that it is not enough simply to dismiss or venerate those figures from the past whose lives and art were entangled in the complexities, contradictions and complicities of their times, and in which the present remains all-too-often caught. In facing the race relations that pull together colonialism and the contemporary, Hollinghurst brokers a re-reading of the past's legacies as part of the unfinished matter of a complex moral and ethical critique.

Notes

1 Alan Hollinghurst, 'Saved by Art: The Shy, Steely, Original Ronald Firbank', *Times Literary Supplement* 17 November 2016, 12–15: 13.
2 Ronald Firbank, *Valmouth* (1919) in *Five Novels* (London: Duckworth, 1949) 1–123: 42.
3 Ibid. 42, 38, 42.
4 Ibid. 43.
5 Ibid. 39.
6 For a critical exploration of the relations between the judicial mechanics of the state and the prejudicial production of personhood, see Colin Dayan, *The Law is a White Dog: How Legal Rituals Make and Unmake Persons* (Princeton: Princeton University Press, 2011).
7 I have used 'postcolonial London' previously to describe the changing social and cultural environment of the British Empire's metropolitan headquarters in the latter decades of the twentieth century during the period of decolonization in Africa, the Caribbean and South Asia, and the dissident forms of literary activity established there by migrants and their descendants in the midst of violence and prejudice. See John McLeod, *Postcolonial London* (London: Routledge, 2004).

8   Brenda Cooper, 'Snapshots of Postcolonial Masculinities: Alan Hollinghurst's *The Swimming-Pool Library* and Ben Okri's *The Famished Road*', *Journal of Commonwealth Literature* 34.1 (1999) 135–57: 138.

9   For more on Bill Richmond, see Peter Fryer, *Staying Power: The History of Black People in Britain* (London: Verso, 1984) 445–6; and John Whale, '"Imperfect Sympathies": The Early Nineteenth-Century Formation of Responses to Black Fighters to Britain', *Moving Worlds: Journal of Transcultural Writings* 12.1 (2012) 5–18.

10 The rendering of the colonized subject as a fetishized ambivalent figure of desire and derision is a well-known proposition made by Homi K. Bhabha in *The Location of Culture* (London: Routledge, 1994) 66–84.

11 David Dabydeen, 'On Not Being Milton: Nigger Talk in England Today' in *Tibisiri: Caribbean Writers and Critics*, ed. Maggie Butcher (Coventry: Dangaroo, 1989) 121–35: 121.

12 Ibid. 121.

13 Judith Butler, 'The Force of Fantasy: Feminism, Mapplethorpe, and Discursive Excess' (1990) in *The Judith Butler Reader*, ed. Sara Salih with Judith Butler (Oxford: Blackwell, 2004) 183–203: 192.

14 Ibid. 197.

15 Paul Gilroy, '*There Ain't No Black in the Union Jack*': *The Cultural Politics of Race and Nation* (London: Routledge, 1995 [1987]) 78.

16 Alan Hollinghurst, '"The Stranger's Child": An Exchange', *New York Review of Books* 12 January 2012, www.nybooks.com/articles/archives/2012/jan/12/strangers-child-exchange/ (accessed 19 January 2016). Daniel Mendelsohn's essay is reprinted in his collection *Waiting for the Barbarians: Essays from the Classics to Pop Culture* (New York: New York Review of Books, 2012).

17 Alan Hollinghurst, 'Robert Mapplethorpe: 1970–1983' in *Robert Mapplethorpe: 1970–1983* (London: Institute of Contemporary Arts, 1983) 8–17: 8.

18 Ibid. 10.

19 In thinking of Will as a Jamesian narrator, I have in mind Henry James's exploration of the ambiguities and limitations of narrative perspective, often thematized through acts of reading, in texts such as *The Aspern Papers* (1888) and *The Turn of the Screw* (1898).

20 Allan Johnson, *Alan Hollinghurst and the Vitality of Influence* (Basingstoke: Palgrave Macmillan, 2014) 48.

21 The reference here is to Edward W. Said, *Culture and Imperialism* (London: Chatto & Windus, 1993).

22 Johnson, *Alan Hollinghurst and the Vitality of Influence* 36.

23 Sarah Brophy, 'Queer Histories and Postcolonial Intimacies in Alan Hollinghurst's *The Line of Beauty*' in *End of Empire and the English Novel Since 1945*, eds Rachael Gilmour and Bill Schwarz (Manchester: Manchester University Press, 2011) 184–201: 197.

24 Denis Flannery, 'The Powers of Apostrophe and the Boundaries of Mourning: Henry James, Alan Hollinghurst, and Toby Litt', *Henry James Review* 26.3 (2005) 293–305: 302.

25   Scarlett Baron, 'An Interview with Alan Hollinghurst', *Oxonian Review* 4 June 2012, www.oxonianreview.org/wp/an-interview-with-alan-hollinghurst-draft/ (accessed 19 January 2016).

5

The Stranger's Child and *The Aspern Papers*: queering origin stories and questioning the visitable past

Julie Rivkin

What Hollinghurst's *The Line of Beauty* did for England in the 1980s, the decade of both Thatcher and the AIDS crisis – that is, unmask a triumphalist public narrative and reveal its terrible costs and distortions, particularly in the lives of its queer characters – *The Stranger's Child* does for England over the longer span of the twentieth century. Again, Hollinghurst's target is cultural mythmaking, and he exposes the practice of constructing such legends by showing the dubious foundations on which they rest. 'Two Acres', the name at once of a suburban London home, a poem that takes the home as its inspiration, and a version of England for which the home is the metaphor, is just that dubious ground. It is where the novel opens, and it works retrospectively in the narratives that follow as a mythic past almost within reach. At the centre of this mythic past is the figure of Cecil Valance, a Rupert Brooke-like poet who dies early in the Great War and in the novel, leaving in his wake not just his mediocre yet irredeemably *English* poem 'Two Acres', but a tantalizing project of recovering the precious truth that his lost life and fading legacy evoke for English culture.

In tracing Valance's afterlife, *The Stranger's Child* explores the political power of institutionalized memory, the power of the archive, even as the novel reveals its necessarily arbitrary and contingent nature. As Valance is revised from patriotic poet of the Great War to queer icon of the 1980s, England is somehow always at stake, even if ironically, as in the overblown claims of the queer 1980s Valance biography, *England Trembles*. Yet the project of history-making, driven by the wish to either seal up or fling open the closet door, always misses its subject, invariably drawing attention to what eludes representation, be it the evanescence of experience or the deliberate erasures of the closet.

The novel is densely intertextual, with Hollinghurst drawing on a vast array of writers and composers engaged in the memorial arts. At the centre of these intertexts is *The Aspern Papers* (1888), Henry James's tale of an archivally obsessed biographer convinced that the truth of the past is recoverable and that the life behind the poem harbours a meaning more valuable than 'the riddle of the universe'.[1] A phrase associated with this conviction is the '*visitable* past' (*AP* xxxi), James's term for an era proximate enough to one's own to occasion survivals and overlaps. Extending the span of the '*visitable* past' in a series of adjacent narratives that span the twentieth century, Hollinghurst multiplies the Jamesian biographer into a host of memoirists, historians, biographers, and antiquarians, all of whom variously pursue their projects of possessing, memorializing, or reviving a mythic literary past. Converging on 'Two Acres' (both poem and site of its inspiration) with purposes belied by its modest dimensions, they expose in their inevitable failure the delusive promise of a sacred origin story, the kind of origin story that captivates James's biographer. *The Stranger's Child* plays with the desire to witness an *ur*-scene of passion between poet and muse behind the art that grounds a nation, but the way in which it queers that origin story is not just a matter of replacing a Daphne with a George as the lover in the garden. Rather, the novel works to unsettle any story of definitive origins for the poem and, by extension, the myth of nation it supports. In its place, I submit, the novel offers a figure of uncertainty, a figure conjured up in the novel's title – 'the stranger's child'. This other intertext, taken from section 10 of Tennyson's *In Memoriam*, works with the Jamesian visitable past to body forth a temporality that undoes the project of cultural mythmaking.

In focusing on temporality, my reading intersects with a topic central to recent queer theory. At least since Lee Edelman's 2004 *No Future*, temporality has come to be important in queer studies, as recent roundtable discussions in *GLQ* and at the MLA among theorists like Edelman, Judith Halberstam, Elizabeth Freeman, Carolyn Dinshaw, Annemarie Jagose, Roderick Ferguson, and others attest.[2] At the risk of simplification, if 'straight time' is seen as 'linear, teleological, reproductive, future oriented',[3] underwriting everything from reproductive futurity and capitalist productivity to national sovereignty, queer time does none of the above. According to Ferguson, queer temporality is peopled 'with figures outside the rational time of capital, nation, and family'.[4] For Edelman, it is in the name of the child, of reproductive futurity, that not only politicized 'family values' but meaning itself is invoked. 'Far from partaking of this narrative movement towards a viable political future, far from perpetuating the fantasy of meaning's eventual realization, the queer comes to figure the bar to every realization of futurity, the resistance, internal to the social, to every social structure or form'.[5] The false promise figured by the child is the promise of redemptive meaningfulness: in what Edelman call a 'Ponzi scheme of reproductive futurism', people keep trading in the promise of future gains until they discover that what they've invested in rests on nothing, is bankrupt.[6] By contrast, queer theorists call for other temporalities, everything from Dinshaw's 'queer historical touches ... affective contact between marginalized people now and then'[7] to Munoz's 'archive of the ephemeral'.[8]

The Stranger's Child might not at first blush seem a candidate for queer temporality. In fact, it might even be said to resemble a traditional historical novel of the familial, genealogical sort. But we need to look again. Although Hollinghurst might have an allergic relation to queer theory – witness the opportunist academic parodied in the novel's last section – the novel probes the same tender places explored by Edelman, Halberstam et al. That is, the novel not only registers the ordinary presence of queer lives across time, queer lives often lived below the threshold of visibility, but it also disrupts linear narrative and its use of a genealogical paradigm to locate past and future. This claim might at first seem surprising, given that the title *The Stranger's Child* seems to invoke the very figure that Edelman associates with a heteronormative reproductive futurity. But, I argue, the way Hollinghurst invokes the Tennysonian figure of the child actually aligns with Edelman's critique and with the novel's own failed Jamesian quest for the archive. Obsessively preoccupied with memory, the novel nonetheless emphasizes the ephemeral, particularly ephemeral desires that exceed or escape record and that cannot be traced or contained. In spite of its apparent traditionalism and antipathy to Theory, the novel is actually an active contributor to the conceptualization of queer temporality. In the sections that follow, I explore the different ways in which *The Stranger's Child* could be said to queer straight time, a set of strategies aligned with the novel's intertextual recoveries and re-enactments.

The visitable past

Told in a sequence of five narrative segments separated by no more than decades so as to permit significant survivals and overlaps, *The Stranger's Child* offers, as I have claimed, the tempting sense that the past is '*visitable*', that this mythic time might be within our grasp. The term comes from the preface to *The Aspern Papers*: James traces his tale to the discovery that Byron's lover Jane Clairmont was still living in late nineteenth-century Florence. Had James known in time, he could have visited her and touched the hand that touched the legend (*AP* xxix). This is the conceit of the visitable past, that one can have access, through a survivor, to the legendary life of a bygone era. In James's fictive version, Byron becomes Jeffrey Aspern, Jane Clairmont is called Juliana, her home is moved from Florence to Venice, and the narrator is a biographer who pretends to be in need of lodgings in order to gain access to her papers (the Aspern papers), which he values, as I've already noted, more highly than 'the riddle of the universe'. Spoiler alert: he doesn't get them. They get burned. And so, one might say, does he.

In an article titled 'Literary Forensics, or the Incendiary Archive', Eric Savoy argues that there is something in the archive that wills its own destruction, or, to put it another way, the desire to conserve is countered by an equally compelling desire that seeks to leave no trace.[9] Savoy builds on Derrida's exploration of this tension in *Archive Fever*,[10] and he finds it most compellingly enacted in James's archival story par excellence, *The Aspern Papers*.[11] For James, the fire in the archive has a biographical as well as a fictive referent; in 1909, decades after *Aspern*, James burned a large collection of personal papers, thereby destroying the evidence of his own 'private life'. But this destruction of the 'evidence' ironically made space for the biographical projects that would fill in that blank, the construction of everything from Leon Edel's Master to the Queer James of our own era. Hollinghurst's novel follows a similar biographical trajectory, his elusive Cecil Valance converted into a patriotic monument and then reclaimed for a different, though no less political, agenda. Secrets are invariably sexual secrets, Eve Kosofsky Sedgwick has convincingly argued,[12] and Hollinghurst makes explicit what James makes only possible, that the secret is a queer secret from the start. Not surprisingly, then, in Hollinghurst's novel, the fire in the archive overlaps with that other crucial figure for queer secrecy, the closet. The two come together at the conclusion of *The Stranger's Child*: a literal closet door from the past is opened, but the contents of the closet have been burned. Public history and private memory meet in this potent image; by 2008, the closet door is open, the queer lives of 1913 no longer in hiding. But as that image suggests, the exposure of the queer secret still leaves a vacancy. While on the one hand, the novel traces the emergence of queer culture into visibility and power over the course of a century, on the other, it refuses to make the queer secret a new ground of truth or justification for narrative teleology.

The opening book of *The Stranger's Child* features an anecdote similar to the one that gives rise to *The Aspern Papers*, and one that similarly complicates the promise of the visitable past. Seeking to impress her son's aristocratic Cambridge classmate and clandestine lover Cecil Valance, Freda Sawle tells a story of encountering Tennyson on a ferry to the Isle of Wight when she was on her honeymoon. Hollinghurst's comment on this anecdote, which he says he always knew he would include, is that it 'illustrat[es] that to her generation certain towering Victorian figures were still within living memory'.[13] Yet Freda Sawle's narration of the encounter paradoxically undermines the sense of immediacy it is intended to produce. Presenting the incident as one would unveil a family treasure, she underscores how the story has become habitual, the original experience effaced by frequent narration. 'You know we met him, of course ...?' Freda advances, before arriving at 'the bit of the story she knew best, knew word for word from her earlier tellings' (*SC* 44–5):

'It was a tall old man, even then he was taller than [my husband], though I believe he was eighty. I can see him now, he had a cloak over his clothes and' – here she always made large swooping gestures above her head – 'an extraordinary, very wide hat, and from behind –' (*SC* 59)

Her ritualized performance is complete with gestures and voice effects ('she always dropped her voice' at the part when she noted his hair was *'filthy'* (*SC* 59)), and even her children know their lines. Hubert dutifully provides a title: 'The Poet Laureate of England!' and when Freda hesitates at some rough language, Daphne ventriloquizes 'in a gruff and approximately regional voice' Tennyson's admonition: 'We need more *bloody*, young man. ... Less *awfully*, young man, more *bloody*!' (*SC* 60). But this would-be oracular moment with its message of raw truth-telling, this animation of the Victorian poetic voice through living memory, ironically emphasizes its remove, Daphne's copied performance of her mother's repetition of her father's report of Tennyson making a comedy of Daphne's attempt at authenticity. 'Living memory' proves to be strangely staged, its vitality an increasingly displaced performance.

Underlining the oxymoronic temporality of 'living memory', Daphne's delivery of the Tennyson speech seems to illustrate what she will state aphoristically much later in her life: that memories are always memories of memories. Everything about this anecdote draws attention to its well-worn telling, the figure of Tennyson receding in this family memorialization. In fact, the performance of the Tennyson story resembles the playing of music on the gramophone, another entertainment in the novel's opening section and an early technology of memory. Designed to capture the living voice, the gramophone, like other technologies of memory in the novel, seems more associated with malfunction than with preservation or animation. The gramophone recording omits crucial strophes of an aria; in later sections, a tape recorder stops working during the most important interviews, and a microphone intended to amplify the voice of a memorialist instead distracts with its own staticky interference. Such efforts seem as clunky as the project of 'Poets Alive!

Houndvoice.com', a website alluded to in the novel's last section that animates still photographs of Victorian poets so as to make the past live again, but that achieves no more than a 'fish-like gaping of the poet's lips and the rhythmical flicker of his eyebrows' (*SC* 549) . The name of the website, 'Hound Voice', is an allusion to a Yeats poem about the voice of memory.[14] Using the latest technology to make the dead speak can be as futile and embarrassing as Cecil's mother's spiritualist sessions in the library, in which she attempts to recover her son after his death through messages in books. Indeed, the updates on the book – the technologies that succeed it – do less to make the living voice present than to condemn it to distortion and inaudibility.

What the opening section does with Tennyson, aligning him with the impossible visitable past, the remainder of the novel does with the poet who succeeds him, Cecil Valance. Cecil Valance becomes Tennysonian not so much in his poetry as in the way his absent presence functions in the lives of those who knew him. As if preparing for this melding of Valance with Tennyson, the first section includes a public reading in which Cecil moves almost imperceptibly from performing his own verse to reciting *In Memoriam*. Those present at this performance might be like Freda on the ferry, garnering their own anecdotes of contact with a 'certain towering ... figure' for future auditors of their own. As the novel moves forward through time, it is equally emphatic in marking the terminus of 'living memory'; about a half century later, a character interested in writing a biography of Cecil Valance wonders whether 'the era of hearsay' is almost over and 'about to give way to an age of documentation' (*SC* 363). By the last section, set in 2008, the detachment from 'living memory' is complete; the protagonist is a dealer in antique books, and the section offers for its chilling epigraph a line from Mick Imlah's poem 'In Memoriam Alfred Lord Tennyson': 'No one remembers you at all' (*SC* 517).

As with *Aspern*, it is just when living memory teeters on the brink and the survivors of the legendary era reach their mortal limits that the lure of the visitable past exerts its greatest magnetism. The novel's fourth section, set in 1980, offers the most direct re-enactment of James's novella, with biographer Paul Bryant openly identifying with James's narrator and envisioning the Valance archive as 'bundled haphazardly in a large locked bureau like the one in *The Aspern Papers*' (*SC* 395). Daphne is his Juliana, and like Juliana she offers the prospect of vicarious intimacy with the mythic poet himself:

> She was a Victorian, she had seen two wars, and she was the sister-in-law, in a strange posthumous way, of the poet he was writing about.

To Paul her natural habitat was an English garden ... Poems had been written for her, and set to music. She remembered intimacies that by now were nearly legendary. (*SC* 372)

Living in the midst of her accumulations, as Juliana does, Daphne is both the precious guardian of a priceless treasure and a figure as decrepit as the 'astounding chaos of junk' (*SC* 471) that surrounds her. Paul's conviction that 'under the tablecloths and blankets in this room were Valance heirlooms, little dusty things that Cecil might have owned and handled' frustrates him with a feeling of both proximity and inaccessibility: 'The sense of the whole unexamined terrain of Cecil's life lying so close and yet so stubbornly out of view came over him at times in waves of dreamlike opportunity and bafflement' (*SC* 507). Daphne's response to his inquiry about a Valance inheritance – 'I didn't get much. I got the Raphael' (*SC* 507) – sounds disingenuous, but when she points out that the Raphael is only a copy, the parallel with Cecil begins to suggest itself. A dirty canvas depicting a 'pale young man with ... a snooty expression' (*SC* 482) that Paul saw stored in the loo is the painting in question, and its dual identity as artistic treasure and forged copy, sublime value and mere waste, conveys the status of Cecil Valance in Daphne's life. The other object inherited from the Valances, a silver ashtray inscribed with Cecil's brother Dudley's mean anticipatory joke – 'Stolen from Corley Court' – adds to this suggestion of inauthenticity the further insult of theft. Not only is the legendary past in Daphne's possession reduced to waste and ashes, but her claim on it is challenged as illegitimate.

This deflection of Daphne as a medium or incarnation of the legendary poetic past is exacerbated by the presence of other living sources. *The Stranger's Child* offers the biographer not the singular Juliana but a small host of survivors, all in their way intimates of the legendary poet. Cecil's brother Dudley, Daphne's brother George (Cecil's classmate and lover), and the Sawles' servant Jonah are all targets of the biographer's inquiry. But it is not only that the presence of multiple survivors challenges Daphne's role as Cecil's medium and oracle; it is also that the particular version of the past she enshrines is at odds with what the others reveal. The Daphne who appears in the novel's first section is a believer in her apparently muse-like relation to the poem. Reading the lines Cecil inscribed in her autograph book, she marvels at the poetic alchemy that has turned prosaic conversation into splendid verse; she feels 'thrilled, and a little bewildered, at being in on the very making of a poem, and at something else magical, like seeing oneself in a photograph' (*SC* 103). But what George and Jonah reveal, each in their different ways, is that it is George more than Daphne who has been 'in on the very making of a poem' and whose image resides within it; it is George and not Daphne who is Cecil's muse. Jonah has retained a once-discarded explicitly queer version of the poem that makes George's presence visible, and George himself, disinhibited by dementia, makes overt the erotic connection that Paul intuits. Touching Paul in much the way that Cecil must once have touched him, George confirms the love affair in a form more immediate than words. These encounters all work to challenge Daphne's role as the prime representative of the visitable past, however much history has assigned her that role.

While these meetings might be said to confirm a queer origin for 'Two Acres' in a manner that disrupts heteronormative convention and satisfies Paul's quest for the truth, they queer the very project of seeking truth. Hollinghurst's presentation of the interviews draws attention to impediments rather than immediacy: for example, the interview with Jonah Trickett is presented not directly, but as the transcription of a recorded interview typed up by his landlady, complete with the frequent parenthetic notation 'inaudible' (*SC* 408–12). Listening to one portion of the tape that he associates with a viewing of photographs, Paul can hear only 'murmurs, grunts and rueful laughs like the sound of some intimacy from which he was now bizarrely excluded' (*SC* 412). His sense of exclusion from 'some intimacy' has more to do with Cecil Valance than with Jonah Trickett, of course, and in this meeting Paul – and the reader – get no more than a glimpse of the revelatory papers in Jonah's possession. Access is even more qualified in Paul's interview with George. This time the tape recorder has stopped working entirely, and instead of a transcribed interview, there are Paul's hastily scrawled notes recorded in a diary after the fact. Left without 'documentary proof of the most important material so far', Paul can only comment, 'Astounding revelations (if true!)' (*SC* 453).

The novel makes us wait a good quarter of a century to learn the fruit of Paul's labours, and we do not hear the fate of his reputation-shaking book *England Trembles* until it is on the remainder pile. Because the 'astounding revelations' come as old news in more senses than one (after all, the reader already knew from earlier sections something of what Paul discovers), the novel blunts and ironizes the narrative drive towards discovery. It is not that the visibility or invisibility of queer lives does not matter, but the past cannot be opened like a closet door. A dismissive comment at a 2013 memorial service puts Paul Bryant's tell-all biography in its place, itself now a dated relic of the superseded 1980s: 'Well, outing gay writers was all the rage then, of course' (*SC* 525).

The monument and the closet

If the pursuit of the visitable past produces, ironically enough, not the past but a consummate creation of the present, an age of opening the closet door, that creation nonetheless needs to be understood in relation to the project of an earlier era, that of building the closet. The second section of the novel, set thirteen years after the novel's opening section and a little more than a decade after Cecil's death, is that of 'boxing in', the building of structures that function as both closet and, interestingly, monument. ('Boxing in' refers to the practice of hiding the ornate walls and ceilings of Victorian rooms behind modernist facades.) Hollinghurst's treatment of the closet draws attention as much to what it makes visible as to what it hides. In emphasizing the closet's paradoxical heightening of visibility, Hollinghurst shares an insight with Sedgwick, who explores this apparent inversion – the closet as spectacle – in the last chapter of *Epistemology of the Closet*.[15] But Hollinghurst takes the 'closet as spectacle' in a particular political direction, tracing the work it performs in the service of nation and empire. This section of the novel hews close to the Rupert Brooke story, exploring what is at stake when an individual life – or afterlife – is drafted to serve as a national story. The exposure of how and why the past gets enshrined, the building of the closet as monument, could be deemed another of the novel's queer temporalities.

The setting for the exploration of the monument is the Valances' country house, Corley Court, a grandiose Victorian pile that works much like the 'towering figure' of Tennyson as an emblem of national culture. (Cecil used to say 'the word "Corley" as other men said "England" or "The King", with reverent briskness and simple confidence in his cause' (*SC* 20).) George Sawle, visiting the effigy of his former lover in the chapel at Corley, takes the political measure of the process of memorialization. Although he initially hoped to feel 'alone with his old pal again, almost as though he'd come into a hospital ward rather than a chapel' (*SC* 152), instead he feels the recruitment of the living Cecil into the project of history-making, enshrining long-existing hierarchies of class and power:

> It struck George, as the chapel itself had on that first day, as a quietly crushing assertion of wealth and status, of knowing what to do. It seemed to place Cecil in some floating cortège of knights and nobles reaching back through the centuries to the Crusades. George saw them for a moment like gleaming boats in a thousand chapels and churches the length of the land. (*SC* 153)

The terrible irony is that George will join that project, covering up his passionate affair with Cecil and taking on the neutralized persona of the academic historian, co-author with his wife of the school text *An Everyday History of England*. His marriage, like the history text, makes its own monument out of the closed closet door, 'G. F. and Madeline Sawle' becoming as familiar as the version of English history they tell. Paul Bryant, Cecil's future queer biographer, will remember 'the title-page on which he had boxed the name G. F. SAWLE and MADELINE SAWLE in a complex Elizabethan doodle' (*SC* 306), their paired names an inscription akin to the Latin words in Gothic plaited lettering carved on Cecil's tomb.

The history text that George will write aligns with the other text underway in this visit to the monument, the official 'Life and Works of Cecil Valance'. Sebastian (Sebby) Stokes, the official biographer, is a statesman, and just as he 'seem[s] to speak from the world of discreet power, of committees and advisers' (*SC* 161), he aligns the project of representing Cecil with that of governing England. Still Sebby is moved to serve as Cecil's biographer, George surmises, not just by patriotic sentiment, but by a feeling more akin to George's for Cecil, one he needs to conceal to the very degree that it motivates him to undertake this project. As Sebby discreetly presses George for more – uncollected letters, uncollected poems, unspoken memories – George senses not only Sebby's guess about his own relations with Cecil, but Sebby's own unstated emotion. Although George has memories that do not accord with the monument – 'images less seen than felt, memories kept by his hands, the heat of Cecil, the hair-raising beauty of his skin, of his warm waist under his shift, and the trail of rough curls leading down from his waist' (*SC* 155) – he will join Sebby in the project of keeping history in the closet. Sebby's edition will become a patriotic monument akin to the effigy, one that converts the man they both desired into the English soldier-poet Cecil Valance, a canonical figure who 'will be read as long as there are readers with an ear for English music, and an eye for English things' (*SC* 162).

In its focus on the conversion of Cecil into a national monument, this portion of the novel follows the Rupert Brooke story, with a particular role for Henry James. Edward Tayler, in a review of *The Stranger's Child* titled 'The Rupert Trunk', traces the parallels: just as Cecil Valance is based on Rupert Brooke, Sebastian Stokes is based on Edward Marsh, characterized by Tayler as a 'promoter of Georgian poetry by night and private secretary to Churchill by day'.[16] Marsh worked to create a version of Brooke that suited the Churchillian agenda (a 'poster-boy for self sacrifice'[17] designed to recruit others to the war effort) and he even managed to draft Henry James into this patriotic project. James, moved not only by his own war horror but also by his warm feelings for 'the Rupert' after an earlier Cambridge visit in 1909, agreed at Marsh's insistence to write a preface to Brooke's *Letters from America*, thereby making his own contribution to the Brooke legend.[18] The review's title 'The Rupert Trunk' points to another dimension of the James connection; even while James contributed to the official biography, his novella *The Aspern Papers* offered the conceit of a life behind the life, 'precious papers' that would tell a different tale. And, indeed, in the case of Rupert Brooke, there was just such a trunk of papers. The contents of the trunk, which in this instance were *not* burned, were not disclosed until many years later, in a biography rather like the one Paul Bryant publishes about Cecil Valance.

Secret throbs

If the statue of Cecil is intended as a patriotic monument but is also a closet, how might it also be part of a coming-out story? A visit to Cecil's tomb in the third section of the book, which takes place in 1967, on the eve of the Sexual Offences Act (which decriminalized private sexual acts between men over the age of twenty-one) provides new lovers with an erotic occasion that draws on the statue's buried meaning. The setting is Corley Court, now turned into a boarding school for boys, and the meeting between teacher Peter Rowe and Paul Bryant, a clerk at the local bank managed by Daphne's husband. For Peter and Paul, Cecil becomes 'a codeword' for their attraction to one another, Peter's invitation for 'just a quick peek' suggesting something licentious about the marmoreal figure (*SC* 347). The statue has been subjected to some mild defacements over the years, with 'boys fix[ing] pretend cigarettes between the poet's marble lips' and one boy even having 'carved his initials on the side of the chest' (*SC* 349). Their talk of Cecil is similar to these revisions of the monument: 'I think Cecil was probably queer, don't you?' (*SC* 356), Peter remarks, and cannot help thinking it 'funny how Paul had been turned on by Cecil's tomb' (*SC* 362). In duplicating George and Sebby's meeting over Cecil's tomb in Section 2, Paul and Peter unwittingly copy the even earlier meetings of George and Cecil in Section 1. The section concludes with a ghostly brush of the past, one that recalls the two earlier lovers. Peter thinks he feels a 'hand strok[ing] the back of his neck', only to recognize it as the 'kite-like form' of a bat (*SC* 363). But as it heads to the roof of Corley to join its fellow, the two indistinct figures they form – 'strangely antique, ... of uncertain size and height ... flow[ing] like oily shadows themselves, in dressing-gowns left open like cloaks' (*SC* 363) – recall George and Cecil in their roof-top assignations.

This ghostly touch in the dark is aligned with another of the novel's temporalities, neither visitable past nor political monument, but something fleeting, not necessarily visible, a sensory and erotic experience not fixed in the novel's various memorializing tropes. Interestingly, it is Daphne, moving in the dark in the novel's opening scene, who first evokes this temporality in her reference to 'secret throbs'. She has been reading Tennyson in the hammock and awaiting Cecil and George, but as the sky darkens she rises to wander the garden. The dusk obscures the words on the page, but the obscurity brings something hidden into focus, drawing her attention to 'the hint of a mystery she had so far overlooked' (*SC* 3). As the 'hedges and borders' grow 'dusky and vague, ... anything she looked at closely, a rose, a begonia, a glossy laurel leaf, seemed to give itself back to the day with a secret throb of colour' (*SC* 4). The effect is Keatsian, nightingale-ready, reminiscent of the speaker's heightened sensory state when he 'cannot see what flowers are at [his] feet'.[19] Daphne seems able to feel even more than see the flowers, to sense synesthetic 'secret throb[s]' that are aligned with the novel's concealed queer eroticism.

The novel traces an alternative history of 'secret throbs', a history of sensory pulses that might be said to begin with Daphne and continue right through the flicker of a text message signalling a new assignation in the novel's final sentence. It is interesting that Daphne is first associated with this language of 'secret throbs', as they might more naturally seem to belong to the clandestine lovers George and Cecil. Yet Daphne, both naive and curious, is somehow folded into their affair right from the start. Her eagerness to try the cigar that Cecil and George are smoking, to join the two of them in the hammock (which Daphne compares to a conjugal bed), and to pursue them into the wood and unwittingly interrupt them in the sexual act all express her erotic fascination. The actions anticipate the way she will make a place for herself in the poem as muse and lover. Although one way to read Daphne's presence in the scene and in the poem is as part the heterosexual cover story, it is actually more in keeping with the novel's treatment of desire to see her as part of a queer erotic triangle, part of what makes desire exceed definition and representation (as Joseph Ronan's chapter explores). George and Daphne's relations with Cecil each have an aspect of cross-dressing, with Daphne literally wearing George's coat when Cecil kisses her in the garden, and George figuratively wearing Daphne's attire when an unnamed lover appears in the poem 'Two Acres'.

Although replacing George with Daphne might seem to turn 'Two Acres' into a version of the closet, the poem also has the capacity for strange life, for producing queer throbs of its own. In the last section, at the memorial service for Peter Rowe, lines of poetry awkwardly read by bereaved husband Desmond puncture the ceremony with a pulse of grief and longing. And who is the author of these poignant lines, a guest wonders. 'Uncle Cecil' (*SC* 535), his seatmate and descendant of the Valance family replies, 'Two Acres'.

The stranger's child

The poem that claims this life most directly is the one that gives the novel its title. First recited in the opening section, *In Memoriam*, like 'Two Acres', takes on new life at the end. In the quoted verse, the speaker laments that the world will become familiar to a strange new generation, and while the natural world will keep on renewing itself, those who know it now will neither endure nor be remembered.

> Till from the garden and the wild
> A fresh association blow,
> And year by year the landscape grow
> Familiar to the stranger's child—
>
> As year by year the labourer tills
> His wonted glebe, or lops the glades;
> And year by year our memory fades
> From all the circle of the hills.[20]

The landscape both 'grow[s]' and 'grows / Familiar' to a new and alien generation, but while natural growth produces a renewing harvest, the change of generations creates nothing but loss. Commenting on this Tennyson passage in an interview, Hollinghurst says that what it evokes so musically and powerfully is 'the unknowability of the future'.[21] But the verse laments less the unknowability of the future than the way it ushers in the loss of the past. There is no child in the future who will recollect what is now familiar; the stranger's child signifies the loss of meaning in time. Such a figure, I posit, aligns with Lee Edelman's concept of *No Future* and the queer refusal to 'perpetuat[e] the fantasy of meaning's eventual realization'. Like Edelman, Hollinghurst finds no redemption in the figure of the child.

In the book's closing scene, Hollinghurst literalizes the Tennysonian figure when he has a child assist his mother, a stranger, in the burning of the archive. Rob, the protagonist of the last section and a bookseller, hot on the trail of further Valance papers, finds his way to the house of the Sawles' former neighbour and possible Valance lover even as it is facing demolition. But the woman tasked with emptying the house has done her job all too well. 'Rubbish, no use to anyone', she comments, 'god, it's Victorian, some of this stuff!' (*SC* 562). What she disparages as Victorian 'rubbish' had once, of course, been the stuff of legend. Even more than the woman, it is her young son who performs the action of the Tennyson verse. Sorting objects into piles for preservation or destruction, sometimes moving 'an item ... from one pile to the other with the proper arbitrariness of fate' (*SC* 562), he is both literally and figuratively 'the stranger's child'.

In the previous section, Daphne had commented on memory as just such a sorting process, marvelling at the arbitrariness of what gets preserved from 'the great backward and abyss' (*SC* 489). (Her own misquotation of Shakespeare – 'the dark backward and abysm of time'[22] – only underscores her point about the untrustworthy workings of memory.) Reflecting on a recent memoir, she marvels at how one undistinguished, if quirky, person is pulled forward into celebrity, while another is simply forgotten. In terms of the Cecil Valance story, there may be no better illustration of this arbitrariness than the role played by former servant Jonah Trickett. Like the 'stranger's child', he too had a hand in what was preserved and what discarded, what was deemed treasure and what eliminated as 'rubbish'. Saving the crumpled pages of verse Cecil Valance threw away, Jonah unwittingly makes a name for himself as well as Cecil in the archive as the contributor of 'the Trickett MS ... an unpublished part of one of the poems ... a sort of queer manifesto, except in tetrameter couplets ... [w]ritten in 1913, quite interesting' (*SC* 541). Through a 'trick', some trace of Cecil's queer life made it into the archive. But it might just as easily have gone the other way, its survival just the whim of a stranger's child.

Emphasizing that trick or whim, the novel closes with the fate of the papers on the other pile, the ones destined for burning. In the novel's final sentence, the book collector's hands hold no precious papers, but only the smell of smoke, the evidence of a conflagration in the archive. The burning of the archive says as much about a future as a past; it speaks to the absence of a future revelation. The past is not stored up to be discovered or recovered, to bring fulfilment to a quest, and in refusing to provide his novel with such a denouement, Hollinghurst, in an interview, sounds not entirely disjunct from Edelman:

> I was weary of the kind of plot in which there is a secret – something knotty which has to be *denoué*. I became rather suspicious of the

device – it just didn't seem to me to be enough like life. That's why there's much less of an attempt to untie, to reveal, and to tidy up in *The Stranger's Child*. The book has its own kind of plot of course, but it's a plot made out of a desire to escape from a certain conception of plot and a certain degree of contrivance ... .

I have always been interested in the degree to which people fail to know themselves or to understand their situations. And am rather resistant to the idea that the machinery of a book will necessarily bring them to a state of understanding.[23]

In refusing the plot based on the discovery of what lies at the origin of the poem, the novel also refuses the plot of self-discovery. The 'machinery' of narrative is not there to generate artificial self-knowledge, any more than it will open a future based on an excavation of the past.

In the novel's last section, the Valance descendant Jennifer Keeping drily mocks Paul Bryant's revelations, which are precisely about these truths of origins, both familial and poetic.

[A]ccording to Paul Bryant everything I've just told you is untrue. Let me see ... My aunt wasn't really Dudley's daughter, but Cecil's, Dudley was gay, though he managed to father a son with my grandmother, and my father's father wasn't Revel Ralph, who really was gay, but a painter called Mark Gibbons. I may be simplifying a bit. (*SC* 524)

When Rob queries, 'And this wasn't the case?' Jennifer replies, 'Oh, who knows?' (*SC* 524). Her response is not that these statements are false, but that their truth or falsity is somehow not the issue. For Jennifer the truth of family origins is no more to be settled than the truth of the poem's origins, neither one of which will produce narrative closure. The point is not to replace Daphne with George as Cecil's true muse in the origin story of 'Two Acres', any more than it is possible to establish the definitive list of Cecil's lovers – a list that may or may not include George's neighbour. Instead, in the final section, the smoke from the burned closet is linked to the flame of renewed desire, the text message that flickers across the screen, the secret throbs that lead to the next assignation. Even as Rob turns away from the burned papers, he turns towards the new text in his hand, a message from the unknown lover who awaits him, an alternate incarnation of the stranger's child.

Notes

1 Henry James, *The Aspern Papers and Other Stories*, ed. Adrian Poole (Oxford: Oxford University Press, 1983) 2. Hereafter, this work is cited parenthetically as *AP*.

2 See, for example, Elizabeth Freeman's 2007 special issue of *GLQ*, *Queer Temporalities*, and particularly (in that issue) 'Theorizing Queer Temporalities: A Roundtable Discussion', *GLQ* 13.2–3 (2007) 177–95. See also Robert Caserio, Lee Edelman, Judith Halberstam, Jose Esteban Munoz, and Tim Dean, 'The Antisocial Thesis in Queer Theory', *PMLA* 121.3 (2006) 819–28. Some influential works on queer temporality include Annamarie Jagose, *Inconsequence: Lesbian Representation and the Logic of Sexual Sequence* (Ithaca, NY: Cornell University Press, 2002); Lee Edelman, *No Future: Queer Theory and the Death Drive* (Durham, NC: Duke University Press, 2004); Judith Halberstam, *In a Queer Time and Place: Transgender Bodies, Subcultural Lives* (New York: New York University Press, 2005); José Esteban Muñoz, *Cruising Utopia: The Then and There of Queer Futurity* (New York: New York University Press, 2009), and Elizabeth Freeman, *Time Binds: Queer Temporalities, Queer Histories* (Durham, NC: Duke University Press, 2010).

3 Annamarie Jagose in 'Theorizing Queer Temporalities' 186.

4 Roderick Ferguson in 'Theorizing Queer Temporalities' 180.

5 Edelman, *No Future* 4.

6 Ibid.

7 Carolyn Dinshaw in 'Theorizing Queer Temporalities' 178.

8 Jose Esteban Munoz, 'Ephemera as Evidence: Introductory Notes to Queer Acts', *Women and Performance* 8.2 (1996) 5–16. Cited in Halberstam, *In a Queer Time and Place* 161.

9 Eric Savoy, 'Literary Forensics, or the Incendiary Archive', *boundary 2* 37.3 (2010) 101–22.

10 Jacques Derrida, *Archive Fever* (Chicago: Chicago University Press, 1996).

11 Savoy, 'Literary Forensics, or the Incendiary Archive' 108 ff.

12 Eve Kosofsky Sedgwick, *Epistemology of the Closet* (Berkeley: University of California Press, 1990) 11.

13 Scarlett Baron, 'An Interview with Alan Hollinghurst', *Oxonian Review* 4 June 2012, www.oxonianreview.org/wp/an-interview-with-alan-hollinghurst-draft/ (accessed 19 January 2016).

14 William Butler Yeats, 'Hound Voice' in *The Collected Works of W. B. Yeats Volume I: The Poems*, ed. Richard J. Finneran (2nd edn; New York: Scribner, 1997) 367.

15 See Eve Kosofsky Sedgwick, 'Proust and the Spectacle of the Closet' in *Epistemology of the Closet* 213–51.

16 Christopher Tayler, 'The Rupert Trunk', *London Review of Books* 28 July 2011, www.lrb.co.uk/v33/n15/christopher-tayler/the-rupert-trunk (accessed 19 January 2016).

17   Ibid.
18   Quoted in Tayler, 'The Rupert Trunk'.
19   John Keats, 'Ode to a Nightingale' in *Complete Poems*, ed. Jack Stillinger (Cambridge, MA: Harvard University Press, 1982) 279–81.
20   Tennyson, *In Memoriam*, Canto CII, ll. 205–12, quoted in *SC* 68.
21   Baron, 'An Interview with Alan Hollinghurst'.
22   William Shakespeare, *The Tempest*, ed. Virginia Mason Vaughn and Alden T. Vaughn (London: Bloomsbury, 2011) 1.2.58.
23   Baron, 'An Interview with Alan Hollinghurst'.

6

Ostentatiously discreet:
bisexual camp in *The Stranger's Child*

Joseph Ronan

Alan Hollinghurst has suggested that there is 'a lot in *The Stranger's Child* which is rather liminal ... there's quite a lot of bisexuality'.[1] Despite this, the words 'bisexual' or 'bisexuality' appear exactly never in the novel's 564 pages. A number of characters display what we might reasonably consider bisexual behaviour yet bisexuality in this novel is unnamed, perhaps unnameable. Similarly, many responses to the novel, even those which do describe some characters as bisexual, have tended to position its explorations of history, memory and literary tradition in relation to homosexuality or gayness. Such readings mistake the activities of the characters within the text for the activity of the text itself. They erase the significant amounts of bisexual behaviour in evidence throughout it and situate the novel in precisely the gay context which, I argue, it undermines.

Rewritten as gay, queer or an immature transitional identity, the text's unnameable bisexuality speaks to a contemporary moment in which bisexuality largely remains culturally illegible, subsumed under different narratives. This chapter advances a reading of *The Stranger's Child* that puts its bisexualities in dialogue with its campness to reveal the novel's interactions with the mainstreaming of gay culture, the advance of queer theory, and what Kenji Yoshino describes as the 'epistemic contract of bisexual erasure' between gay and straight discourses that ensure that bisexuality remains invisible.[2] I argue that *The Stranger's Child* takes the cultural illegibility of bisexuality and runs with it, making an outrageous camp excess out of its absence and structuring its narrative through the supposed irresolvabilty of bisexuality as an identity position.

Robyn Ochs notes that due to a lack of bisexual visibility outside a limited set of behaviours (such as having simultaneous partners of different genders), 'many people equate bisexuals with promiscuity ..., untrustworthiness, horniness and hypersexuality. Bisexuals who are not currently engaging in one of these behaviors are seen as ("well-behaved") straight, lesbian or gay people'.[3] Phoebe Davidson also shows that a linear sexual narrative bolsters a perception of bisexuality as immature. Since 'sexuality is perceived as a maturation process ... bisexuality could be perceived at the beginning, in infancy, but it certainly has no place at the end of this process, in adulthood'.[4] As Marjorie Garber states, this narrative is based on 'the idea that it is "normal" to reach a settled sexual identity, and that that "identity" is either heterosexual or homosexual'.[5] Moreover, Esther Saxey's analysis of the mechanics of the gay coming-out narrative reveals that it typically 'uses the exclusion of any bisexual potential as one of its key ...incidents',[6] an exclusion which 'becomes the climax of an ethical battle between enforced, inauthentic heterosexuality and redemptive gay honesty'.[7] Elsewhere she explains that 'the key cultural story we have for understanding same-sex sexual desire' has therefore 'excluded the possibility of a character with self-aware, ongoing desire for both sexes', and has therefore cast bisexuality as an unresolved, transitory position en route to a fixed and authentic monosexual identity.[8] In addition, Clare Hemmings notes that some queer theorists refuse 'to recognize bisexuality as a valid and enduring sexual identity and bisexuals themselves as authentic subjects'.[9] This can lead to subsumption into a queer discourse which is supposedly inclusive but, as David Halperin has noted, in practice has often 'subsided into a mere synonym of gay', effacing specifically bisexual experiences and perspectives.[10]

The Stranger's Child rehearses all of these positions although not as a further unfortunate act of bisexual erasure. Rather, this chapter reads the novel as a camp critique of the personal and cultural narrative processes that lead to such erasure in the first place. Georges Letissier notes 'the potentialities of "camp" as a countercultural impulse within Alan Hollinghurst's aesthetic' more generally;[11] I posit this camp impulse in *The Stranger's Child* as a specifically bisexual one, countering the culture of erasure fostered by straight, gay and contemporary queer discourses. 'Trying to define Camp is like attempting to sit in the corner of a circular room', as Andy Medhurst memorably observes. 'It can't be done, which only adds to the quixotic appeal of the attempt.'[12] That said, 'most of us know it when we see, hear, feel or do it'.[13] For Medhurst,

> Camp is a set of attitudes, a gallery of snapshots, an inventory of postures, a modus vivendi, a shopful of frocks, an arch of eyebrows, a great big pink butterfly that just won't be pinned down. Camp is primarily an adjective, occasionally a verb, but never anything as prosaic, as earth-bound, as a noun.[14]

While remaining difficult to define, camp is traditionally understood to have specific historical connections to (primarily male) homosexuality.[15] This is not to say that that bisexuals do not already do camp, or have not been part of this history, but rather that camp is primarily understood through its relation to homosexuality rather than to bisexuality – which may be in part because bisexuality has been consistently rewritten as gay. Fabio Cleto agrees that many

> questions remain to some extent unsettled: about how camp might be defined and historicised, about its relation – be it ontological or happenstantial – to homosexuality (is it an exclusively gay cultural mode of representation, or what? If so, how subversive is it and how much does it comply, or has it historically complied, with the compulsory heterosexual, and both gyno- and homophobic, dominant structures of interpellation?), where and in what forms it can be traced, and about its relation to postmodern epistemology and theories of textuality/ subjectivity.[16]

These questions are particularly pertinent to bisexuality, which has an equally uncertain relationship to straight, lesbian and gay identities and to queer theory. A camp which 'hasn't lost its relentless power to frustrate all efforts to pinpoint it down to stability'[17] aligns with bisexuality's 'unresolved definitional uncertainty [which] points to a larger uncertainty about what sexuality is and how it should be understood'.[18]

While many characters in *The Stranger's Child* exhibit bisexualities, my focus is on Cecil Valance, the young aristocratic poet who, in the first section, comes to visit his secret lover George and his family. During this visit he writes a poem, 'Two Acres', which later becomes well known and is said to have 'entered the language' of the nation (*SC* 172). 'Two Acres' is ostensibly written for George's younger sister Daphne (with whom Cecil later has a sexual relationship) although there are also unpublished sections written for George that are rediscovered after Cecil's death. Over the course of the novel's five sections (which span 1914 to 2008 with significant gaps in time between them) characters try and fail to piece together various truths about the poem and the past: a process that involves their writing about Cecil. Among the texts published are: Daphne's memoir detailing her relationship with Cecil; gay writer Paul Bryant's scandalous biography outing Cecil as gay; and queer theorist Nigel Dupont's edited edition of Cecil's poetry in which the previously lost 'queer' verses are made public.

As characters write *about* Cecil they also rewrite Cecil and his bisexuality as immature, gay or queer. As such, they are shown to be agents of gay/queer and heteronormative practices which overwrite bisexuality. By the end of *The Stranger's Child*, Cecil stands in for the bisexuality rewritten as gay, the bisexuality subsumed by queer theory, and the bisexuality invalidated as an immature phase en route to a normative straight life marked by marriage and children. What his bisexuality is not allowed to be is the bisexuality that is named, and names itself bisexuality. Attempts by various characters to rewrite Cecil in these ways expose what Daniel Mendelsohn identifies in the novel as an 'exploration of the way in which the stories we tell ourselves can occlude (comically or tragically) the real story – how "our" truth ends up obscuring "the" truth, whether in poetry, history or biography'.[19] So, despite Cecil's agency in the brief period he is alive, the rest of the text concerns characters training their various other lenses on him, repurposing his bisexuality and writing monosexual maturity or queer radicality on top of it.

Cecil functions fundamentally as a threshold – as the adolescent bisexuality out of which people, gay or straight, must mature in order to (attempt to) achieve adulthood. The normative straight story, the gay story and the queer story are all imposed on his bisexuality. For Daphne, ostensibly the straight character in the novel, he is no more than a gateway to monosexual maturity.

> 'Really Cecil means nothing to me – I was potty about him for five minutes sixty years ago. The significant thing about Cecil, as far as I'm concerned,' said Daphne, half-hearing herself go on, 'is that he led to [first husband] Dud, and the children, and all the grown-up part of my life, which naturally he had no part in himself!' (*SC* 500)

Well, naturally. How could Cecil, as a figure of bisexuality, have any part in the grown-up part of a life when a life can only be read as 'grown-up' by invalidating its bisexuality? In trying to downplay his significance, however, she also owns that without him the grown-up part of her life as it is would not have been possible. Bisexuality here is what maturity must reject in order to be read as such, and yet is simultaneously that which brings about that maturity in the first place. Note also the disjuncture between internal and external voices; Daphne only half-hears herself go on. We may assume then that this disavowal is not complete, however much she may outwardly attempt to rewrite Cecil as a fully invalidated immaturity.

Paul's attempt to rewrite Cecil as gay takes a strategic and knowing form. In conversation with a minor character, Jake, Paul explains his project, thus:

'I'm writing a biography of Cecil Valance,' said Paul firmly...
'So he was gay too was he?'
'Again ... among other things.'
Again Jake was delighted. 'They all were, weren't they?' he said.
Paul felt he should be a bit more cautious: 'I mean, he did have affairs with women, but I have the feeling he really preferred boys. That's one of the things I want to find out.' (*SC* 420)

While acknowledging (but not naming) the bisexual nature of Cecil's actual sexual practices, it is still Paul's feeling that he really preferred boys. There is an ambiguity here as to what, precisely, Paul wants to find out: *whether* Cecil preferred boys, or *that* he did? While 'affairs' may be an accurate way to describe Cecil's relations with both men and women, the word's use in connection with only the latter implies a hierarchy in which relations with men are less trivial, more authentic; this is what enables Paul to read Cecil as gay. Marcin Sroczyński rightly notes that

> Paul Bryant's quest to prove to the world that Cecil and Dudley Valance were gay receives harsh criticism in the book. The character is denounced at the end of the novel as a rather repellent figure with an ambiguous past...This seems to be Hollinghurst's warning against too fervent a gay activism which may consist in building an artificial 'gay heritage.'[20]

The warning here is, I think, more specifically against activism that not only finds gayness where it is not, but that actively installs a gay identity at the expense of other, bisexual possibilities.

Paul's work to make Cecil gay directly opposes Nigel Dupont's work to make him queer, which once again lays claim to Cecil at the expense of his bisexuality. While Paul researches Cecil's life for the biography, Dupont prepares his edition of the poems. For Dupont, the 'unpublished part' of 'Two Acres' turned out 'to be a sort of queer manifesto, except in tetrameter couplets' (*SC* 541), although from what the reader sees of it to 'walk the ... wild dark path of love' (*SC* 52) hardly seems enough on its own to constitute a queer manifesto. Where Paul has claimed Cecil for gay, acting on a 'feeling that he preferred boys', Dupont has claimed Cecil for queer with a particular reading of his poem. By the end of the novel, 'the Valance work seemed a distant prolegomenon to far more sensational achievements' (*SC* 540): namely his 'milestone works in Queer Theory' (*SC* 528). Cecil, as prolegomenon, provides the introduction to Dupont's later, queerer work.

Underneath the discarded lines of verse on the rediscovered manuscript 'was a very dense crossing out, as if not only Cecil's words but his very ideas had had to be obliterated' (*SC* 52). We do see the obliteration of Cecil's 'very ideas' in the novel, through their subordination to Paul's 'gay' and Nigel's 'queer'. Cecil obfuscates something in the poem that he considers unnameable and that subsequent readers (must) find illegible. For Paul this is understood as gay, and for Dupont queer: each installs a nameable subject in place of the figurative and literal illegibility and unintelligibility of Cecil's bisexuality. In each of these cases bisexuality is the necessary preface to what becomes differently fixed as straight, gay or queer: the immature gateway to a normative hetero-reproductive future and the prolegomenon to two separate writing careers – the tenacious biographer who outs gays and the successful but pompous queer theorist. Cecil and his bisexuality function as the starting point out of which these other identity positionings mature and the 'achievements' of gay and queer writers, presented as a straightforward linear advancement towards commercial success or prestige, rely on the erasure or subsumption of an originary bisexuality.

This rewriting of bisexuality is not confined to the novel; it also characterizes many critics' responses to it. For Mendelsohn, for instance, *The Stranger's Child* is 'about the way in which the true, gay story behind a poem ... is elided over time'.[21] James Wood similarly asserts that 'the real subject of Paul's biography, as is the real subject of Hollinghurst's novel, is the hidden homosexuality of [Cecil,] this now idealized literary representative'.[22] There are a number of problems with situating the text in this way. First, it signals and contributes to the erasure of bisexual representation in contemporary culture more generally. Secondly, reading the text in terms of a hidden 'true gay story' risks repeating the process through which (particularly male) bisexuals are commonly believed to be 'confused' and 'really gay',[23] by asserting the authenticity of a gay identity over a transitory bisexual one. But this novel is precisely not about revealing the 'true gay story'. Rather, it demonstrates how the development of that story can impose gayness on other, more ambiguous sexual possibilities. Thirdly, a gay reading of the novel performs the same interpretative mistakes on the novel as its characters do with the poem the within it. Theo Tait describes the novel as:

a sort of ironic meditation on the evolution of literary memory. It shows how the poem and the original incident behind it are mythologised, and the myth is made official. Later comes the revisionist version .... The myths are partially corrected, but new myths replace some of the old ones, and new fashions unbalance the historical record just as the old ones did.[24]

Cecil is subject to various misreadings and rewritings. He functions not only as a fictive origin to which all subsequent sections of the novel return, but also as an elusive and allusive stand-in for the 'real' literary past and the processes of re-reading and reinterpretation which literary texts inevitably undergo.

But while the influences of other literary texts are made clear in the abundance of allusion, quotation and quasi-pastiche, *The Stranger's Child* is as concerned with Hollinghurst's own position in the text as it is with the novel's intertexts. According to one interviewer, Hollinghurst, 'refuses to engage with ... whether he is still pigeonholed as a gay writer'.[25] 'I spent 20 years politely answering the question, "How do you feel when people categorise you as a gay writer?" and I'm not going to do it this time round. It's no longer relevant,' Hollinghurst says. Elsewhere he suggests that he is actually 'not writing such completely gay [novels] anymore',[26] even though 'there is a particular kind of gay reader who would like me to keep writing the same book over and over again, which I've never had any interest in doing'.[27] *The Stranger's Child*, as a not-so-completely-gay text, responds to and rebukes the particular kind of reader Hollinghurst describes here and, more specifically, the novel's bisexualities stage a camp critique of their inevitable (mis)interpretation within the context of the 'gay' novel.

One of the key historical functions of camp has been as a coding practice that communicates queerness to those in the know, while remaining hidden (or at least plausibly deniable) to mainstream culture. But the world in which *The Line of Beauty* wins the Booker Prize is markedly different from the world where same-sex desire once needed to operate through codes and secret languages. Historically, camp can be understood as a gay response to, and method for coping with and critiquing, the straight culture that oppresses it. It is 'a survival mechanism, a form of queer resistance in a world where the systems surrounding gender and sexuality are rigidly policed'.[28] But mainstream gay culture, in its reliance on the fixing of an authentic identity, polices its own rigid systems which work to erase bisexuality. What I identify as bisexual camp therefore operates as a site of specifically bisexual resistance to this monosexist gay culture. According to Jonathan Dollimore, camp 'negotiates some of the lived contradictions of subordination, simultaneously refashioning as a weapon of attack an oppressive identity inherited *as* subordination, and hollowing out dominant formations responsible for that identity in the first instance'.[29] Bisexual camp therefore refashions the uncertainty, unresolvedness and hypersexualization of stereotypical constructions of bisexuality as weapons with which to attack contemporary gay discourse.

Perhaps inevitably, elements of Hollinghurst's previous novels fostered expectations which influenced the reception of *The Stranger's Child*. In particular, Tait observed that Hollinghurst seemed to have taken 'vows of chastity', and 'radically cut down on the sex, which is mostly shielded by soft focus or euphemism' in place of the explicit detail for which he is known.[30] Take the first incident of sex in the novel, between Cecil and George, and the way it is (explicitly not) represented:

> Cecil stopped and shrugged with pleasure, slipped off his jacket and hung it on the upraised claw [of the branch] above him. Then he turned and reached out his hands impatiently.
>
> 'That was very good', muttered Cecil, already standing up – then walking off for a few paces as he roughly straightened his clothes. .... He had a way of distancing himself at once, and seemed almost to counter the bleak little minute of irrational sadness by pretending that nothing had happened. (*SC* 78)

After seventy-seven apparently chaste pages, the sex for which Cecil (and the reader) waits 'impatiently' is consigned to the blank space of a paragraph break and followed by an abrupt 'distancing'. In this way Hollinghurst plays with the expectation of explicit sex and overtly refuses to deliver it. But just like Cecil, he is only pretending that nothing has happened. To perceive this as chastity misreads what happens to the sex: it has not been removed, it has been dissolved into the rest of the text at the level of language such that the entire work is built upon a sexualized textuality that simultaneously withholds and indulges in it. Mendelsohn thinks that 'there is something tame' about this novel and that 'by the time you reach the last of its ... pages, you wonder whether a certain vital organ is missing'; for him the book comes to be defined by 'an absent penis'.[31] This particular omission is announced when Paul Bryant looks at pictures by the bisexual artist Revel Ralph (who feels 'there is room in the world for more than one kind of beauty' (*SC* 141)) and notices a set of drawings 'of a naked young man, ... everything about him wonderfully brought out, except his cock and balls which were consigned to the imagination by a swoop of the pencil, ostentatiously discreet, pretending it wasn't the point' (*SC* 510). Just like the genitals in these drawings, the sex *has* happened and *is* the point. Like Revel and Cecil, Hollinghurst is only pretending otherwise. Bisexuality, as Michael du Plessis notes, 'seems to lend itself to exaggeration – all or nothing; everyone is bisexual or no one is'.[32] This can be a further way in which bisexuality is delegitimized as a distinct identity experience or perspective (if everyone is bisexual then it loses any specificity, becoming synonymous with all sexuality; if no one is then it does not exist): here 'all or nothing' is repurposed through the text's representations of sex as all *and* nothing, everywhere and nowhere. Commonly, bisexuality is either rendered invisible (rewritten as gay, queer or immature) or else hypersexualized (visible only through promiscuity);[33] the unrepresented sex in *The Stranger's Child* – which is then made conspicuous by its absence – parodies both of these mechanisms. Eric Banks suggests that 'there's a primness to the sex here that feels ironically shocking in its blatant modesty';[34] it is in the ironic shock of Hollinghurst's ostentatious discretion that we encounter bisexual camp.

As the characters' lives are shaped by Cecil's absence, so the text becomes sexualized by the apparent absence of explicit sex; sex is found instead in near-constant innuendo. In one scene Daphne (aged twenty-six) and the designer Eva Riley are in the garden:

> 'Can I tempt you?' said Eva .... The nacreous curve of her cigarette case gleamed like treasure in the moonlight.
>
> 'Oh ...! hmm ... well, all right ...'
>
> Up flashed the oily flame of her lighter. 'I like to see you smoking', said Eva, as the tobacco crackled and glowed.
>
> 'I'm starting to like it myself', said Daphne. ...
>
> [Eva] slid her arm companionably round Daphne's waist.
>
> 'Let's try not to fall into the fishpond', Daphne said, moving slightly apart.
>
> 'I wish you'd let me make you something lovely', said Eva ... [and she] snuggled against her again cajolingly .... 'I wish you'd let me make you happy.'
>
> Daphne said ... 'I'm really rather cold, I'm most frightfully sorry.' She jerked herself away, dropping her cigarette on the path and stamping on it. (*SC* 214–15)

Describing this to Revel a few moments later, Daphne declares: 'I'm absolutely certain she was making love to me' (*SC* 218). Daphne's interpretation indicates the way the absent sex permeates the rest of the text: the act of sex becomes an act of language (as indeed the more explicit sex of Hollinghurst's early writing often was). The novel repeatedly foregrounds coding and innuendo: Paul, for instance, ponders the real meaning in Daphne's memoir 'of Cecil preparing for a "mighty thrust"' (*SC* 469) as well as 'the matter of Cecil's massive tip' given to servant Jonah (*SC* 417). Indeed, at one stage 'it seemed Cecil had already become' a 'codeword' for sexual encounters between Paul and lover Peter Rowe (*SC* 340). By repeatedly announcing the ways in which language stands in for conspicuously absent sex, the text actually enables sex to be found almost everywhere throughout it. Being less explicit than Hollinghurst's other novels does not make it less sexual; indeed, its bisexual camp effect makes the ostensible absence of sex outrageously sexualized.

The cigarettes in the passage above are an obvious innuendo that has been set up in the opening section (sometimes a cigarette is not just a cigarette). Daphne, aged sixteen, goes into the garden in the dark, looking for Cecil and George; near the hammock she detects 'the gentlemanly whiff of Cecil's cigar' and overhears them wondering whether George and Daphne's older brother Hubert is a 'womanizer' (*SC* 32–3). This is their word for heterosexual, and so it situates what follows in the context of coded sexual language: Cecil 'pulled on his cigar' and Daphne sees 'the scarlet burn of its tip' as it twitches and fades (*SC* 34). Daphne feels 'a simple urge to climb in with' the two men. 'She had shared the hammock with her mother, when she was smaller,' but now 'she was mindful of the hot cigar'.

> The cigar tip, barely showing, dithered in the air like some dimly luminous bug and then glowed into life again, but now it was George's face that she saw in its faint devilish light. 'Oh, I thought it was Cecil's cigar,' she said simply.
>
> George chortled in three quick huffs of smoke. And Cecil cleared his throat – somehow supportively and appreciatively. 'So it was,' said George, in his most paradoxical tone. 'I'm smoking Cecil's cigar too.'
>
> 'Oh really ...' said Daphne, not knowing what tone to give the words. 'Well, I shouldn't let Mother find out.' (*SC* 34)

This passage establishes the bisexual triangle between these characters. Daphne, in her relations with Cecil, is more than 'a transvestic stand-in, an improvised George'.[35] That sort of reading, necessary to assert Cecil's gayness, sidelines those parts of the text where it is made clear that Cecil *does* have interest for Daphne, or for other women; those points for instance at which it is revealed that he does not share George's 'fastidious horror at the mere idea of a cunt' (*SC* 72), and indeed 'would fuck anyone' (*SC* 456). A reading that subordinates the relationship between Cecil and Daphne to a supposedly more authentic homosexual desire for George therefore recalls attempts to rewrite bisexuality as 'really gay'.

Reading this bisexually takes us closer to the kinds of ambivalent sexuality which are being represented here. It also points to the novel's preoccupation with time, memory and narrative, all of which are as conflicted as its relationship to bisexuality. Explaining the prevalence of bisexuality in the novel, Hollinghurst states that 'one of the ideas of the book is about the unknowability or uncategorisability of human behaviour, and I was rather tempted into those ambiguous sexual areas'.[36] He explicitly links the unnamed bisexuality with the novel's broader engagement with unknowability: characters' attempts to uncover truths, gay or otherwise, ultimately fail. He suggests that he had

> just become tired of that model ... where a book contains a secret which, when finally revealed, makes everything make sense. And it seems to me ... life's not like that .... I wanted to create uncertainty in the reader; the reader shares the uncertainty and ignorance of a lot of the characters themselves about what actually happened between people they knew quite well in the past. ... My subject was much more to do with not so much remembering as forgetting and the way so much about the past, about our own lives, is sort of irrevocably lost to us.[37]

This structural uncertainty aligns with the forgetting posited by Judith Halberstam as integral to a queer project to think about 'an opportunity for a non-hetero-reproductive future'.[38] Halberstam proposes 'a notion of queer forgetting within which the forgetful subject ... lives to create relationality anew in each moment and for each context and without a teleology'.[39] I see similar possibilities in the ways in which *The Stranger's Child* imbricates narratives of sexuality, identity and literary tradition and repeatedly stages their failures.

'One's own life doesn't naturally have a shape', Hollinghurst has said in interview, 'one is constantly imposing a shape on it; constructing the narrative'.[40] *The Stranger's Child*, structured around unknowable gaps in time, exposes the limitations of these narratives and our reliance on their continuity by frustrating our desire to see *how* characters have arrived at each position. He explains that he 'loved the idea of leaving the characters at one point and then joining them 10, 15 years later without any real explanation; making the reader work out what's happened'.[41] Hollinghurst excises lines of continuity and fills in gaps only through the explicitly fallible and contradictory memories (or rather, forgetting) of those characters. What 'the reader is ultimately presented with', according to Elsa Cavalié, is 'a distinctly postmodernist mosaic of non-congruent portraits and texts, which simultaneously denounces the quest for an irrevocable and fictitious past while enhancing [their] fascination for it'.[42] These discontinuities expose and frustrate the desire for congruence and the desire for fulfilment through resolution.

In its very early stages *The Stranger's Child* was to be a series of short stories.[43] The idea that the different sections of the novel are separate books, with different archives of literary influences, persists in their failure to fully and finally cohere. This facilitates a form of forgetting that defers and frustrates all 'attempts at finality or wholeness' and thus 'withholds fulfilment'.[44] The withholding of both sexual and narrative fulfilment again converges in Cecil, *The Stranger's Child*'s absent centre. The novel opens with a delayed arrival: Daphne, in the hammock, excitedly awaits Cecil and George, but Cecil 'must have missed his train, or at least his connection' (*SC* 3). Their eventual arrival becomes apparent when she hears 'an unfamiliar voice, with an edge to it, and then George's laugh. ... She couldn't really hear what they were saying, but she was disconcerted by Cecil's voice' (*SC* 4). Remembering that 'edging' is a term for the sexual practice of intentionally delaying orgasm, Cecil's disconcerting voice then references the refusal to climax or resolve that is present in the broader structure of this narrative which has dissolved bi-sex into its language. The entire narrative becomes analogous to the holding plateau before orgasm: focused not on the one climactic arrival but on the extended experience. The (non)orgasmic structure of the narrative seems to have been felt by Hollinghurst himself: 'Normally, I do have a brief but acute sort of depression when I finish a book ... but I was so desperate to get this thing off that I seem to have escaped that'.[45] Perhaps he escaped his usual come-down – 'that bleak little minute of irrational sadness' (*SC* 78) – after a novel by constructing one which never 'gets off' at all but comes to embrace this frustration as the necessary failure of life and literature to cohere with finality, to split into all or nothing, this or that. Instead, *The Stranger's Child* has it both ways.

Notes

1   Stephen Moss, 'Alan Hollinghurst: Sex on the Brain', *Guardian* 18 June 2011, www.theguardian.com/books/2011/jun/18/alan-hollinghurst-interview (accessed 19 January 2016).

2   Kenji Yoshino, 'The Epistemic Contract of Bisexual Erasure', *Stanford Law Review* 52.2 (2000) 353–456.

3   Robyn Ochs, 'Why we Need to "Get Bi"', *Journal of Bisexuality* 11.2–3 (2011) 171–5: 172.

4   Phoebe Davidson, '"Her Libido Had Flowed in Two Currents": Representations of Bisexuality in Psychoanalytic Case Studies' in *The Bisexual Imaginary: Representation, Identity, and Desire*, ed. Bi Academic Intervention (London: Cassell, 1997) 58–72: 64.

5   Marjorie Garber, *Vice Versa: Bisexuality and the Eroticism of Everyday Life* (New York: Simon & Schuster, 1995) 343.

6   Esther Saxey, *Homoplot* (New York: Lang, 2008) 10.

7   Ibid. 130.

8   Esther Saxey, 'Desire without Closure in Jaime Hernandez' Love and Rockets', *ImageTexT* 3.1 (2006), www.english.ufl.edu/imagetext/archives/v3_1/saxey/ (accessed 19 January 2016).

9   Clare Hemmings, *Bisexual Spaces: A Geography of Sexuality and Gender* (New York: Routledge, 2002) 4.

10 David Halperin, 'Thirteen Ways of Looking at a Bisexual', *Journal of Bisexuality* 9.3–4 (2009) 451–5: 454.

11 Georges Letissier, 'Alan Hollinghurst/Ronald Firbank: Camp Filiation as an Aesthetic of the Outrageous', *Études britanniques contemporaines* 45 (2013), http://ebc.revues.org/742 (accessed 19 January 2016).

12 Andy Medhurst, 'Batman, Deviance and Camp' in *The Many Lives of the Batman*, ed. Roberta E. Pearson and William Uricchio (London: BFI, 1991) 149–63: 154.

13 Andy Medhurst, 'Camp' in *Lesbian and Gay Studies: A Critical Introduction*, ed. Andy Medhurst and Sally Munt (London and Washington: Cassell, 1997) 274–93: 276.

14 Medhurst, 'Batman, Deviance and Camp' 155.

15 Fabio Cleto, 'Introduction: Queering the Camp' in *Camp: Queer Aesthetics and the Performing Subject – A Reader*, ed. Fabio Cleto (Edinburgh: Edinburgh University Press, 1999) 1–42: 5.

16 Ibid. 2–3.

17 Ibid. 2.

18 Halperin, 'Thirteen Ways of Looking at a Bisexual' 451.

19 Daniel Mendelsohn, 'In Gay and Crumbling England', *New York Review of Books* 10 November 2011, www.nybooks.com/articles/archives/2011/nov/10/gay-and-crumbling-england/ (accessed 19 January 2016).

20 Marcin Sroczyński, 'The Stranger's Child: Alan Hollinghurst's Subversive Englishness', *Acta Philologica* 43 (2013) 77–86: 82.

21 Mendelsohn, 'In Gay and Crumbling England'.

22 James Wood, 'Sons and Lovers', *New Yorker* 10 October 2011, www.newyorker.com/magazine/2011/10/17/sons-and-lovers-james-wood (accessed 19 January 2016).

23 Shiri Eisner, *Bi: Notes for a Bisexual Revolution* (Berkeley, CA: Seal Press, 2013) 39.

24 Theo Tait, 'The Stranger's Child by Alan Hollinghurst – Review', *Guardian* 17 June 2011, www.theguardian.com/books/2011/jun/17/strangers-child-alan-hollinghurst-review (accessed 19 January 2016).

25 Moss, 'Alan Hollinghurst'.

26 Alice O'Keeffe, 'Alan Hollinghurst', *Bookseller* 28 July 2011, www.thebookseller.com/profile/alan-hollinghurst (accessed 19 January 2016).

27 Scarlett Baron, 'An Interview with Alan Hollinghurst', *Oxonian Review* 4 June 2012, www.oxonianreview.org/wp/an-interview-with-alan-hollinghurst-draft/ (accessed 19 January 2016).

28 John M. Wolf, 'Resurrecting Camp: Rethinking the Queer Sensibility', *Communication, Culture & Critique* 6.2 (2013) 284–97: 286.

29   Jonathan Dollimore, 'Post/modern: On the Gay Sensibility, or the Pervert's Revenge on Authenticity' in Cleto ed., *Camp*, 221–36: 224.

30   Tait, '*The Stranger's Child* by Alan Hollinghurst – Review'.

31   Mendelsohn, 'In Gay and Crumbling England'.

32   Michael du Plessis, 'Blatantly Bisexual; or, Unthinking Queer Theory' in *Representing Bisexualities: Subjects and Cultures of Fluid Desire*, ed. Donald E. Hall and Maria Pramaggiore (New York: New York University Press, 1996) 19–54: 19.

33   Eisner, *Bi* 37–8.

34   Eric Banks, 'Love Is a Battlefield', *Bookforum* September–November 2011, www.bookforum.com/inprint/018_03/8281 (accessed 19 January 2016).

35   Greg Graham-Smith, 'Sexuality and the Multicursal Maze in Alan Hollinghurst's *The Stranger's Child*', *Scrutiny 2* 17.2 (2012) 7–12: 10.

36   Moss, 'Alan Hollinghurst'.

37   Michael Cathcart, 'Alan Hollinghurst on *The Stranger's Child*' (video), *Big Ideas*, www.abc.net.au/tv/bigideas/stories/2012/04/16/3476838.htm (accessed 19 January 2016).

38   Judith Halberstam, *The Queer Art of Failure* (Durham, NC: Duke University Press, 2011) 70.

39   Ibid. 80.

40   Angela Meyer, 'Pleasure, Memory, Decay, and *The Stranger's Child*: An Interview with Alan Hollinghurst', *Literaryminded* 11 April 2012, http://literaryminded.com.au/2012/04/11/pleasure-memory-decay-and-the-strangers-child-an-interview-with-alan-hollinghurst/ (accessed 19 January 2016).

41   O'Keefe, 'Alan Hollinghurst'.

42   Elsa Cavalié, '"A Book Persisted as a Coloured Shadow at the Edge of Sight": Englishness and Influence in Alan Hollinghurst's *The Stranger's Child*', *Revue Interdisciplinaire 'Textes & contextes'* 7 (2012), http://revuesshs.u-bourgogne.fr/textes&contextes/document.php?id=1765 (accessed 19 January 2016).

43   Cathcart, 'Alan Hollinghurst on *The Stranger's Child*'.

44   Graham-Smith, 'Sexuality and the Multicursal Maze in Alan Hollinghurst's *The Stranger's Child*' 8.

45   Moss, 'Alan Hollinghurst'.

7

Hollow auguries: eccentric genealogies in *The Folding Star* and *The Spell*

Robert L. Caserio

The purpose of history, guided by genealogy, is not to discover the roots of our identity but to commit ... to its dissipation. (Michel Foucault)[1]

Alan Hollinghurst's novels take inspiration from the era of literary modernism, and his characters invariably discuss writers and works of the period. Yet the literary origins Hollinghurst solicits for his novels – and *in* the novels themselves – don't have the prominence that might straightforwardly explain their relevance. The novels also express unease with a modernist genealogy. If the publication of *The Waste Land* and *Ulysses* in 1922 marks the crest of the modernist wave, then Hollinghurst's references to this era are a bit out of line. His fiction mostly refers to lesser figures who overlap with the modernists but who are labelled Edwardian or Georgian because they are considered not modernist enough. The canon of Hollinghurst's references constitutes an alternative literary-historical 1922. It comprises the last *Georgian Poets* anthology (1920–2), which includes Robert Graves and D. H. Lawrence, A. E. Housman's *Last Poems* (1922), Thomas Hardy's *Late Lyrics and Earlier* (1922), Gordon Bottomley's verse plays, *King Lear's Wife* (1915) and *Gruach* (1921), Ronald Firbank's *The Flower Beneath the Foot* (1923) and *Sorrow in Sunlight* (1924), and John Masefield's *Collected Poems* (1923). Does Hollinghurst want his readers to research his literary-historical allusions? To some extent, yes. But filling in the allusions might make readers miss a leading suggestion in Hollinghurst's fiction: that the tradition, whether centric or eccentric, should be let go, or must be let go. The strange character of the genealogy results from Hollinghurst's use of the past in his novels, including the uses of literary history, with a simultaneous gesture of rejection. While soliciting a literary-historical source and lineage, Hollinghurst reminds one of Nietzsche: like the philosopher, the novelist addresses 'origins' with 'the kind of dissociative view that is capable of decomposing itself'.[2]

The novelist's backhanded, dissociative tendency is signalled in Hollinghurst's introduction to his 2005 selection of A. E. Housman's poems for Faber's 'Poet to Poet' series. When he notes that over the course of thirty years 'there is little sense of development in Housman's poetry',[3] he suggests Housman's subordination of causal or historical unfolding to an interest in decomposition as well as dissociation. What stays the same in Housman is the poet's subject matter: mortality and death. 'The search for descent is not the erecting of foundations',[4] Foucault also says of Nietzsche's genealogical project. The subversion of foundations is a constant in Housman's verse.

Because of that changelessness in Housman, for Hollinghurst to revive Housman 'poet to poet' is for him to engage a contradiction-filled project. There is death in every turn of Housman's verse, and the poetry therefore equates the past with what is irrevocable and non-generative; with death, not with living influence. 'The creation of life has no place in [his] universe', Edmund Wilson writes of Housman's poems, because 'he can only repeat the same bitter experience over and over and draw from it the same bitter moral'.[5] Hollinghurst is in tune with Wilson when he remarks that Housman himself regarded his poetry as 'a morbid secretion'.[6]

Hollinghurst's note about the absence of Housman's 'development' is followed by a remarkably ambiguous assertion about Housman's relation to literary genealogy. In addition to being fecundated by morbidity, 'Housman was spontaneously literary too', Hollinghurst writes, and he adds: 'and the resources of tradition came to him as readily and as aptly as a cry of pain'.[7] The latter clause means that cries of pain and the resources of tradition – of literary history – came to Housman's poetry separately but with equal ease and fit. But the latter clause also, thanks to a slippery *as*, suggests that the resources of tradition express, readily and aptly, a cry of pain. Whose cry is it, the past's or the present's, Housman's or Hollinghurst's? If the cry belongs to both times, it expresses a different significance for each author. For Hollinghurst it might express the pain of carrying on the past, even the crying hope that those genealogies of the present called *history* and *literary history* are now among the departed, equivalents of Housman's fallen personae.

If the cry of pain does express Hollinghurst's lament for the resources of literary history and simultaneously a valedictory drive to let go of tradition, his motive would have everything to do with his role as an historical novelist and a novelist of manners – of gay manners. His fiction represents the advent of an historical sea-change: the transformation of homosexuality's status, its new legitimacy and tolerance in many contexts.

Because of that change, the artistic traditions that have been the space of homosexual self-recognition (aside from sex, but in defence of sex) are no longer the centres of representation that they were. *The Folding Star* and *The Spell* dramatize the plight of characters deeply troubled by genealogies of gay life, hence by the very generators of their tradition. What comes after the tradition – besides the enactment of sexual desire in newly accepting contexts – remains unknown. Nevertheless, whatever the future is, Hollinghurst's figures often want to lay to rest the past's shaping of their lives. They suggest their author would too. His attraction to Housman enforces the suggestion, because the poet insists on endings. If his insistence 'is sour', Housman writes, 'the better for the embittered hour'[8] – for the hour that, personally or culturally, must be recognized as a last one. Hollinghurst's fiction enacts such recognitions.

Hollinghurst inclines to and might also identify with writers unlike Housman. Another of them is Firbank, three of whose novels Hollinghurst introduced in a Penguin re-issue in 2000. Hollinghurst does not come near Firbank in wit or tone, or in intensity of feeling combined with lightness of construction. When Hollinghurst's 'Introduction' to *Three Novels* contrasts Firbank's formal inventiveness with '[t]he massive prosecution of a system of cause and effect, so characteristic of the Victorian novel',[9] one is reminded of a neo-Victorian 'prosecution' of cause and effect in *The Folding Star*. Yet when Hollinghurst's novel, as will be seen, also prosecutes – in an adversarial sense – its own genealogical cause-and-effect construction, one is put in mind of Firbank's inspiration.

A reminder of Firbank in *The Folding Star* is the play with names of churches and schools (St Vaast, St Narcissus, St Opportune) and the camp title of a book, *Careful, Mary!*, written by the protagonist's great-aunt, who would have been a contemporary of Firbank's. But the melancholy of the novel's narrator, Edward Manners, is the narrative's most Firbankian echo. It reminds us of the ends of Firbank's Laura di Nazianzi, whose disappointment in love causes her to retreat from her glamorous world into a cloister. It reminds us also of his Miami Mouth, whose disappointment causes her to join a band of itinerant penitents. Both heroines mortify themselves by cutting clear of their origins and their original desires. *The Folding Star* and *The Spell* tell of their protagonists' similar mortification. Their experience argues their need to surrender to unknown future prospects by letting go of the past altogether, even if the withdrawal hurts, and even though – and even because – the resources of tradition include Housman and Firbank ('Life's bound to be uncertain when you haven't got your roots!' says a Firbank flower).[10]

The cul-de-sac of genealogy

Why does thirty-three-year-old Edward Manners arrive in Belgium at the beginning of *The Folding Star*? And why does he decide to make seventeen-year-old Luc his erotic object even before encountering him? The withholding of answers underlines the diffusion of aims that makes Manners, the novel's narrator, refer to his life as 'an empty vortex' (*FS* 135). But Hollinghurst presents a counterweight by shaping the narrative as a progressive disclosure of the reasons behind his narrator's actions. The second segment ('Underwoods') of *The Folding Star* promises to be the personal and historical genealogy – here in the sense of an explanation (a conventional rather than Nietzschean one) – of Manners's compulsive distractions. He is recalled to England on the occasion of the death in an automobile accident of his first lover (from public school days), a man nicknamed 'Dawn'. The nickname derives from an association with a poem by Gordon Bottomley that celebrates morning. Manners has been thinking of his own middle season of life as the onset of life's evening (hence the star of the novel's title, borrowed from Milton's 'Lycidas'). 'Underwoods' brings Manners back to the sunrise of his desire, as if to illuminate its confused aftermath.

The explanatory origin is Housman-grim. 'Underwoods' discloses that in Manners's beginning is his end, and the end of others. 'Dawn' suffered from a HIV-related illness, but was improving as a result of AZT treatment; but there was no medicine for the fatality of the accident, and there is no medicine that can return Manners to Dawn, since whom 'Nothing [has been] quite the same'; 'everything' after Dawn has been 'in some way melancholy, frantic or foredoomed' (*FS* 200). 'After' is misleading, however; the contrast between matutinal light and folding star collapses, because doom seems to have struck at the advent of Dawn.

The reader has already been told, in the first part of *The Folding Star*, that Manners maintains a lasting tenderness for his father. The son still tells time by his father's watch: on a weekend when he is to spy on Luc around the clock, he notes 'the vestigial gleam of my father's watch-dial – "illuminous" I had called it as a child' – and he measures by his father's timepiece 'the worst wastes of the night at last admitting the possibility of [the] dawn' (*FS* 110) – of his voyeurism. From the explanatory perspective of 'Underwoods', Manners's spying on the seventeen-year-old seems to constitute a way of returning erotically to his younger self, indeed as a way of spying on himself at the same age of his love for Dawn. And the reference to the father's timepiece implies that Manners wants his father to share watching his boy-self and to watch with desire. Hence the glow of his father's relic predicts what 'Underwoods' will shine more light on: the likelihood of an incestuous cathexis as the origin of Manners's 'empty vortex'. Death along with incest are mixed with the origin and the highpoint of Manners's love of Dawn. The mortal illness of the father, a musician and singer who died in his fifties at a moment made sadder by a failing career, intruded itself into the start of Manners's love life. After the father's death, the young couple one night camped in a tent on their town common. Edward, wandering out of the tent, encountered, and was propositioned by, a thirty-three-year-old man. As Hollinghurst portrays it, Edward's confused response to the proposition compounds sexual attraction to the man (old enough to be his father), sudden tears about the loss of the elder Manners, and aggressive fag-baiting (as if to ward off attraction to the father-figure). Those overwhelming cross-currents, brought into high relief by the chance encounter, mark the beginning of the end of the relationship with Dawn – and the start of Manners's subsequent, largely frustrated, erotic quests. Revealing this part of the past, 'Underwoods' implies that Manners at thirty-three now has become the man on the common, intending to lure his youthful alter ego Luc into a liaison. Because the liaison is a daddy–boy one, it keeps the dead father alive by continuing to mourn him, by simultaneously resurrecting him as his son Edward, and by projecting young Manners onto Luc.

Manners himself recapitulates the explanatory gist of 'Underwoods' when he belatedly articulates his frustration as 'a kind of futile force – ... the anger of bereavement hugely delayed' (*FS* 311). The delay will be permanent, unless the deadlocked antagonists – mourning and morning and eros – are decisively separated. One might think that the long final segment of the novel will consummate the separation. Instead, all but flaunting its structural redundancy, Hollinghurst's finale does 'Underwoods' one better. It interfuses the etiology of Manners's personal deadlock with motives that transcend any single sexual orientation and that are global-historical. The reader has already discovered that Manners's 'vortex' resembles a similar emptiness in the life of a 'straight' Belgian artist who is a central reference point: the artist, Edgard Orst, who died during the German occupation of Belgium in the 1940s. The gap between his time and Manners's will appear to be a continuity nevertheless. The novel's last third implies that the Second World War is to be included in Manners's genealogy.

The narrative vehicle of the genealogical tie is Paul Echevin, the father of another student whom Manners is tutoring. Echevin, another man old enough to be Manners's father, is an art historian dedicated to Orst. The artist's work, dating from the Symbolist era, expresses his passion for two women, the first of whom he lost to death, the second of whom he tried to make a replica of the first. Edward Manners's loves clearly double Orst's (both men are Eds). Manners is further bound to Orst when he becomes Echevin's assistant in constructing a *catalogue raisonné* of Orst's *oeuvre*. Now, in the finale, Echevin confesses to Manners a secret sexual history that attaches Orst's eros and Manners's to the more comprehensive genealogy whereby a perplexed gay love in the 1990s becomes involved with the Second World War. Echevin in his adolescence, a resident of Nazi-occupied Belgium, aided the ageing, blind Orst. At the same time Echevin began a secret homosexual affair with a Belgian old enough to be *his* father. He learned belatedly that his lover was a Nazi collaborator – too late for Echevin to disengage himself or to win the lover away from collaboration, and too late to prevent the murder of the artist and his caretakers by the Germans, perhaps by the lover. Although Echevin's parents harboured Jewish children in their home, the bravery of his family has never offset his guilt about his politically nefarious paramour. His curatorial aim to continue the life of Orst's work displaces the death which darkened his erotic dawn.

Echevin's confession bids for a renewal of his homosexual life, with Manners as the non-fascist heir of the soldier. It also renews for the reader – if not for Manners's immediate consciousness – the scene of young Manners's crisis on the common. How is one to read this extraordinarily, even fantastically, over-determined repetition, whereby Hollinghurst brings together widely separated stories as if they demand comprehension by a shared genealogy? Manners has once read a fabliau about a murderous erotomaniac. He identifies with the character because its obsession reminds him of his fidelity to Luc. And he explains that 'My love-struck need for shapes and portents was eased by the curving together of two stories' (*FS* 178), one of them being his own. He likens such 'curving together' to the convergence of the cheeks of Luc's *cul* (and to the palindromic fusion of name and noun). Yet the climactic convergence of Echevin's and Manners's stories inspires a reaction of distaste. Manners had already only recently – and belatedly – learned the history of Echevin's most familiar friends: they are the grown-up Jewish orphans who were saved during the war. In response to the knowledge, he remarks that 'It was hateful of me, but I began to be irritated by the ubiquitous power of the unsaid' (*FS* 388). All those weighty pasts! When Echevin begins his confession, Manners squirms at the prospect of a 'curving together': the similarity of his experience with Echevin's will make him feel 'robbed' of the 'force and singularity' of his own experience. Then, once the confession is complete, he admits that 'the long perspective of [Echevin's] revelations made him faintly unattractive to me'. He wants to 'politely dissociate our ... predicaments' (*FS* 415).

Behind his narrator's back, Hollinghurst suggests that Manners is too polite. The author has submitted his narrative structure, his protagonist, and his reader to a surfeit of genealogical explanation in order to provoke a cold reaction, not merely a polite one. The reader is more free than the narrator to respond to the author's provocation. The author himself, to be sure, is not without self-division. Hollinghurst praises Firbank for avoiding the Victorian novel's 'massive prosecution of a system of cause and effect'; yet, as if he wants his fiction to be tied back to the Victorian form, Hollinghurst makes the last third of *The Folding Star* an exercise in cause and effect. Under the surface, though, the modernist inspiration of Firbank, producing an ironic dissociation of form from substance, wins out. If Manners does not fully seize the dissociative opportunity because he thinks it unmannerly (or hateful) to resist a supposedly explanatory convergence of past and present tales, it is because he is not as aware as the reader is of his moribund tethering to the past. The origins of his frustrated desires (and the origins of Echevin's) are a cul-de-sac, a no-outlet in which politeness and passion are trapped. It is worse for Manners, more inhibiting rather than less, that he has been recalled to the past by Dawn's funeral. The ill of ties to an originary past is signalled early in the novel by Hollinghurst when he links genealogical explanation – the very thing that his structure will exploit – to absurdity. Luc's family traces its lineage to the Virgin Mary and to Jesus' half-brother, St James the Less. Manners countenances the absurdity, for the glamour it adds to Luc, even though genealogy smacks of the bitter cross-currents of what one might call Manners's Dawn-complex. He needs to contest genealogical thinking. Yet when he comes close to doing so, he tends to deflect the occasion. Apropos of Orst's erotic history, he remarks: 'My own obsessions made it hard for me to grant the force of someone else's – besides [Orst's obsession] was long ago and part of the never fully plausible world of heterosexual feeling. I started trying to convert it to my own terms' (*FS* 292). The conversion attempt (where one might expect a dissociation attempt) insures that Manners will stay fixed on 'long ago', and that – despite his gay snark about heterosexual feeling – he will conform his world of homosexual feeling to the never fully plausible object, Luc.

The final segment of the novel, in which Echevin's confession appears, is titled 'A Merry Goose Hunt'. The phrase is a Belgian student's garbled version of a wild goose chase. As a boundary line between 'Underwoods' and the finale, the title gives a first-time reader pause. In addition to its immediate oddity, does the title and its garbled nature reflect back sceptically on the explanatory purport of 'Underwoods'? Was that excursion into the past a pointless search? The title is apt once the finale becomes a baffled chase after Luc, who has fled home and his hopeless love (for a petty thief and pornographer with whom Manners is sleeping!) in order to begin an indefinite life in England. But the title also insinuates that the novel's commitment in its final third to genealogical explanation – the sort that Echevin's confession exemplifies – will amount also to a wild goose chase, an error, a dark joke (a Firbank-inspired formal joke on pre-modernist fiction, one might add). Perhaps a hunt for explanations will lead nowhere because they will make no practical difference to present predicaments.

That possibility appears to be borne out. The threads Echevin tries to connect are less a system of causes and effects than they are a line of analogies – more like fiction than fact. Echevin realizes something of this (or makes it possible for Hollinghurst to make the reader realize it), even as he involves himself, Orst, Manners, and Luc in one erotic-historical cause-and-effect net. The causal explanation might inspire responsibilities: of the present to the past, of the young to the old, of heirs to traditions. Yet Echevin admits: 'How does one know what one is responsible for? ... [A] youngster cannot know. He picks up an older person's life and then ... he's no idea what he's doing – lets it drop' (*FS* 414). That is what he did in regard to Orst and his first love. Yet he wants to pick things up again, to interconnect them. Manners suddenly gets a clue. He wants to 'dissociate our two predicaments'. Not responding to Echevin's invitational embrace, to his desire 'to keep us looking after each other' (*FS* 415), Manners finally lets a father-figure drop.

In the last paragraph of *The Folding Star* Manners has caught up with Luc at Ostend. The reunion is an enigma. The two men seem invisible to each other; their connection is severed. Might this be, after all, a happy ending? Their pasts, and the longer pasts (Orst's, Echevin's) encapsulated in their brief history, have come to a terminal point. The termination promises a better dawn than those that have dragged Manners and Echevin (and the novel) back along the lines of fruitless explanation. To understand the past as merely a dead end, not as 'love-struck shapes and portents' and 'long perspective[s] of revelations', does indeed end it.

One of Housman's strongest poems asserts that

> The troubles of our proud and angry dust
> Are from eternity, and shall not fail.
> Bear them we can, and if we can we must.[11]

There are moments when Hollinghurst makes Manners mind what Housman harps on. On the night of Dawn's funeral he meditates on 'the odd economics of time, the way waste [of time] demanded more waste'

(*FS* 240) because one has no foreknowledge if the waste will be fruitful or additionally sterile. Facing waste in this way, Manners confronts the essential human dust that is his common trouble, and the trouble with genealogies. If our troubles are from eternity, to historicize their origin is defensively to obscure their changelessness, and to shirk their resistance to intelligibility. By suggesting that explanatory origins and subsequent effects are a wild goose chase, Hollinghurst has had the nerve to face the prospect that history is so much dust.

'The odd economics of time, the way waste demanded more waste' affects *The Folding Star*'s implications for the literary past – for its specific 'dawn' in Housman, Bottomley, and Firbank – as well as for the historical past. 'The way waste demanded more waste' suggests that the literary tradition, however rich, is in regard to the present a wasted common or common place, a waste land. The cynosure of modernism makes its appearance, after all. The best escape from the cul-de-sac it exemplifies is to inhabit a present, or to wait for a future that has let the past go.

The novelist's insertion of Gordon Bottomley into a dream that Manners has while pursuing Luc at the novel's end signifies the backhandedness about literary genealogy that doubles the narrative's self-divided perspective about other genealogies. In the dream, Bottomley is composing an unfinished, interminably long verse play, and Manners and he talk about a poem by Bottomley that might have been set to music and that Manners's father might have sung. The dream brings the father and his son, Dawn, and Luc the new Dawn, back to Manners's favourite period of poetry, the Georgian, in which Bottomley first made his mark. Quotations of Georgian poets – Graves and Masefield – come readily to Manners during his wild goose chase. For Manners to return to that era, however, is for him (and his creator) to return to literary history with customary divided feelings. Early on, while browsing in a bookstore, Manners describes his favourite works in terms of 'the melancholy secrecy of reading' (*FS* 45). The reader learns the reason for the epithet *melancholy*; but why 'secret'? The answer indicates a fact that the narration mostly suppresses before 'Underwoods': Manners's poetic ambition. An aspiring poet at fifteen, he had used the common, before Dawn, as a place where he felt 'in direct contact with the Muse', especially when he waited there to see 'the folding star' (*FS* 212), in hope of adding himself to the literary tradition. His ambition failed, but not before he felt it confirmed by Sir Peregrine Dawlish, a surviving Georgian poet (unlike Bottomley, Dawlish is Hollinghurst's invention). A friend of the family, and no doubt gay, Dawlish read Manners's early poems, blessed them, and predicted a great literary future. 'I took a nearly erotic pleasure in' Dawlish's approval, Manners remembers: 'I felt as if I'd been received into succession.' But neither succession nor success followed. Dawlish's prediction was 'a hollow augury' (*FS* 215). When the now-ancient Dawlish turns up at Dawn's funeral, Manners notes, 'there was something moving and irrelevant in his having come' (FS 255).

There is something moving and irrelevant in all the returns to the past in *The Folding Star*. Housman's emphasis on terminations strikes the keynote of what the novels reiterate. The emphasis is underwritten by the constant allusions to Bottomley. *King Lear's Wife* and *Gruach* are dramatized genealogies: prequels to the careers of Lear and Lady Macbeth (Gruach). Bottomley's plays extend the lives of the figures backwards, thus enlarging their history and presenting a genealogy of what the characters 'later' enact in Shakespeare's plays. Nevertheless, Bottomley twins the genealogical enlargement in each play with counterbalancing constraints. Gruach makes her first encounter with Macbeth an occasion for her freedom to 'burn the past' and not be 'shut back into the cast-off life' dominated by her enemies.[12] But because her future in Shakespeare is not free, Bottomley's drama shows genealogical vision to be a false dawn; not the pledge of a liberated future, but a dead end. Bottomley's Lear is similarly caged. He rids himself of his wife for the sake of a mistress, then indirectly uses his daughter Goneril to rid himself of the paramour. His aim is to guarantee his future; but the past Bottomley invents for Lear is only a hollow security, a mad waste that predicts Lear's scenes on the heath. At the end of *The Folding Star* Manners, whose journey to Belgium and back to his 'underwoods' enlarged his vision of his own wasting, pursues his well-beloved to Dorset, where, unless he parts with the past, waste lies ahead.

Hollow auguries

For Hollinghurst *The Spell* lies ahead. Yet it repeats the genealogical narrative of *The Folding Star*, by again emphasizing generational differences. In the 1990s the youth of twenty-year-olds apparently causes them to be different from forty-year-olds, and their middle age in turn apparently causes them to be different from sixty-year-olds. *The Spell* also refuses these differences and dizzyingly eroticizes them. If we can see Paul Echevin and Manners as daddies wanting son-like lovers, *The Spell* delivers more starkly than the previous novel the suggestion of familial – and quasi-incestuous – gay relations. It does so by compressing what appears to be a span of three generations into less than thirty years.

Underlying the generational drama is another literary genealogy: Hollinghurst's relation to Thomas Hardy. *The Spell* is set largely in

Dorset. It is more than a matter of setting. *The Spell's* protagonist, Robin Woodfield, points out locales mentioned in Hardy and reads Hardy. He cites him blunderingly (he names a Hardy poem that doesn't exist) but the very title of the poem he refers to at one point – 'An Assignation – Old Style' (*S* 122) – would fit poems in *Late Lyrics and Earlier* or in Hardy's other volumes of verse. The Hardy text that matters most to *The Spell*, however, is *The Well-Beloved* (1897; thematically tied to the novel, a poem of the same title appears in *Poems of the Past and Present* [1901]). The genealogies that are in play in *The Spell* require laying out before I come to Hardy's ghost in them.

The novel's genealogical compression is conveyed by the sexual entanglements of the characters. Robin, a married gay man in the 1960s, fathers a son, Dan, who is also gay, and who in the novel's present (1996) is about to turn twenty-three. Robin, a divorced man nearing fifty, has previously been the partner of Simon, who died of AIDS. Robin has found a new lover (younger by fifteen years), Justin, who has left his recent lover of the same age, Alex, for Robin. When Alex pays Robin and Justin a visit, he discovers Dan, and begins a rapturous affair with him, a recovery of youth (he thinks). Alex still desires Justin, nevertheless (Dan is patently a younger Justin). When Alex and Dan sleep in Robin and Justin's bed, Alex feels uneasy: 'I suppose it's a further twist on not being able to imagine your parents having sex'. Dan responds, 'I can imagine him and Justin only too well' (*S* 161). His imagination is helped because Justin desires him too, and others: unknown to Robin, Justin sleeps with a local rent boy, Teddy, who also sleeps with Dan. Dan likes Alex well enough, but he is attracted to older men and prefers forty-year-old Gordon to the slightly younger Alex. So Dan breaks off with Alex, who has now been thwarted by Robin's son as well as by Robin's capture of Justin. Justin is scarcely a permanent captive. He initiates a trial separation from Robin, whereupon Teddy seduces Robin (Teddy will subsequently tell Dan that Simon, unknown to Robin, used to 'abuse' Teddy). By the novel's end Robin, who has prided himself on never having been left by anyone, is back with Justin; and Alex, with an older, hence presumably more trustworthy lover in tow, is visiting Robin and Justin again. In *The Folding Star* Manners once remarks about an object belonging to his father: 'I remembered it so well, your things took the place of your father's, you became a kind of couple in your turn' (*FS* 145). In *The Spell* such familial coupling happens with a vengeance.

What is one to make of this endogamous cluster of gay relations, in which everyone's past is at once everyone's present, and in which intimacies therefore are smotheringly close? Within two weeks of knowing Dan, Alex feels he is 'under a beautiful spell' (*S* 107). But earlier he 'felt the incongruity of chasing after Robin's son. He wasn't sure if he was taking a devious revenge on Robin for stealing Justin, or if he was helplessly joining Justin under the spell of the family' (*S* 70). The two spells – erotic and familial – have contradictory effects. Thanks to the spell of Dan, who introduces Alex to drugs and raves, Alex feels liberated from his routine government job and London life. Dorset – where gay men now feel at home as much as they do in London – adds to the liberation effect. But the familial spell, whereby every new love treads on the heels of a more original one, becomes claustrophobic, a new closet. Dan wants to escape his father. Robin commits an action that suggests his violent desire to open a way out of what he senses is closing in on itself. Impulsively he nearly drives a vehicle in which Justin, Alex, and Dan are passengers over the edge of a Dorset cliff. The characters wonder indignantly what this action is about. So does a reader, who (indignant or not) wonders all the more at the event's unexplained intrusion because the last pages of the novel repeat the action, albeit in a tempered way: as non-risky access for Robin, Justin, Alex, and Alex's new lover to a view of the 'grey' sea and the 'curling silver roads' of its currents (*S* 257). Despite prominently treating the event twice, and as a finale, the text does not explain the motive for the treatment.

The motive appears to be the author's desire to dramatize a jettisoning of the past, no matter how near, how familiar it is, even if it is the gay past. The impulse to unload history at first seems contradicted by Robin's vocation: he is an architect, and a restorer (as Thomas Hardy originally was). Robin's cliff-hanging aggression immediately follows the four men's visit to an ancient estate house that Robin is to work on. He is to remediate 'the buckling of one of [the] strainer arches' in the estate's pyramidal family crypt, whose inside is 'both mysterious and claustrophobic' (*S* 57). But Robin can't imagine how to work on the strainer arches without their falling down – and on him. The drive to the cliff's edge is preceded by a description of the cliffs – 'the crumbling cross-section of the line of hills' that makes the landscape part of the mausoleum (*S* 62). The past, one gathers, suddenly seems a killing genealogical force for Robin: it is too much with him. Rather than be passively crushed, he wills to meet his end, and to enforce ending on the others.

The novel's last scene inhibits such self-destruction, just as the characters finally draw back 'a prudent distance from the crumbly edge' (*S* 256) of additional break-ups and ingrown liaisons. Yet the cliff-side vision survives, because *The Spell* generations are by the novel's end looking at a radical lover's leap: the future of gay life after the liberation exemplified by the novel's figures. Dan is a scion of the future, and not a heartening one. He relies on drugs, he can't hold a job, he is described by Alex as 'a great lover, that would be his career, though he knew next to nothing about love' (*S* 243), he permits the theft during a sexual orgy of an heirloom necklace (hence a heritage and its history) given to him by Alex. He callously treats the gay past, even his own father's, by opposing 'the muddled commitments of this group of older men' to the 'thought of himself as a free person' (*S* 225). If Dan is the future of the past, one might well look forward to the crumbly edge. Even more so in the light of an older 'youth', Gordon (he is thirty-six), who predicts a gay future with less attractive aspects than Dan's. Turning up at Dan's birthday party, Gordon talks with Robin, who sees him as a puritanical antithesis to Dan, a distasteful 'evangelist of change' (*S* 139). As part of the change, in response to Robin's attempt to talk with him about Hardy, Gordon reports having spiritual contact with Arthur Conan Doyle ('one of the higher spirits working for world change'), who has told Gordon that he is 'not really gay', and who leads Gordon to distinguish between being gay and 'living as a gay man' (*S* 139–40). According to Gordon, and Conan Doyle, 'living as a gay man', rather than being one, can mean heterosexual marriage as part of the 'living as' repertory, which might include women's return to subordination to men.

Robin is repelled by Gordon, is censorious too of Dan's choice of lovers, although Dan looks better in comparison to Gordon. But if the gay future looks like a bad break with its genealogy, the novel refuses to line up with the past. The man whose estate Robin is refurbishing dies, after being torn between 'dogged love of the place and his new [financial] need to let it go' (*S* 175). Robin also lets go. Hollinghurst harks back to 'letting things drop' in *The Folding Star*. Robin's bafflement about how to preserve the mausoleum results in 'a paralysing sense of responsibility' that he can't any longer enact (*S* 178). Whether or not Dan and Gordon exemplify the shapes of eros to come, the older protagonists' last look at the ocean discovers the colours of age (grey and silver). They are seeing their history as achieved, not to be forwarded. The earlier glimpse of the sea from the cliff revealed 'a vast unconscious arc of silver green', however (*S* 63). The green, youth's colour, must still be there; and the sea, being Aphrodite's birthplace, must hold future erotic spells. For the spells already risen from the sea-foam have their genealogy in a prior termination: the castration of Uranus by his son Chronos. The father's severed testicles, landing in the ocean, generated the goddess. Now the gay fathers too are being cut off in Hollinghurst's texts. Their shaping literary history might therefore be only hollow auguries of the future, from which they must retreat (as Firbank's heroines do), or which they must recognize with Housmanesque resignation.

A lesson along such terminal lines is to be seen in Hardy, a literary father who exhibits eros as drastic magic for all sexual orientations, and who also dramatizes an end of art. If Hollinghurst allows *The Spell* to conjure *The Well-Beloved*, it is perhaps because Hardy's protagonist, the sculptor Jocelyn Pierston, sets the pattern for the erotically claustrophobic interplay of generations in Hollinghurst. Pierston unsuccessfully pursues three generations of women, the first of whom is the mother of the second and the grandmother of the third. Each generation is the spitting image of the other. Pierston courts each when each is the age he was to begin with: twenty. As he advances towards forty and then sixty, 'His record moved on with the years, [but] his sentiments stood still', as Hardy's narrator says.[13] He refers to Pierston's passion as 'genealogical' and 'historic' – 'if its continuity through three generations may be so described'.[14] It is the same 'historic' predicament that Manners and the protagonists of *The Spell* suffer by the obsessive, retrogressive circularity of their desires. Hence 'it seemed [to Robin] like one lover could become another, like the smoothly metamorphosing figures in dreams' (*S* 190).

Unfortunately, the years count. Although Pierston finally marries a woman with whom he cohabited before the succession of well-beloveds began, he experiences overall the odd economics of time, the waste demanding more waste. His marriage is without erotic drive. It is also without art, because he deliberately renounces sculpture to escape from the past. It is a termination of the kind I have pointed to in Hollinghurst's backhanded use: a rejection of literary forebears, each of whom constitutes a hollow augury of the future because each in his work accepts the immitigable fact of endings.

The Spell's acceptance of the fact is accompanied by an odd tonality, difficult to catch: not elegiac, not celebratory, not a bitter moral, but disinterested and somehow flat. That uncertain tone is its principal deviation from Hardy, whose novels and poems are more generically and more tonally definite. Might this be another sign of Hollinghurst's refusing to give his work an unqualifiedly identifiable lineage? If one cannot quite tell the tonal or literary-historical centre to which his stories might be referred, Hollinghurst gains another possibility of cutting his fiction (and us) loose from the very past that inspires him.

Notes

1   Michel Foucault, 'Nietzsche, Genealogy, History' in *Language, Counter-Memory, Practice*, ed. D. F. Bouchard (Ithaca, NY: Cornell University Press, 1977) 139–64: 162.

2   Ibid. 153.

3   Alan Hollinghurst, 'Introduction' in *A. E. Housman: Poems Selected by Alan Hollinghurst* (London: Faber, 2005) vii–xii: vii.

4   Foucault, 'Nietzsche, Genealogy, History' 147.

5   Edmund Wilson, *The Triple Thinkers* (New York: Harcourt, Brace, 1938) 87, 99.

6   Hollinghurst, 'Introduction' in *A. E. Housman* vii.

7   Ibid.

8   *The Collected Poems of A. E. Housman* (London: Cape, 1945) 89.

9   Alan Hollinghurst, 'Introduction' in Ronald Firbank, *Three Novels* (London: Penguin, 2000) vii–xxiv: x.

10   Ronald Firbank, *The Flower Beneath the Foot* in *Three Novels*, 101.

11   A. E. Housman, Poem IX of *Last Poems* [1922] in *A. E. Housman: Poems Selected by Alan Hollinghurst* 42.

12   Gordon Bottomley, *Poems and Plays* (London: Bodley Head, 1953) 204, 199.

13   Thomas Hardy, *The Well-Beloved* (London: Macmillan, 1975) 103.

14   Ibid. 169.

8

Some properties of fiction: value and fantasy in Hollinghurst's house of fiction

Geoff Gilbert

'What would I do with the Clerkenwell building?' said Nick sulkily. 'You'd own it,' said Wani. (*LB* 440)

The solid spatial reality of Hollinghurst's worlds, and the vitality of the buildings and spaces through which his plots unfold, are a source of pleasure. Some accounts have associated this pleasure with the continuity of the world and the durability of traditional forms of fiction – either celebrated as vital truth, or upheld as value against forces of erosion.[1] I see how those thoughts work, but I want to propose that this location of literary value fails to understand the persistent interaction of sexual desire and space, and keeps describing Hollinghurst's prose apart from the work that it is doing. My account of the pleasure taken in reading the solid spaces of *The Line of Beauty* involves two related claims: first, that spatial solidity and spatial continuity in Hollinghurst's work are underpinned by the concept of property and property value; second, that the sex scenes in his work are not separable realist acts that take place in distinct physical spaces, but are part of a fantasy constitution of space and place within the field of property that my argument will associate with modernism – good sex is what places are for and an index of their living continuity, but good sex and the enabling persistence of live spaces are trammelled and defeated by the domination of the law of value over the fact of place.

Property, reading, and the sex scene

I want to start with the first, glorious, sex scene that opens *The Line of Beauty*. Nick Guest is the smitten lodger, 'in residence, and almost, he felt, in possession', in the grand Notting Hill house of Gerald Fedden, 'rising' Tory MP in the Thatcher government and father of his university friend and occasional lust-object Toby. He is undeflected by the indifference of the house, which addresses itself in a 'glazed' manner to the terraces on the other side of the square, and of Toby, who 'had never perhaps known why he and Nick were friends', although he 'quite liked his rower's body to be looked at. It was the easy charity of beauty' (*LB* 6). It is 1983, Nick is twenty, and he is meeting Leo, whose personal ad has described him as 'Black guy, late 20s, v. good looking, interests cinema, music, politics, seeks intelligent like-minded guy 18–40' (*LB* 9). After their date, when they realize they cannot go back to either of their homes, Nick suggests that they go to the private communal gardens at the centre of the square, closed to all but the keyholders, inhabitants of Kensington Park Gardens.

These gardens are special, charged for Nick with the exorbitant fantasy of luxurious central possession, accessed through the awkwardness of his current and chronic insider–outsider status. They are uselessly glamorously huge and discreet, 'as much a part of Nick's romance of London as the house itself' (*LB* 15). He knows his way to the 'little compound of the gardeners' hut', hidden material sign of the labour necessary to maintain picturesque display, where they kiss. Immediately, confusingly, a 'sex scene' has begun, for the reader and for Nick. 'He was gasping from the rush of reciprocity, the fact of being made love to. ... He'd never seen it described in a book. He was achingly ready and completely unprepared' (*LB* 38).

This is first-time sex, for Nick, for the novel, and for readers for whom it works. It is a hot scene. Ostensibly, the passage recounts what Nick remembers the next day, but quickly that distance is overcome, so that event and recollection and representation and reading are tightly proximate. Sex in memory, narration, reading, is as alive as it was when happening; the details are arrayed less in an exposition of what is happening than as props for the escalation of desire, in the scene and in its recounting and reading. The fact that Leo wears his sister's shirt 'made Nick love him much more, he couldn't say why' (*LB* 40). Something has been 'switched on', and the world is electrified in an arousal shared between reader and character.

This is perhaps risky, for a literary novel. The scene is seductive for the reader, and the more I am seduced into it, the more I am likely to drift into a world of my own imagining. The engagement the scene solicits is in danger of taking me away from its place within the novel, such that the writing is elided altogether. Later in the novel and in his affair with Leo, Nick will describe something like this problem. He is writing a graduate thesis on style in Henry James and other writers, which he fears he will never complete. One of the reasons for this is that Nick's mind keeps wandering from the page towards memories and fantasies of sex with Leo:

> nothing much was being done, and through most of Nick's library days his eyes wandered just beyond the page in a deep monotonous reverie about Leo: the great unfolding sentences of Meredith or James would slow and fade into subliminal parenthesis, half-hour subordinate clauses of remembered sex. (*LB* 139)

The properties of the scene – the compost, the enclosed park, the sister's shirt – serve as broad encouragement to free elaboration, expropriation, distortion. Katy Terruga, in her manual for aspiring writers of pornography, notes, of the most basic pornographic forms, that

> there needs to be some reason for the characters to be in this situation, after all. … It's basically just a way for your characters to get to their goal, which is, of course, sex. All you really need to do is to set them up so they can do so.[2]

The risk of the sex scene is that all of its singularity, all of that writing, will be roughly appropriated to the service of the undifferentiating desires of the reader.

These potential porn-scenes are not just perfunctory ways of getting characters to 'the goal, which is of course sex'. Through them – the words on the page opening to spaces 'just beyond the page' – character and reader find themselves necessarily in the world, without that world being given or familiar. Nick is regularly breathless in his scenes of desire, or his recollection or narration of scenes of desire, as though the metabolism of self and world (where I inhale and exhale the air that surrounds me) has become fraught or deliciously tendentious. This is what Nick is realizing and failing to realize in thinking about style and the way James's sentences host his fantasy, his absorption and his distraction. Scenes, to Nick, are inhabited in a mode of transformation because they are important to him, because he is sexually interested. And the hallucinatory clarity and solidity of the spaces in Hollinghurst's novels are attachments to and through the act of reading, which is also an engagement with the world. In a perfunctory porn scene – say, the plumber coming in to fix the washing machine – the engagement of desire makes visible the thresholds between the domestic and the public, or accounts of labour time and class distinction, which have silently circumscribed and regulated the relation between the subject and the world. As a 'scene' emerges, a 'setting for desire' in the words of psychoanalysts Laplanche and Pontalis (to whose work this chapter will return), these circumscriptions and regulations become affectively charged.[3] The fit between the subject and the world is unsettled, and the scene becomes – as it arouses us and implicates us into distraction and absorption, and as it becomes generic and objective – both strangely exterior and foreign and resonantly interior and constitutive of the self.

Nick and the novel align this interest in the world-as-sex-scene with the fact that he does not own anything. He knows about – and notices as props for his desire and fantasy, as part of the differentiated *hotness* of the world – the objects of the rich and powerful people by whom he is surrounded, exactly *because* he does not own them. His parents' distance from the world of the Feddens, and his father's role as an antiques dealer, sponsors his outsider proximity to value and evaluation. His position is distinct from that of possessors, like Toby. At the Feddens' *manoir* in France, Toby, framed in an archway, is seen to be

> born to use the gateway, the loggia, the stairs without looking at them or thinking about them. And something else came back ... a sense that the house was not only an enhancement of Toby's interest but a compensation for his lack of it. (*LB* 295)

The scene frames Toby's desirability for Nick; but it also replaces his subjectivity, makes him more interest*ed*, more implicated in the world he does not need to register. His sexy property – like the wriggling of the hips by which characters in two of Hollinghurst's novels carelessly divest themselves of trousers[4] – is absolutely and constitutively part of his nature. But it is also alienated from him, arriving from elsewhere and before, activated only through the attentiveness and desire of Nick.

Toby is picturesquely *part* of the scene of which Nick is connoisseur; desire displaces between them. Nick's exploration mixes vicarious possession with a kind of scouting for hidden sites for sex, like the pool-house where he 'would have had Wani ... if Gerald hadn't been hanging, even snooping about' (*LB* 311). He recognizes that he is

> poking and memorizing, possessing the place by knowing it better than his hosts. If Rachel had said, 'If only we still had that pogo stick!' Nick would have cried, like a painfully eager child, 'But we do, it's in the old shed, with the broken butter churn and the prize rosettes for onions nailed to the beams.' It struck him that a sign of real possession was a sort of negligence, was to have an old wood-yard you'd virtually forgotten about. (*LB* 310)

A range of key concerns for the novel are opened in this distinction between the act of possessing through poking and memorizing, and the structural negligence of 'real possession' in which your things take over some of the functions of your subjectivity, and you become part of a scene.

Affective positioning in the world is objectively relative to patterns of value and property, tracing borders and barriers that give form to space and subjectivity, in collective as well as individual ways. The world is made hot and cold, sexually zoned for Nick and for the novel, according to these patterns, which compel the reader 'beyond the page'. This is the method through which the novel investigates the story both of an individual subjectivity and of the historical determination of a collectivity. 'Thatcherism', as one name for the context of this novel, is a libidinal arrangement – 'heterosexual queenery' (*LB* 382) – for many of the characters. And if Thatcher is the historical name for this structure of feeling, Gerard's father-in-law Lionel, and his bank, are the best images of its material specificity. His ownership and command of traditionally beautiful things – Cézannes, aged stone, handsome servants' labour time – while it is traditionally anchored in inheritance and class, is mediated by new economic modes. The financial instruments created within Lloyds and similar institutions, inside the panelled room held within the steel structure, allow some people to get rich in new ways. Such instruments freshly mediate the old hierarchies of wealth.[5] And they will arrange people in surprising and englobing patterns of debt and profit which become spatial and social relations in the era of 'property-owning democracy'.

So the 'scene of desire', a libidinal arrangement severed from and linked to real possession, is determined objectively from without and articulated with social histories of property and value. But nothing in this structuring can quite explain why and how it should be experienced as the form and scene of desire and subjectivity. *The Line of Beauty* provides a second line of approach to the relation between subject and scene. Nick describes his attentiveness as that of a 'painfully eager child'. The childishness of his exploration looks original, learning particular spaces as though for the first time and discovering a singular self in the response to them:

> All his life he'd looked at furniture from odd angles, and he still had his childhood sense of tables and sideboards as elaborate little wooden buildings that you would crawl into, ... their rough undersurfaces retaining a dim odour of the actual wood. (*LB* 109)

The childish desire to know the world of the negligent Feddens in order to attach interest to them looks like a repetition of an original moment. Nick notes that the furniture at odd angles to which he had found himself drawn as a child would often be gone the next day, sold in obedience to the directive tug of 'London prices, which had always been the family code for extortion' (*LB* 266). His parents' world appears to be innocent of the forces that emanate conjointly and jerkily from the centres of finance and politics, from Lionel and Gerard. But as the gradient of property prices becomes more important than the alienation of long commutes, as the idyll of 'rural life' becomes economically rational for wealthier Londoners, new houses are built, blocking his parents' view, and making the dividend that accrues to their own property impossible to ignore. Comfort is redefined and brought into the orbit of finance: the lifeworld is capitalized (see *LB* 265).

Hollinghurst rehearses some ways of imagining a queer child's relation to space in his 1982 *Confidential Chats with Boys*. The first two poems in that pamphlet imagine a child in spaces thick with sexual confusion and possibility. In the title poem the space is a 'fashionable hotel' in which the boy narratee is advised to be on his guard, ready for violence, against 'those men who avoid / real men'. The second poem inhabits the scene of an 'upstairs junkroom / where I made my houses', and in which that making butts up against the stuff of the room, including a reproduction of Sickert's painting *Ennui*, which is imagined to have been so stilled for so long by dreary afternoons, that the woodworm have 'drilled what mother called / unmentionable places' (*CCB* 1).

The third poem is perhaps the most interesting in its handling of motifs that will appear in the fiction. A child lives 'over the bank'; after the cleaners are gone, it becomes a play-space. Play repeats work, 'swivelling stools / at the locked tills', but also appropriates the secrets held back from work, 'the cashiers' little oddities' (*CCB* 3). This exploratory inhabiting is doubled inside the home, where the child has a 'dressing table drawer / called Banking Business' in which mysteries and dissociations parallel with those of the bank are enacted (*CCB* 3). He keeps copies of *Geographics*, we presume for the images of nakedness there, and 'cuttings that matured their hard-core / innocence as we slept' (*CCB* 3). This closed drawer of value, modelled on the locked spaces in the bank, is where sexuality will have been (where maturing 'hard-core innocence' will find that all along it was 'interest'), in a structure of belatedness that the forward child projects himself unknowingly into. But the psychic and sexual processes, far from being organic, are already inscribed within a space and time governed by the mysterious scene of 'banking business'.[6]

The nationwide price index of beauty

My description of Hollinghurst's novel has begun to connect a number of disparate elements: the sense of luminous charged spatial solidity, the traditional pleasure in inhabiting a fictional but meaningfully physical world, the positioning of characters in acute awareness of the boundaries of property value. Together these inform the 'sex scene' of Hollinghurst's writing. I move now to a more formal description, constructed on Laplanche and Pontalis's account of fantasy as a 'setting' for desire, through which the origins of the subject are staged.

For Laplanche and Pontalis, in their reading of Freud's account of *Urphantasien* – primal and originary fantasies – 'psychic reality' is relatively autonomous from reality, but not opposed to it; it signals the fact that reality and the subject have never been in unmediated relation. The primal fantasies depend upon a relation to a primal scene. In that scene, sounds or significations from the outside bear a material pressure that marks them as already affective, and which allows them to rip through the 'continuity of perception'. Here meaning *'fait signe'*, makes itself known. This is both a structural effect and a historically contingent one; it inheres both in the damaged structural autonomy of the subject vis-à-vis the world, and the ungovernable historical contingency through which we inherit our place in the world.

This scene originates the story of the subject and the ways in which the matter of the world will constitute her psychic reality. As scene, it has multiple entry points, it does not indicate where the subject will locate herself, but rather what syntax and disposition of positions and activities are possible and compelling. In the Freud case 'A Child is Being Beaten', on which Laplanche and Pontalis draw, the scene 'a child is being beaten', discovered within a series of analyses, did not suggest that the analysand was in the position of the child, nor of the person doing the beating, but in both of those positions, and watching, and in the syntax of the scene itself. The scene models a 'setting for desire'; it does not represent a given subjectivity or particular desire.

There is no direct passage from psychoanalytic theory towards the world outside the analytic situation. But Laplanche and Pontalis's formulation allows me to imagine what is happening in the experience of reading Hollinghurst. The scene of the luminous world and the positions arrayed with it provides a setting for desire. Nick has grown into that setting through charged intrusions of meaningfulness which present themselves as a puzzle still to be solved. And the power of that scene, for the reader as well as for Nick, is structural, in that it appears to be quite generally a question of individuation, of being both *of* a world which exists before you and somehow *separate from* that world such that you can be affected by it. It is also historically contingent, in that the weight of meaning is representative of gathering 'Thatcherism'.

The Line of Beauty both explores and organizes psychic reality in a world – *this* world – of value. One account of the modernist challenge to the realist novel is that its innovations mark a shift in the scene of fantasy. Particularly, the novel in the moment of modernism struggles with propertied spaces.[7] To give one example: Virginia Woolf, in 'Mr Bennett and Mrs Brown' (1924), argues that properly modern fiction requires the destruction of houses. The problem with existing novels – specifically those of Bennett, Wells, and Galsworthy – is in what they conflate: they 'have laid an enormous stress upon the fabric of things. They have given us a house in the hope that we may be able to deduce the human beings who live there.' Character is obscured by the details of property: in *Hilda Lessways*, for example, 'we cannot hear her mother's voice, or Hilda's voice; we can only hear Mr Bennett's voice telling us facts about rents and freeholds and copyholds and fines.' There is a failure of integrity which betrays a lack of interest 'in character in itself; in the book in itself'.[8]

Woolf's modernism strives to save the autonomy of the artwork and the autonomy of the person; the buildings as properties have to go:

> At whatever ... damage to valuable property Mrs Brown must be rescued, expressed .... And so the smashing and the crashing began. Thus it is that we hear all round us, in poems and novels and biographies ... the sound of breaking and falling, crashing and destruction.[9]

She may imagine this noise as transitional, but the making visible of property, and thence its erosion, is a constitutive strain in Woolf's aesthetic. For example, in *To the Lighthouse* (1927), darkness floods into the holiday home of the Ramsays:

> Nothing, it seems, could survive the flood, the profusion of darkness which, creeping in at keyholes and crevices, ... came into bedrooms, swallowed up here a jug and basin, there the sharp edges and firm bulk of a chest of drawers. Not only was furniture confounded; there was scarcely anything left of body and mind by which one could say 'This is he' or 'This is she'.[10]

The confounding of furniture and the effacement of personhood look set to take the whole house with it. Of course, the house is restored; and the redemptive aesthetic enclosure and the corresponding rescuing and expressing of Mrs Ramsay are pointedly dramatized. But an alignment persists of the vision of the novel with the forces which would have houses and forms collapse. Lily herself articulates it: 'One wanted most some secret sense, fine as air, with which to steal through keyholes and surround her where she sat knitting, talking, sitting silent in the window alone.'[11] This secret sense follows closely the path of the flood of darkness which had effaced body and furniture. The idea that getting rid of the house would give us 'the person' and the 'complete' artwork disavows this alignment, where the aesthetic sense of the whole person is the same destructive dark force that will bring the house to nothing. Personhood and property do not adequate mutually, but inhabit a scene full of the conflicted energies of fantasy.

There is a material determination for this scene. In 1878, according to José Harris, land constituted one quarter of the national wealth, by 1914, less than one twelfth.[12] Land had been the ground of social hierarchy in Britain: wealth, power, and land ownership circumscribed congruent constituencies. So we might expect the collapse in land values to have led to a confounding of economic and social distinction; but access to property in Britain at the end of this period was probably more unequal than at any time in national history (and any comparable European country). The dematerialization of capital did not have democratizing effects. So, to take an example which situates the tropes of Hollinghurst's tradition within the modernist moment, a journal like *Country Life*, launched in 1896, was designed to represent the continuity of English rural spaces. Initially photographs included images of gardeners, figuring the labour that maintained the vistas the viewer enjoys; gradually they were removed because they were historically marking, 'interfering' with the invitation to step into the past.[13] But construction of continuity aimed to bring continuity within the marketplace. Malcolm Kelsell suggests: 'it might be said that the cry that the country house is in danger has been but another act of mystification to conceal the facts of economic power. England has changed merely to stay as it was.'[14]

James Wood suggests in his critique of *The Stranger's Child* that in *The Line of Beauty*, 'Hollinghurst may have seemed at times to be secretly in love with the world of Gerald Fedden ... as Evelyn Waugh was in love with the Marchmains', but the novel is saved from this by its moral stance: 'Nick's lower-middle-class alienation from that privileged world stiffened the book's moral fibers.'[15] For Robert Macfarlane, 'Hollinghurst reveals himself to be more in love with the ... languid beauty made possible by wealth, than he can acknowledge or even sense'; uncertainty over whether to 'despise or crave' beautiful possessions scuppers the moralist ambitions of the novel, as desire and writing together have escaped authorial control and even what the author can 'sense'.[16] These readings strike me as hasty, bearing something of the confused accusation of a 'politics of envy' with which class critique was met in the Thatcher era. *Of course* I crave Gerald Fedden's beautiful home, which is delightful and comfortable, filled with objects on which skilled labour has been lavished, and through the gorgeous quiddity of which we can imagine the redemption of that labour. These are things we all should have together: the problem is not in the having of beautiful things, but that the fact of value thrusts them out into a realm where I can only wish for them impotently. This is the topic of Hollinghurst's novel: political economy rather than morality is its field; its affect and its modal instability derive from the heavy presence of that barrier in value. Questions of style are not gauges of identity category nor ciphers for affiliation, nor evidence of failure of control. Rather, the scene of urgent modernist reading in Hollinghurst's work, which takes the reader just beyond the page into distraction and absorption, is a scene in which the ongoing origination of the subject in a world of value is explored.

A Marxian Hollinghurst is a stretch, perhaps. But his novels are irreducibly imbricated with the contemporary history of value in London. *The Line of Beauty* is set in the years – 1983 through 1987 – that mark the steep slope of the first London property boom. This is also the moment of the writing and publication of Hollinghurst's first novel, *The Swimming-Pool Library*, published in 1988. Property prices rose until 1989, but then fell and stabilized at a lower level, so that at the time of the publication of his next novel, *The Folding Star* in 1994, London property cost 40 per cent less than in 1987–8. The year 1995 saw the start of the inflation of the new property bubble, in relation to which much of London life is still arranged in the second decade of the twenty-first century. The Nationwide house-price index graphs London property prices, calculated quarterly, against a baseline in 1993 of 100. On the publication of *The Spell* in 1998, prices were indexed at 160; *The Line of Beauty* was published against the background of an index of 352, and by the time of *The Stranger's Child* in 2011, prices were nearly four and a half times their 1993 level. At the time of writing, the index has risen to around 660, and the politics which that index dictates are ever more divisive and acute.[17]

I do not want to insist on a direct correlation between the trajectories within Hollinghurst's *oeuvre* and the vicissitudes of the property market. The relation is more fine-grained than that, ramifying through subjective space and social relation and the field of literary production, which have temporalities and relative autonomies and relations to consciousness – the stuff of the novel – which are not directly captured in property prices. But when Hollinghurst suggests that the 1980s 'seems to have determined so many things about the way we live now',[18] some of the forces that shape that world are visible through the graph. As Gerald Fedden puts it at Toby's birthday party, Dr Johnson's definition 'What are acres? What are houses? Only dirt, or wet and dry', is *'far* from suitable advice to the grandson and nephew of great bankers, or for any young person coming of age in our splendid property-owning democracy' (*LB* 67–8).

The world of the property boom that is explored in *The Line of Beauty* is the same world that is written in *The Swimming-Pool Library*. In that novel, *rentier* William Beckwith's narration announces very early that he 'belong[s] to that tiny proportion of the populace that indeed owns almost everything' (*SPL* 3). This disarming acknowledgement is part of what makes him obnoxious and sexy. The enormous vague extent of his property allows history and life to pass through him without his registering very much. This is the dynamic of the novel and the logic of the first-person narration: irony will gradually impinge upon the 'romance of myself' that Will has been indulging (*SPL* 5). Will does discern, in a narration that is fraught with his own projections, that his friend James's apartment, because it has not been decorated into sociological stability or expression of personality, has 'a sense of valuelessness despite the climbing prices and the mortgage' (*SPL* 214). But he is 'coltish about recognizing [the] provenance' of the apartment which was 'more or less bought' (*SPL* 98) for him by his grandfather, patriarch and villain in the plot; Will has no need to articulate provenance with value.

That is: the gay history and gay identity that is offered in this novel – a history of traditions and legal and cultural cruelty – informs spaces, and is played out in places, that are innocent of the contemporary history of property. Thus the novel tends brilliantly towards a historical and cultural narrative of homosexual identity, where *The Line of Beauty* finds that the fantasy origins of sexuality – the unfinished relation between sex and the world – are coincident with urgent contemporary concerns.

But within *The Swimming-Pool Library* there are a few moments in which the narration of (and within) gay history is held in proximity with property questions. First, there is Nantwich's house, which reminds William of 'the invalidish world of Edwardian ghost stories', in the narrow streets down near Southwark bridge, surrounded by 'semi-derelict buildings' and, because of the 'narrow gauge of its alleyways', by 'somnolent trades' (*SPL* 70). Here open interest in the story of the acquisition of the house is set against Will's ignorance about the history his family shares with Nantwich. And while we move through a brief account of property as value towards the capacious figured Roman baths in the basement, from the constitution of knowledge of the contemporary history of sexuality within value towards culturalist and legal stories of homosexuality that are felt to be deeper, the ante-room is still present in the scene of narration.

The second kind of moment that interests me is when William meets ugly spaces. His pursuit of Phil takes him around the back of the hotel where he works, and into its staff quarters, through 'a horrible area of store rooms, rumbling boilers and stacked wicker laundry baskets' (*SPL* 103). When Phil, in the staff canteen at the hotel, has said 'I love you', Will begins a set of interior movements which find themselves reflected and distorted in the space:

> It was much more of an avowal than I'd asked for, and the tears came to my eyes and I grinned ..., and looked anywhere but at him – around the horrible, narrow but disproportionately tall room, which had obviously been made by splitting some more generous space in two. (*SPL* 194)

Subdivision is a vandalism done on the 'generous space' of the tradition, as it is in other places in Hollinghurst's work (like Dan's room in *The Spell*, still bearing the traces of the property's conversion to a rooming hotel; or the work that Robin is doing in that novel to transform his neighbour's quirky Victorian property for multiple occupation (*S* 52–4, 177), or the covering and effacing of detail in Corley Court in *The Stranger's Child*). It is a material sign of the pressure of value in and on space, and thence on the arrangement of people. The affective ugliness of the space produces a kind of parallax – like the perspective across the hall and up the long mirrored stairway by which Will's 'mood of atrocious egotism' is alienated (*SPL* 117), or like reading about himself in James's diary (*SPL* 216) – through which Will is positioned within the setting, and the priority of the setting over his romance is established. Like Toby's for Nick, the interest of Will in his property becomes present through these angles.

Will is beaten up – and his desirability and invulnerability compromised – in another ugly space, a housing estate consisting of 'prefabricated units slotted and pinned together, [which] showed a systematic disregard for comfort and relief, for anything the eye or heart might fix on as homely and decent' (*SPL* 169). This is the kind of place where Arthur and others of his black British lovers live; he is attractive to them in the bars partly for the simple reason that his flat is central and they 'had no way, if they failed to score ... of getting home' (*SPL* 192). The act of violence establishes the reality of the ugly space as abstraction and as real. That is, being beaten up as he hopes to cruise is an instance of 'homophobic violence', but its location and Will's way of experiencing the violence is already pre-positioned in the subjective-objective setting. Will narrates – with some of the surging affect that attends Nick's retelling of sex with Leo, with some of the compulsion of a porn scene – the rising consciousness that 'it was actually happening. It was actually happening to me' (*SPL* 174).

In this novel the relations among the experience of reading, the solidity of space, the idea of value, and the question of property are only implicit. They are not quite a thematic concern as they are in *The Line of Beauty*. But they inform the edge of the narration, in the underpinning and undermining of the 'almost everything' that Beckwith owns. As he has learned about his implication in the history of sexuality, and after two experiences of sex which have not allowed him to absorb, own, or control them, he is walking home through his expanded or shattered world. Will notices a crowd of city people, 'youngsters in pinstripes from the City fanning out from the gates, jackets here and there hooked over a shoulder, smart clippety-clop of old-fashioned City shoes', and reflects upon himself:

> In many ways they were like me; yet ... they were an alien breed. And then I was a loafer who hardly ever actively earned money, and they were the eager initiates, the coiners of the power and the compromise in which I had unthinkingly been raised. (*SPL* 268).

Thus the novel ends aware, with some disaffected precision, of the financialization which is at the bottom of the distribution of spaces and feelings under Thatcher, and which is churning away within the money and property Will has without 'ever actively earn[ing]'. This also suggests that *The Swimming-Pool Library*'s rich culturalist and historical account of gayness needs some supplement in political economy. This need became more evident at the time of Hollinghurst's writing *The Line of Beauty*, in the second property boom.

Foreclosure on the house of fiction

Traditional forms of realist fiction have been born into a world that they confirm and challenge. The shape given to the novel and the world by the act of closure both reproduces and critically pressures the given-ness of the world. There has been a great deal of attention paid to the extraordinary ending of *The Line of Beauty*: two paragraphs which stretch the narrative mode considerably. It has been seen both to offer an account of freedom for Nick that is aligned with the aesthetic as a democratic force,[19] and to blankly undercut the claim of the aesthetic by having to locate its avatars in the propertied objects of the world.[20] The novel charts the gradual removal of loving – or even enlivening – sex from Nick's world, the looming possibility of a positive HIV diagnosis for him, and the commodified failure of any aesthetic accommodation of the subject to the world of Thatcher's power. We can read this as Lukácsian critical bourgeois realism, in which the totality of historical processes is concentrated concretely through the protagonist's action; and in which a critical response is evoked which would help concretely to mediate political response in the world.[21] And we can see that this shaping grasps something important about the Thatcher era.

This account of a sense of the ending is challenged by a complicating factor. Wani has left Nick a property, an office building constructed on the site of a corner block of Victorian properties in Clerkenwell.

'What would I do with the Clerkenwell building?' said Nick sulkily.
'You'd own it,' said Wani. 'It'll have thirty thousand square feet of office space. You can get someone to manage it for you and you can live on the rent for the rest of your life.' (*LB* 440)

Nick remembers his first encounter with those 'solidly built' buildings, before they are destroyed and the new building constructed. He notes and remembers the 'blackened brick which showed up plum red when they were knocked down', displaying a heightened apprehension of details, listing the 'doorbells of moribund trades'. His 'whole impulse was to do them up and live in them', and he projects a life of friends and parties and dancing. The exploration and the wish feel infantile and blocked: '[h]e felt like a child whose desperate visionary plea has no chance of persuading a parent'. His ideas are discounted, and the building destroyed and converted into Baalbeck House: '[a]nd now this monster lego house, with its mirror windows and maroon marble cladding, was to be Nick's for life' (*LB* 443–4).

Woolf's modernism and Nick's suspended position at the end of the novel register how economic value impinges upon childlike subjectivity and constricts social habitation. For Georg Lukács, the modernist text does not exist actively in relation to history because the position through which the world is understood is both humanly and formally excluded from the world it has narrated. An 'abstract' rather than a 'concrete' totality is constructed; the modernist subject that seems to know the world is pathologically foreclosed. Hollinghurst's novel suggests that this modernist pathology is entirely realistic: the abstractions which block movement between the world and the subject are a recognition of a world of value under capital. Any reading of the ending that concentrates on the inheritance highlights the abstractions of value, inscribed as the ongoing phantasmatic origination of Nick's subjectivity. But rather than palpitating in desirous relation to impossible novelty, that subjectivity is propertied within the world of value and excluded from the concretions of social relation: like Will, Nick is in uncertain relation to the 'coiners of the power and compromise' which are the condition of his life. The vision that Nick has of preserving and inhabiting the property must be coloured, for a reader at the time of the novel's publication in 2004, by a knowledge that he would have been beautifully ahead of the curve. While loft conversions were already currency in the 1980s in St Katharine Docks and Wapping, the re-purposing of Clerkenwell's industrial spaces would have to wait until the mid 1990s.[22]

So while the aesthetic preference for beauty over ugliness appears to be moral and to attach itself to an idea of a healthy moment of the subject, distinguishing between two visions of the building's future will not take us beyond the scene of fantasy in the field of property. We may feel an opposition between two ways of wishing the world to be, in 1987 – a world in which maroon marble signals a terrible resignation to the logic of a Thatcherite economy that tramples over history, ornament, and life. This would be a reading of the novel as a moralist fable guided by the aesthetic as flickering beacon. But Nick's redeeming fantasy – a setting for socially and sexually integrated desires that attaches itself to the plum red emerging from the demolition of blackened bricks – is at least tainted, if it is not rendered positively auratic, by the sense that the building itself not only promised a world that could have been home, but would have coined it in as well: it would perhaps be even more valuable now than 'meretricious' Baalbeck House.

Notes

1   See, for example, Bart Eeckhout, 'English Architectural Landscapes and Metonymy in Hollinghurst's *The Stranger's Child*', *CLCWeb: Comparative Literature and Culture* 14.3 (2012), http://dx.doi.org/10.7771/1481-4374. 2042 (accessed 19 January 2016); Sarah Brophy, 'Queer Histories and Postcolonial Intimacies in Alan Hollinghurst's *The Line of Beauty*' in *End of Empire and the English Novel since 1945*, eds Rachael Gilmour and Bill Schwarz (Manchester: Manchester University Press, 2011) 184–201; Robert Macfarlane, 'Alan Hollinghurst, *The Line of Beauty*' in *The Good of the Novel*, eds Liam McIlvanney and Ray Ryan (London: Faber, 2011) 170–85.
2   Katy Terruga, *It's a Dirty Job: Writing Porn for Fun and Profit: Includes Paying Markets* (Bradenton, FL: Booklocker, 2001) 169.
3   Jean Laplanche and J-B Pontalis, 'Fantasy and the Origins of Sexuality', *International Journal of Psychoanalysis* 49.1 (1968) 1–18.
4   Cecil does this in *The Stranger's Child* 4; Dan does the same in *The Spell* 71.

5   See Andrew Eastham, *Aesthetic Afterlives: Irony, Literary Modernity and the Ends of Beauty* (London: Continuum, 2011) 196–7.

6   Hollinghurst's father was manager of a local branch of Lloyds; the figure of the local bank manager – as opposed to the bankers of the financial instruments of the 1980s boom – is also central to *The Stranger's Child*. See Alan Hollinghurst, 'The Art of Fiction No. 214', *Paris Review* 199 (2011), www.theparisreview.org/interviews/6116/the-art-of-fiction-no-214-alan-hollinghurst (accessed 19 January 2016).

7   The argument which follows is developed at greater length in Chapter 1 of Geoff Gilbert, *Before Modernism Was: Writing and the Constituencies of History* (London: Palgrave Macmillan, 2005).

8   Virginia Woolf, 'Mr Bennett and Mrs Brown' in *A Woman's Essays*, ed. Rachel Bowlby (London: Penguin,. (1992), 69–87: 82, 80, 77. Wells and Galsworthy's fiction is marked in several places by property plots, in which the speculative wealth produced in the novel cannot be realized in architectural form.

9   Ibid. 84.

10   Virginia Woolf, *To the Lighthouse* (London: Penguin, 1992) 137.

11   Ibid. 214.

12   José Harris, *Private Lives, Public Spirit: A Social History of Britain, 1870–1914* (Oxford: Oxford University Press, 1993) 97.

13   Michael Hall, *The English Country House: From the Archives of Country Life, 1897–1939* (London: Beazley, 1994) 12.

14   Malcolm Kelsall, *The Great Good Place: The Country House and English Literature* (New York: Harvester Wheatsheaf, 1993) 155.

15   James Wood, *The Fun Stuff* (New York: Farrer, Straus and Giroux, 2012) 313.

16   Macfarlane, 'Alan Hollinghurst, *The Line of Beauty*' 182.

17   See Nationwide House Price Index, www.nationwide.co.uk/about/house-price-index (accessed November 2015).

18   Interview with Stephen Moss, quoted in John Su, 'Beauty and the Beastly Prime Minister', *ELH* 81.3 (2014) 1082–10: 1096.

19   See Eastham, *Aesthetic Afterlives* 202.

20   See Macfarlane, 'Alan Hollinghurst, *The Line of Beauty*' 185.

21   Georg Lukács, 'The Ideology of Modernism' in *The Meaning of Contemporary Realism* (London: Merlin, 1957) 17–46.

22   Chris Hamnett, *Unequal City: London in the Global Arena* (London: Routledge, 2003) 144.

9

Cinema in the library

Alan O'Leary

The visual is *essentially* pornographic, which is to say that it has its end in rapt, mindless fascination .... Pornographic films are thus only the potentiation of films in general, which ask us to stare at the world as though it were a naked body. (Fredric Jameson)[1]

In August 1908 Leo Tolstoy received a visit from a handful of early cinematographers. Surrounded by their cameras, he made a prediction: 'this little clicking contraption with the revolving handle will make a revolution in our life – in the life of writers. It is a direct attack on the old methods of literary art. We shall have to adapt ourselves to the shadowy screen and to the cold machine.'[2] According to Julian Murphet and Lydia Rainford, with these words Tolstoy 'foretold the crisis of the greatest narrative form of the nineteenth century – the realist novel – and the supremacy of a new mechanical one in the twentieth.'[3]

The realist novel has survived and Alan Hollinghurst's *The Swimming-Pool Library*, the novel I discuss in this chapter, is evidence it has thrived apparently untroubled by the incorporation of the cinema into the cultural-economic ecosystem. Still, my argument will be that *The Swimming-Pool Library* is *not* untroubled by cinema. The appeal of *The Swimming-Pool Library* resides not only in the powerful vision it offers of its world and the brilliant way that vision is realized through the musings of its narcissistic narrator (and the 'extracts' he reads from Lord Nantwich's journals), but also in the formal unity of the book. Discerning this formal unity is a readerly pleasure that manifests itself in parallel to the thrust of the tale, as one infers the discreet seeding of detail to be reaped as signification further on in the novel and the sense that *The Swimming-Pool Library* is the cunning account of its own genesis.

The challenges to the novel's unity are the key theme of this chapter. My interest is in the extent to which certain elements in *The Swimming-Pool Library* exceed the novel's unifying forces in the same way that history exceeds and forecloses the story's suspended temporalities. History is the Other to the novel's enchanted summer, 'the last summer of its kind there was ever to be' (*SPL* 3). History is also HIV, the ghastly virus present but unidentified, ready to spread its appalling blossom through the utopia of sex beyond book and summer's end. Like this history, the cinema in *The Swimming-Pool Library* must be held at bay. Cinema is an excessive element that resists integration into the middlebrow poise of *The Swimming-Pool Library* and the cool surfaces of its realist prose.

For Roland Barthes, the effect of reality is achieved in the novel by the 'futile detail', the element in the descriptive *mise-en-scène* that seems to carry no denotative or symbolic ballast. What such elements connote, in their extraneousness as mere information, is precisely 'the category of "the real"'.[4] In a later essay on cinema, Barthes glosses similar details as 'obtuse', a word he uses to indicate how such elements refuse to carry meaning in the surface narrative and resist integration into the text's symbolic superstructure.[5] Barthes's commentators have preferred the term 'excess'. As the scholar of cinema Kristin Thompson writes in an essay that builds on his work, 'excess is not only counternarrative; it is also counterunity.'[6] In other words, excess works against the design of a text, against those features that serve to achieve or give the impression of narrative and formal coherence. 'Pretending that a work is exhausted by its functioning structures', Thompson writes, 'robs it of much that is strange, unfamiliar, and striking about it.'[7] Part of what is strange, unfamiliar and striking about *The Swimming-Pool Library* is also sinister, menacing and deadly: the implied presence of HIV is associated with cinema and/as pornography, but in a way that is not systematic. Cinema is an 'obtuse' element, an element of excess. In order to show this, I provide below a list of references to cinema in the novel, annotating where appropriate.[8] If cinema is an element that resists integration in *The Swimming-Pool Library*, then we should not expect to find a consistent role for it in the novel as motif or metaphor. My inventory demonstrates that cinema, as this element of excess, 'forms no specific patterns which we could say are characteristic of the work'.[9]

1 The first mention of the cinema in *The Swimming-Pool Library* occurs before the book begins, in the epigraph taken from Ronald Firbank's *The Flower Beneath the Foot*: '"She reads at such a pace," she complained, "and when I asked her *where* she had learnt to read so quickly, she replied 'On the screens at Cinemas.'"'[10] Georges Letissier

writes of the epigraph that it 'prepares the reader for an inter-semiotic experience' throughout the novel,[11] and indeed ekphrasis is a technique employed throughout.[12] Few books dwell so insistently on images – often photographs, but also drawings, paintings and stone carvings as well as the moving image. Pornographic images, as we will see, are subjects of ambivalent and especial scrutiny. Still, inasmuch as the quoted lines can be read as a statement of Firbank's poetics, suggesting his elliptical modernist style, the epigraph is curiously inapt for *The Swimming-Pool Library*, which is unflappable rather than camp, and cast (as I will argue) in the mode of middle-brow queer.

2   In the book's first visit to the Corinthian Club, we find three mentions of the cinema. 'Corinthian pillars at each corner are an allusion to ancient Rome, and you half expect to see the towel-girt figures of Charlton Heston and Tony Curtis deep in senatorial conspiracy' (*SPL* 11). The allusion is to the camp of 'sword-and-sandal' films, and to the gay potential of ostentatiously heterosexual masculinity, in the case of Heston, along with the prettiness of Curtis. Hollinghurst follows this with a description of the image and caption on a club postcard (said no longer to be available) from after the Second World War. This is parenthetically glossed as follows: 'James had immediately seen that this caption should be read with the clipped, optimistic tone of a Pathé news announcer.' The out-of-time camp of the Pathé tone has often been remarked upon. Finally, in the club's underground swimming pool, 'small, weak spots let into the ceiling now give vestigial illumination, like that in cinemas ...' (*SPL* 12). The comparison suggests there is something to be *seen* (as well as read) in the 'library' of the swimming pool, and it links the pool to the book's other basements: the Brutus Soho porn cinema and the remains of the Roman mosaic in Lord Nantwich's home with its more recent erotic fresco.[13] All function as metaphors for the concealed histories of gay life and its necessarily clandestine practices of pleasure.

3   In the Corinthian Club, Will observes Nantwich enter 'one of the standard hard-on sessions of the shower': 'In a few seconds the hard-on might pass from one end of the room to the other with the foolish perfection of a Busby Berkeley routine' (*SPL* 26). Berkeley was a director-choreographer famous for his geometrically abstract dance numbers, often captured on film with ostentatious camerawork. His work is still seen as a quintessential example of the

so-called 'cinema of attractions' in which narrative is suspended for pure spectacle.[14] As the bodies in a Berkeley routine are subject to the abstraction of the choreography, so the shower hard-on is a motif independent of individual bodies. This is comic but also ominous, in that it is associated with the first sniffs in the changing room of the 'Trouble for Men' fragrance, associated throughout the novel with the HIV virus.

4   At the Brutus, Will goes not 'so much to see a film as to sit in a dark, anonymous place and do dark, anonymous things' (*SPL* 47) including, possibly, having his first sexual encounter with Phil. The passage contains what seems to be the only explicit dating in the book ('the far-off spring of 1983' (*SPL* 48)). The unexpected description of a television nature film of an anteater devouring a termite colony – all too readable as an AIDS metaphor – is accompanied by another mention of 'Trouble for Men'.

Pornography is the object of both particular attention and ambivalence in *The Swimming-Pool Library*. However the porn projected in the Brutus scene is described as 'touching' (*SPL* 50); Will talks of the 'blatant innocence of it all' (*SPL* 52). Most of the prose is expended on the activities in the cinema itself rather than on those onscreen. In this context it is significant that the screen performers mostly seem to be blond: golden haired Californians who contrast with the blackness fetishized elsewhere in the book.

5   Will and his lover Phil encounter Rupert, Will's young nephew, in the street. Rupert canters along before the couple, facing backwards in order to take them in. Will remarks, 'I thought it must be like being filmed, walking towards an ever-receding camera, and I put on silly faces to make him laugh' (*SPL* 155). The scene foreshadows the footage of Ronald Firbank described at the close of the book, which also features children. Rupert's gaze anticipates the more sinisterly angelic character of Gabriel, who also regards Will in the manner of a camera.

6   The porn filmmaking scene in Ronald Staines's home studio contains several references to film. 'It's the very last bit dear', the photographer-pornographer Staines explains to Will. 'It's going to be the most wonderful film ever. We've been doing it for months now – a cast of tens ... I thought you'd like to see us polish it off in this sensationally sensational scene' (*SPL* 187). This is a threesome involving two

young white men and an older black one, all employees at Wicks, Nantwich's gentlemen's club. Nantwich has subsidized the making of the film, which will later be shown in basement cinemas like the Brutus.

The passage stages key issues to do with pornography and exploitation. Will, appalled by the scene's 'achieved bizarrerie which made it normal to the participants, demonic to the outsider' (*SPL* 187), makes his exit in a moralistic huff after noting that the black performer, Abdul, seemed 'like some exquisite game animal, partly skinned and then thrown aside still breathing' (*SPL* 188). Will later challenges Nantwich on representation and race (*SPL* 245), a matter John McLeod discusses in his chapter on 'Race, empire and *The Swimming-Pool Library*'. Working against Nantwich's insouciance is the fact that the old lord had found Abdul and the other young porn actors their jobs at his club, so that they are part of what Will ironically dubs the 'Nantwich feudal system' (*SPL* 137). The degree of coercion exerted on the men to appear on film is unclear but their performance can be inferred to be the expected pound of flesh paid and displayed as part of an economy of gratitude for Nantwich's so-called benevolence. Plainly, race (and empire) does indeed 'come into this'.

7 Speaking to Aldo, one of Staines's models, at an exhibition of the photographer's images of martyrs, Will refers back to the porn filmmaking scene (at which Aldo was present) in the context of a one-sided discussion of porn and representation. Will calls Staines's photographs 'soft porn': 'I honestly prefer to have hard porn – or no porn at all' (*SPL* 231).

8 The farcical scene in the Queensbury hotel room with the Argentinian Gabriel is one of those moments where the book wryly acknowledges its own themes, the relationship between sex and the politics of colonization being prominent among them. The S&M-loving Gabriel offers: 'I could whip you … for what you did to my country in the [Falklands] war.' '"I think that might be to take the sex and politics metaphor a bit too seriously, old chap"', Will responds, 'and I could see the whole thing deteriorating into a scene from some poker-faced left-wing European film' (*SPL* 275). Questions of power and fetishization are comically raised in the passage. Just before, Gabriel puts on a leather mask that obscures his face, and Will thinks: 'Close to I could see only his large brown pupils and the whites of his

eyes, blurred for a split second if he blinked, like the lens of a camera'
(*SPL* 274). Brenda Cooper argues that 'as the mask is assumed, there
is a reverse objectification as Gabriel becomes photographer, clicking
in Will's face'.[15]

9   In Staines's studio, the book culminates with the projection of the
    footage of Firbank in Genzano at the end of his life. The film of
    Firbank has been discovered as part of an auction batch of gay home
    movies. Firbank is described as 'Chaplinesque' (*SPL* 285). The footage
    (apparently Hollinghurst's invention) is minutely described; this
    is cinema as 'a treasured piece of memory'.[16] Firbank has appeared
    previously as a character in the novel (glimpsed in an episode from
    Nantwich's journals) but he is made physically and grotesquely vivid
    to us in this passage as part of an impromptu 'charivari' (*SPL* 287)
    featuring the local children that transforms him into a 'marionette of
    a man' (*SPL* 286).

The foregoing inventory demonstrates that *The Swimming-Pool Library*
richly deploys cinema as a resource for locale, exposition, figure and
allusion. Yet cinema itself is not a distinct theme of the novel and the
motifs and metaphors drawn from it pull in multiple directions. I want
to suggest that the opposition between what I will call (following Jaime
Harker) the 'middlebrow queer'[17] of *The Swimming-Pool Library* and
cinema (as the old vaunted enemy of the realist novel) results in the non-
systematic deployment of cinema as sinister trope.

Firbank's epigraph (discussed in item 1 above) may help explain why.
Cinema, history and heartbreak are conjoined in *The Flower Beneath the
Foot*. Hollinghurst selects his epigraph from the tragic end of what has
been (until then) a comic novel. There, Firbank mentions 'the preparation
of a Cinematograph Company on the parapet of the Cathedral'.[18] As the
film crew is setting up to record the wedding cortège of Prince Yousef,
their preparations and the procession itself are witnessed from afar by
that same Laura who had learned to read 'on the screens at Cinemas'.
She has rejected Prince Yousef, though deeply in love with him, and now
stands high inside the walls of the convent where she has taken orders.
The book ends:

> Laura caught her breath.
>   Already?
>   A shaking of countless handkerchiefs in wild ovation: from rooftops,
> and balconies, the air was thick with falling flowers – the bridal pair!
>   But only for the bridegroom had she eyes.

Oblivious of what she did, she began to beat her hands, until they streamed with blood, against the broken glass ends upon the wall: 'Yousef, Yousef, Yousef ....'[19]

The stream of blood marks the eruption of grief into the comedy of manners and of history: the marriage of alliance between the Balkan prince and the plain English princess. The cinematographic newsreel is the engine and voyeur of this history, its agent, means and emblem. It records the public event for projection and posterity and is implacable in its ignorance and indifference to the tragedy. Cinema is none of these things in *The Swimming-Pool Library*, but it is an excessive element that resists integration to the novel's suave middlebrow. In its pornographic aspect cinema becomes an ambivalent figure of innocence and pleasure. It also represents the threat to being that is HIV/AIDS, the known future history beyond the book.

Signatures of the invisible

If HIV/AIDS is all too well known in the future beyond the suspended summer of *The Swimming-Pool Library*, it remains invisible in the book itself, something that generates a paradox in the novel's construction of a plausible world. Speaking of the cinema, the French sociologist Pierre Sorlin has characterized the idea of a shared perception of reality as the 'visible'.[20] For Sorlin, films do not duplicate reality but provide fragments of the society they portray. The cinema of an age, he says, 'captures a fragment of the outside world, reorganizes it, makes it coherent, and produces, starting from the continuity of the sensible universe, a finished, circumscribed, discontinuous, and transmissible object'.[21] Sorlin argues that a tacit agreement with the audience about what it will accept as true (what viewers will accept 'without surprise') permits a film's fragmentary-as-whole portrayal.[22]

In terms of writing, Sorlin's 'visible' can be understood as that which is accessible to textualization, as 'the perimeter within which it is possible to pose [a society's] problems'.[23] Such ideas call to mind Roland Barthes on verisimilitude, which he describes as 'entirely subject to public opinion'; subject, that is, to an implicit but social consensus on the receivable content of the world.[24] *The Swimming-Pool Library* too has to establish this 'truce' with its readers, but there is a double irony in its treatment of the 'visible'. HIV is invisible in the novel, rendered only as the ubiquitous scent 'Trouble for Men', but it will have been all too present to Hollinghurst's readers in the late 1980s.[25] What is 'visible' – accessible to awareness and textualization, verisimilitudinous – differs for different groups. Taboo and convention may proscribe the communication of that which is perfectly well known by subcultures within a given society.

Viewed from the perspective of what I will call the 'straight mainstream', the novel transposes the regime of the visible from the heterosexual to the male homosexual milieu. Indeed, for Stephen Murphy, the unapologetic portrayal of gay life in *The Swimming-Pool Library* represents the Forsterian ideal of an unashamed, public and 'masculine' homosexual community.[26] Certainly, the book presents as normal what Paul Bailey calls 'a certain kind of man's world from which women are excluded'.[27] This absence of women, recalling a gay male porn scenario in which the female would be a bizarre interruption and an unwelcome distraction, is one of the conventions that renders *The Swimming-Pool Library* specifically or potentially pornographic – a characteristic the book must harness and tame. But for now I want to note that the structuring absence of women functions in a similar way to what Danish filmmaker Lars Von Trier would call an 'obstruction', an arbitrary formal constraint that generates something unexpected.[28] This element is introduced so that it can reach those beyond the constituency it describes. The 'opinable' verisimilitude permits the introduction of the new element into the schema or truce of the visible, and this regime of the visible – realism itself, one is tempted to say – is consolatory: it communicates that the world is as one knows it to be, however disturbing such an assertion must seem in a book that implies the catastrophe of HIV/AIDS beyond its covers. Ultimately, though, the 'visible' for the possible mainstream addressee of *The Swimming-Pool Library* (to whom I will allocate a gender and a sexuality below) has been augmented, so that the book's 'realism', in the colloquial sense of that which is jarring or harsh, is also flattering. The shock of the new is of a piece with the flattery of interpellation. The mode of this receivability, embellished rather than obstructed by the novel's element of surprise, can be described as 'middlebrow queer'.

Straight mainstream and middlebrow queer

The Swimming-Pool Library is a realist novel. Its explicit descriptions of men having sex with men are intrinsic both to this realism and to the book's appeal – an appeal, it has been attested, that goes beyond any 'gay' readership, so that the book has been receivable by what I am calling the straight mainstream. It has achieved this mainstream reception through its employment of the mode of middlebrow queer. In Jaime Harker's work on this mode, Christopher Isherwood is an important, exemplary figure. Harker, though, does not set out to recuperate Isherwood as a high modernist but rather to recuperate the middlebrow itself as a destabilizing concept. For Harker, the term 'middlebrow' shares with 'queer' an initial pejorative status. But, like 'queer', 'middlebrow' has the potential to trouble known categories and established binaries. Reading *The Swimming-Pool Library* from a perspective provided by Harker, I see it as a novel in the middlebrow mode and one, therefore, that both belongs to, and queers, the mainstream.

As such, *The Swimming-Pool Library* deals with the serious questions of love, life and the law in a number of ways: with an immersive story, empathetic characters and a direct and transparently mimetic (though intensely self-aware) narration.[29] With the exception of self-reflexivity, many of these characteristics are disdained by the high culture that modernism shaped, though they are perfectly at home in a national culture dominated by figures like, say, John Galsworthy and Evelyn Waugh. The TV and film adaptations for which writers such as these provided the raw literary material also evince these qualities. Essential to the middlebrow mode, however, is precisely this worthiness, the measured component of challenge to the reader or viewer.[30] In order to distinguish itself from the mere pleasure provided by trash, pulp or lowbrow, the middlebrow needs to contain an improving aspect.[31]

This, ironically enough, is the role of the explicitly described sex in *The Swimming-Pool Library*. Where the *form* of the novel is highly achieved but (in terms of modernist aesthetics) essentially conservative, we find *content* outré enough to be flattering to the reader seeking validation for the middlebrow *plaisir du texte*. Flattering, that is, because the straight reader feels 'man-of-the-world' enough to be above shock (if not revulsion) at the descriptions of man/man sex. If, here, I am deliberately, and in defiance of my own politics, gendering and ascribing a stable and delimited sexuality to this putative reader I do so because some of Hollinghurst's early readers did precisely this, and because the terms of their appreciation explain how a sexually explicit account of gay life is accepted as mainstream literature.

Let us take two early responses to the book: a review by John Lanchester of *The Swimming-Pool Library* and the mentions of Hollinghurst's novel in Nicholson Baker's rumination on writing and reading in his non-fiction *U and I*. What characterizes these accounts is their foregrounding of the sexual aspect of *The Swimming-Pool Library*, their insistence that the descriptions of sex go beyond the salacious to justify themselves in aesthetic and other terms. In Baker's case, the fantasy use of the gay sex in *The Swimming-Pool Library* becomes a discursive gambit between (straight) men. The following quotation is taken from early in Lanchester's review:

> One of the triumphs of *The Swimming-Pool Library* ... is the tonal control it achieves in writing graphically and explicitly about homosexual sex while never seeming flustered or prurient, and never wavering in the amused, ironic control of the narrating voice ... However Dionysian the events depicted – fellatio, sodomy, an erection passing along a line of men in the shower 'with the domino effect [sic] of a Busby Berkeley routine' – the narrator's tone remains, in keeping with his personality, resolutely Apollonian.[32]

Lanchester disavows *The Swimming-Pool Library*'s potential for generating arousal because of the book's style and address. That is to say, the straight reviewer can discount the novel's gay pornographic power by reference to its amused, ironic and unwavering narrative voice, its 'Apollonian' decorum. This last is a taming of the excess that sex itself represents in the novel. Hollinghurst is on record as wanting to celebrate in *The Swimming-Pool Library* man/man sex despite writing in the wake of the AIDS epidemic.[33] Still, sex remained a primary medium of HIV transmission (and so the celebration's ineluctable limit). It exceeded the experience and control of any one body. This excess, as Lanchester notes, is figured by the image from cinema (discussed in item 3 of the list above) tellingly misquoted by the reviewer so that it seems to point to the presence of the deadly virus – one thinks of the Pet Shop Boys single 'Domino Dancing', released same year as *The Swimming-Pool Library*.

Nicholson Baker mentions *The Swimming-Pool Library* several times in *U and I*, once in an imagined conversation with his literary hero John Updike:

> If *I* were golfing with Updike this week, would I tell him, 'Hey, I'm reading Alan Hollinghurst's *The Swimming-Pool Library*, and you know, once you get used to the initially kind of disgusting level of homosexual sex, which quickly becomes really interesting as a kind of ethnography, you realize that this is really one of the best first novels to come along in years and years! The guy does everything – dialogue, scenic pageantry, wit, pathos, everything!'[34]

Even as its potential to arouse must be denied, the ('disgusting') sex in *The Swimming-Pool Library* seems to be the first thing to notice about it, immediately associated with the warrant of the book's quality; only then is the novel also witty, pathetic and so on. This is in part a rather obvious protesting-too-much, so that the explicit sexual description in *The Swimming-Pool Library* has to be acknowledged in order for its threat to be dismissed.[35] What's notable, though, is that the hysterical imperative to array one's straight credentials on the golf links of homosociality is subtended by the sense of privileged access to knowledge. Again this is part of the flattery of address in the book's mode of middlebrow queer. In speaking of 'ethnography', Baker may be following a cue from *The Swimming-Pool Library* itself, picking up on the moment when Will comes across the duty manager of the Brutus porn cinema watching a nature film on the foyer television. One implication is that Hollinghurst himself is training his pen, like the nature filmmakers and their camera, on a variety of 'exotic' species and their behaviour – indeed Will-narrator uses the term 'exotic species' of the assortment of men in the Corinthian Club changing rooms (*SPL* 223). But if this is so, then the question raises itself – exotic to whom? To a different 'species' from that described, presumably: to what I am therefore calling the straight mainstream.

Ethnopornography

The appeal of realism is essential to the address to the straight mainstream in *The Swimming-Pool Library*, and the book's explicit sex is a key component of this realism. But the sex is presented and perceived as 'knowledge' – what can be 'learned' of an 'exotic' way of life by reading the novel. The sexually explicit realism of *The Swimming-Pool Library* must distinguish itself from proximate but less favoured modes. One such mode is the gay art film. Allan Johnson suggests that *The Swimming-Pool Library* offers a 'mischievous parody of [the] pre-AIDS celebration' that is Derek Jarman's *Sebastiane* (1976) in the kitsch photo-tableaux by photographer Ronald Staines.[36] As we have seen, Will considers these tableaux to be 'just soft porn', to which he prefers 'hard porn – or no porn at all' (*SPL* 231). This is a statement of aesthetic preference on behalf of *The Swimming-Pool Library* itself, which is at once hard porn and no porn at all: its uncensored accounts of man/man sex are presented as 'ethnopornography', a kind of natural history that supposedly evades titillation.

Hard porn, however, is treated inconsistently in the novel. When Will storms in his censorious sulk from the porn filmmaking scene at Ronald Staines's home studio, he slams the door ambivalently on behalf of the novel itself. As sexually explicit literary fiction *The Swimming-Pool Library* must distinguish itself both from racialized imperialism and from a certain pornographic quality that, for Fredric Jameson, is cinema's quintessence. It may seem perverse to assert of a book so preoccupied with the corporeal (a topic Angus Brown's chapter explores), but *The Swimming-Pool Library* evades any classification as 'body genre' – Linda Williams's term for film horror, melodrama and pornography, all designed to elicit physical reactions in the viewer.[37] Measured in prose, the body is a *subject* of *The Swimming-Pool Library* rather than its *object* – and pornography is that which must be harnessed by the novel's wry tone, complex narrative structure and formal quilting. Beverley Brown has described pornography as the 'erotic organization of visibility'.[38] The phrase also works as a characterization of Will Beckwith's personal worldview and even the frankness of the book itself. As Letissier writes, 'Hollinghurst's insistence on visibility is … all-pervasive, in particular through the scopic drive prompting the crude depiction of same-sex scenes and, to all intents and purposes, doing away with the refined effeminacy of camp'.[39] Will's worldview and the crudeness of the register must be framed and tamed by another order – the middlebrow queer that means *The Swimming-Pool Library* is received as a respectable book.

Richard Dyer has written that 'the fact that porn, like weepies, thrillers and low comedy, is realized in/through the body has given it low status in our culture':

> Popularity these genres have, but arbiters of cultural status still tend to value 'spiritual' over 'bodily' qualities, and hence relegate porn and the rest to an inferior cultural position.
>
> One of the results of this is that culturally validated knowledge of the body, of the body's involvement in emotion, tends to be intellectual knowledge about the body, uninformed by experimental knowledge of it.[40]

The novel's 'ethnopornographic' exploration – what it teaches of an 'exotic' way of life – is set against cinema's pornographic essence (for Jameson) of mere gaze: a kind of reflex empty voyeurism. However, the book's 'culturally validated knowledge of the body' cannot refuse the history its bodies may be incubating. In the episode of the Brutus porn cinema, the text's sedate ekphrasis of the images on screen disavows (even as it is evoked by 'Trouble for Men') the information held, perhaps, by certain of the horny bodies in the seedy basement: the HIV that some may yet realize.

My argument is not that the cinema is an emblem or harbinger of HIV in *The Swimming-Pool Library*. However, the novel's ambivalent treatment of cinema and/as pornography suggests how a rival medium and proximate mode might resist the novel's formal system, just as the known future history of HIV/AIDS exceeds its 'Apollonian' (and Forsterian) diorama of homosexual virility. Cinema in the novel is, in Barthes's terms, 'obtuse', and the novel ironically confirms Barthes's assertion that the obtuse subverts the whole practice of meaning, appearing 'necessarily as luxury, an expenditure with no exchange'. Barthes explains that this 'luxury does not *yet* belong to today's politics but nevertheless already to tomorrow's'.[41] HIV/AIDS is likewise obtuse: its baleful luxury obeys no intention, partakes of no practice of meaning. Its politics – legislative persecution under Thatcher and the resistance of Stonewall and AIDS activism – are already tomorrow's in Hollinghurst's novel. The 'visible' proposed in the novel via its mode of middlebrow queer is among other things a matter of command over a history that cannot be contained.

Notes

1 Fredric Jameson, *Signatures of the Visible* (London: Routledge, 1990) 1.
2 David Bernstein, 'Tolstoy on the Cinema', *New York Times* 31 January 1937, 158.
3 Julian Murphet and Lydia Rainford, 'Introduction' in *Literature and Visual Technologies: Writing after Cinema*, ed. Julian Murphet and Lydia Rainford (Basingstoke: Palgrave Macmillan, 2003) 1–11: 1.
4 Roland Barthes, 'The Reality Effect' [1968] in *The Rustle of Language*, trans. Richard Howard (Oxford: Blackwell, 1986) 141–8: 148.
5 Roland Barthes, 'The Third Meaning: Research Notes on some Eisenstein Stills' [1970] in *Image Music Text*, ed. and trans. Stephen Heath (London: Fontana, 1990) 52–68.
6 Kristin Thompson, 'The Concept of Cinematic Excess' [1977] in *Narrative, Apparatus, Ideology: A Film Theory Reader*, ed. Philip Rosen (New York: Columbia University Press, 1986) 130–42: 134.
7 Ibid. 134.
8 By my count, there are fourteen distinct mentions of cinema in the book. I omit several in this list for reasons of space.
9 Thompson, 'The Concept of Cinematic Excess' 132.
10 Ronald Firbank, *The Flower Beneath the Foot* in *Five Novels* (New York: New Directions, 1981) 2.
11 Georges Letissier, 'Queer, Quaint and Camp: Alan Hollinghurst's Own Return to the English Tradition', *Études anglaises* 60.2 (2007) 198–211: 200.
12 I think it interesting that Barthes discusses ekphrasis as the 'detachable set piece' that anticipates the surplus/useless detail connoting 'reality' in the realist novel (Barthes, 'The Reality Effect' 143).
13 Letissier, 'Queer, Quaint and Camp' 205.
14 The 'cinema of attractions' is a famous coinage of film historian Tom Gunning that puts the emphasis on the vaudeville origins or conditions of

exhibition of early cinema. For Gunning, this was an 'exhibitionist cinema' characterized by its 'ability to *show* something' rather than its capacity to tell a story. The point is that the excessive, spectacular element of 'attraction' survives the early period and persists in narrative cinema to this day – to be ritualistically deplored, indeed, as 'mere' spectacle by critics who desire precisely that sense of formal unity and integration we may privilege in *The Swimming-Pool Library*. See Tom Gunning, 'The Cinema of Attractions' in *Early Cinema: Space Frame Narrative*, ed. Thomas Elsaesser (London: BFI, 1990) 56–62: 57.

15 Brenda Cooper, 'Snapshots of Postcolonial Masculinities: Alan Hollinghurst's *The Swimming-Pool Library* and Ben Okri's *The Famished Road*', *Journal of Commonwealth Literature* 34.1 (1999) 135–57: 143.

16 Letissier, 'Queer, Quaint and Camp' 200.

17 Jaime Harker, *Middlebrow Queer: Christopher Isherwood in America* (Minneapolis: University of Minnesota Press, 2013). I return below to Harker's concept of the middlebrow queer.

18 Firbank, *The Flower Beneath the Foot* 92.

19 Ibid. 94.

20 Pierre Sorlin, *Sociologie du cinéma* (Paris: Aubier Montaigne, 1977). Sorlin's influential volume has not been translated into English, but his idea of the 'visible' is effectively discussed in Francesco Casetti, *Theories of Cinema 1945–1995*, trans. Francesca Chiostri, Elizabeth Gard Bartolini-Salimbeni and Thomas Kelso (Austin: University of Texas Press, 1999) 129–30. I rely on Casetti and his translators for the quotes from Sorlin used here.

21 Sorlin in Casetti, *Theories of Cinema* 129.

22 Ibid.

23 Ibid.

24 Roland Barthes, 'The Reality Effect', in *The Rustle of Language*, trans. Richard Howard (New York: Hill and Wang, 1986), 141–8: 147.

25 'Trouble for Men' is mentioned seven times in the novel and most commentators agree it is a metaphor for the HIV virus. Tammy Grimshaw is an exception. She sees the fragrance (or its name) as 'an allusion to the gay male's "Trouble with the Law"'. See Tammy Grimshaw, 'Hollinghurst's *The Swimming-Pool Library*', *The Explicator* 64.4 (2006), 242–5: 243. I am grateful to the editors of this volume for pointing out to me that 'The Troubles' had become, by the early 1990s, a slang term for AIDS, particularly as a diagnosis. The term is deployed by Belize, a nurse, in the second part of Tony Kushner's *Angels in America* (1992). 'Guess who just checked in with the troubles?' he says about Roy Cohn, the famously homophobic, and closeted, politician. See Tony Kushner, *Angels in America: A Gay Fantasia on National Themes* (London: Nick Hern Books, 2007) 156.

26 Stephen Murphy, 'Past Irony: Trauma and the Historical Turn in Fragments and *The Swimming-Pool Library*', *Literature and History* 13.1 (2004) 58–75: 70.

27 This phrase is from Paul Bailey's review in the *Observer*, an extract from which is quoted in the front matter to the 2006 Vintage paperback edition

of *The Swimming-Pool Library*. See Paul Bailey, 'Snow Queen', *Observer* 21 February 1988, 27.

28 See *The Five Obstructions*, the 2003 film directed by Von Trier and Jørgen Leith.

29 I am grateful to my colleague at Leeds, Diana Holmes, for sharing with me a book proposal on the middlebrow, the text of which has informed this material.

30 *The Swimming-Pool Library* contains a dismissive reference to Waugh's *Brideshead Revisited* when Will describes Nantwich's journals as containing 'some rather Bridesheady bits about Oxford – though somewhat more candid than that deplorable novel' (177). There are no specific allusions in *The Swimming-Pool Library* to the eleven instalments of the television adaptation of *Brideshead Revisited*, even if they were first broadcast in Britain from October to December 1981, so that the series' portrayal of passionate male attachments and aristocratic and exotic milieus must be on the horizon of *The Swimming-Pool Library*'s 1983.

31 See Pierre Bourdieu, *The Field of Cultural Production: Essays on Art and Literature* (Cambridge: Polity Press, 1993) 128.

32 John Lanchester, 'Catch 28', *London Review of Books* 2 March 1988, 11–12: 11.

33 See Cooper, 'Snapshots of Postcolonial Masculinities' 137

34 Nicholson Baker, *U and I: A True Story* (London: Granta, 1991) 53.

35 I am not discounting Baker's own self-awareness in all this, and the allusion to Hollinghurst in *U and I* forms part of a longer meditation that circles continuously back on its own fixations and modalities.

36 Allan Johnson, *Alan Hollinghurst and the Vitality of Influence* (Basingstoke: Palgrave Macmillan, 2014) 40. Johnson also considers (on pages 40–50) the parallels in *The Swimming-Pool Library* with a screenplay of Jarman's (never filmed and unpublished until 1996) about the same pharaoh, Akhenaten, who is depicted on the stone carving shown to Will by Nantwich, as well as with the well-known Philip Glass opera on the same figure, produced in London in 1985. Though ingenious, Johnson's analysis of these campy but highbrow intertexts seems to me to distract from the essential middlebrow of Hollinghurst's novel.

37 See Linda Williams, 'Film Bodies: Gender, Genre and Excess', *Film Quarterly* 44.4 (1991) 2–13.

38 Beverley Brown quoted in Linda Williams, *Hard Core: Power, Pleasure and the Frenzy of the Visible* (Berkeley: University of California Press, 1999) 30.

39 Georges Letissier, 'Alan Hollinghurst/Ronald Firbank: Camp Filiation as an Aesthetic of the Outrageous', *Études britanniques contemporaines* 45 (2013), http://ebc.revues.org/742 (accessed 19 January 2016).

40 Richard Dyer, 'Coming to Terms: Gay Pornography' [1985] in *Only Entertainment* (London: Routledge, 1992) 138–50: 139.

41 Barthes, 'The Third Meaning' 62–3.

10

Using Racine in 1990; or, translating theatre in time

Denis Flannery

> I felt I'd have to be Racine to keep abreast of this convulsive trio,
> their switches of allegiance that seemed compacted in retrospect
> into little more than a day. (*FS* 398)

> Hoist the red curtain, grind the gears,
> Mysterium mechanicum, prepare the scene,
> A love-and-death spectacle, a veil of tears,
> Classic and tragic, as if penned by Racine![1]

If your name were Jean Racine and if you had an interest in how your *oeuvre* meshed with historical understandings of 'homosexuality', then 1990 really was your year. Setting out to explain the workings of the closet as a major formative force in Western culture, Eve Kosofsky Sedgwick had surprising recourse then to *Esther*, your biblical drama of 1689. And Alan Hollinghurst, the late twentieth century's most striking new novelist of something called 'gay life', found time in 1990, between the publication of *The Swimming-Pool Library* (1988) and *The Folding Star* (1994), to translate what became known as your 'most violent and most frightening play', *Bajazet* (1672).[2] Hollinghurst's version, directed by Peter Eyre, was performed at London's Almeida Theatre in November of your heady year.

As my first epigraph shows, that work of translation found echoes in *The Folding Star*, whose narrator, Edward Manners, jokingly, and with some bitterness, invokes a Racine whose genius can meticulously illuminate the caprices of triangulated desire at the same time that it compacts them 'in retrospect into little more than a day' (*FS* 398). Certainly the 'convulsive trio' of Luc, Patrick and Sibylle from which Manners finds himself excluded at the very moment that he discovers its existence, echoes the convulsively repetitive triangulations of Racine's entire career. *Bérénice*

(1670), which Hollinghurst went on to translate in 2012, centres on the tortured trio of Titus, Bérénice and Antiochus. Such triangles occur in *Brittanicus* (1669), *Phaedra* (1677) and, of course, *Bajazet* with its all-too-convulsive trio of Bajazet, brother of the Sultan Amurat, Roxane (a former slave, sultaness and Amurat's favourite) and Atalide, Bajazet's betrothed and a blood relative who was 'raised together' with him (*Bajazet* 90). Such triangles can produce and mimic others, especially in *Bajazet* where, for Leo Bersani, Racine 'creates the dim outlines of an Oedipal structure ... (Acomat–Atalide–Bajazet) which coexists with the earlier psychic structure of the hero between two women: (Roxane–Bajazet–Atalide)'.[3] A structure of triangular betrayal is central in Racine and, in *The Folding Star*, Racine is also the rich linguistic and affective glue that binds the narrator Manners to his schoolfriend, Graves: 'We egged each other on into a language world of our own,' Manners tells the reader, 'The discovery of French Classical drama was a major step: after a term with our A-level texts we were recycling alexandrines and spoke with a marked sense of the caesura' (*FS* 209).

The boys' combination of Racinian speech and schoolboy erudition enables them to gain protective prestige by channelling ancient and obscure cultural forms into their exclusive present, thereby providing a carapace against the sexual and normative pressures to which they are subject. The channeling of Racine creates what Barbara Johnson calls 'a space of play and risk' between and around the boys.[4] In what follows, I argue that Hollinghurst's first translation of Racine is part of an historical moment where one of the most historically conscious and significant of playwrights was used and adapted at a time that both prided itself on the termination of history as a category even as it sensed new forms of historical pressure.

A Racine who was not too blinded by the odd wave of recognition that 1990 brought might have noticed echoes of his *Bajazet* in the work of the director Derek Jarman, whose 1991 film adaptation of Christopher Marlowe's *Edward II* (1593) echoed many features of Racine's Oriental tragedy: a situation in a confined space, an approaching act of violence that is part-execution, part-political murder. Both also contain allusive references to the first Gulf War and to a particular phase of the AIDS crisis – new, relentless, almost invariably mortal. Written in 1990, Jarman's script trims the near 3,000 lines of Marlowe's original to less than 1,000, closer to the sleek scale of most of Racine's plays, which, generally, come in at about 1,600 lines. Via Tilda Swinton's performance as Queen Isabella, this *Edward II* highlighted a plot of feminine revenge that matched the implacable energy of the Sultaness Roxane. Both women cling to men – Edward and Bajazet – who are fundamentally not all that interested. And both go to murderous lengths when their desires are not reciprocated.

Racine's play is set in a harem, a confined space towards which terrible forces converge and from which only one character, Grand Vizier Acomat, can escape. Jarman's film was shot in a walled world, one that is, like Racine's seraglio as described by Roland Barthes, a 'ceaselessly inverted structure ... a site both smothered and smothering'.[5] *Edward II* opens in a dungeon; the film's action is framed as a series of flashbacks from the time just before the execution of Edward (played by Steven Waddington). With *Bajazet*, too, the order of an execution (of Bajazet, by his brother Amurat) is one of the grounding facts of the play. Racine's play and Jarman's film make much of the approach of an executioner figure (Orcan in *Bajazet*, Lightborn – played by Jarman's boyfriend Kevin Collins – in the film) who is made to take on the eroticized weight of a death drive which all the characters disavow and to which they are devoted. The film also posits a different future for Edward, and for his executioner. Representing, in hellish red light, Edward's death by having a heated poker inserted in his anus, the film also has a more optimistic parallel ending with Edward and Lightborn romantically kissing after Lightborn throws his heated poker into a water-tank.

Giving equal weight to both endings, the film uses Marlowe to open a space of historical reflection and possibility. Jarman, who spoke out eloquently against the Gulf War, has his Mortimer (Nigel Terry) reading a copy of Adel Darwish and Gregory Alexander's 1991 book *Unholy Babylon: The Secret History of Saddam's War* as he lies in bed next to Swinton's Isabella. And in November 1990 few audiences could have sat through performances of Hollinghurst's translation without sensing connections between what they were witnessing onstage and the build-up towards the Western invasion of Iraqi-occupied Kuwait that was to begin the following January. All the play's events take place in an atmosphere of feverishly imagined Oriental war. *Bajazet's* first dialogue – between the Grand Vizier Acomat and his confidant, Osmin – concerns in part the siege of Babylon by the Sultan Amurat, Bajazet's older brother and the man who issues the play's structuring order of execution.

Queer political responses, both to the HIV epidemic and to its ideological marshalling, animate *Edward II*. The king's 'troops' in the civil war sequences were all volunteer members of the group OutRage!, wearing their own t-shirts, holding banners and chanting slogans over and in response to Marlowe's verse. *Edward II* makes clear the connections then being made visible, often in the most exploitative fashion, between male–male anal sex and death that were such a feature of the sexual-political scene in the early 1990s.[6]

A sense of doomed young male life, so ghostly and anticipated in *The Swimming-Pool Library,* so eroticized and mournfully elaborated in *The Folding Star,* is the defining feature of *Bajazet.* For Barthes, Bajazet is 'like those geese stuffed to make their livers succulent'.[7] For Bersani, he has a 'vague death wish'.[8] Certainly he is a target (and a perpetrator) of deadly betrayals. Those to whom he is bound with ties of fraternity or obedience all become manifestations of a death wish that might be vague but is also vast.

The year 1990 also saw another gay writer, Tony Kushner, 'freely adapt' (rather than translate) *L'Illusion Comique* by Racine's predecessor, Pierre Corneille. The second epigraph to my chapter, taken from Kushner's version, represents a very different way in which seventeenth-century French theatre was translated that year: in the published text, Kushner claims that there 'are virtually no lines directly translated from the French'.[9] The epigraph from Kushner also resonates with how, in establishing temporality as a critical term, recent queer scholarship has enabled time to be freshly conceptualized. A key ambition of such work has been to distinguish between 'temporality' and 'time'. For Elizabeth Freeman, the former is considered 'a mode of implantation through which institutional forces come to seem like somatic facts'.[10] As anyone who has ever moved from one culture to another can tell you, the recognition of a particular shared measurement of time is not synonymous with the successful occupation of a culture's framing and making of temporality. Early rising, the psychoanalytic or pedagogical hour, the lunch 'hour', the working day, waiting, Christmas, the future: these sometimes 'shared' and known temporal categories get reworked and, it can appear, attacked as one moves, sometimes pleasurably and often with anguished confusion, between cultures. If such movements and recognitions are affective and cultural, then they are also inevitably political. Freeman has pointed out how our 'need' for eight hours of sleep, now understood as a bodily requirement, comes, rather, from a form of what she terms 'resistance to wage work' as 'nineteenth-century workers in the United States and Europe claimed the eight-hour workday as part of a triad that included eight hours of sleep and eight hours of leisure.' For her, 'time, then, is not only of the essence; it actually produces "essences"'.[11] When it comes to questions of sexuality, reproduction and national personhood, the political making of temporal essences invites conflict and confusion. This temporal making is also accompanied, as Lee Edelman argues in his reading of *A Christmas Carol* (1843), by ranges of violence that are as remorselessly thorough as they are sentimentally disavowed.[12]

Exploring queer temporality has, for Freeman and others, entailed a critical stance towards both 'progress' and linear time. Valuing repetition and alert to what temporalities other than those of Western capitalism have to offer, this field also cherishes the extent to which desire in the present can come from other times.[13] Such senses of time are encapsulated in these lines from *The Illusion* that amount, like the particularities of Jarman's *Edward II*, to a kind of temporal kink. With the phrase 'Classic and tragic, as if penned by Racine', time gets twisted. Kushner has the playwright who historically *preceded* Racine (Corneille was prolific in the 1630s; Racine wrote plays between 1664 and 1690) claim Racine as a model and progenitor.

Unlike Kushner, Hollinghurst stays with direct translation, carefully balancing scrupulous fidelity, pragmatic change and imaginative intervention. Responding, in Act 2, Scene 5, to Bajazet's potentially suicidal refusal to utter false declarations of love to the implacable Roxane, Atalide says:

> She'll be more thirsty for my blood than yours;
> She'll let me stage before your sickened eyes
> The spectacle that you rehearse for me. (*Bajazet* 111)

Racine's original reads:

> Elle aura plus de soif de mon sang que du vôtre,
> Et je pourrai donner à vos yeux effrayés
> Le spectacle sanglant que vous me prépariez.[14]

In his Foreword, Hollinghurst makes an eloquent case for translating Racine into blank verse, that 'staple form of English verse tragedy from the Elizabethan period on' (vii). In making this claim, Hollinghurst's point of reference and contrast is Shakespeare. This translation's most radical aspect is its step away from Racine's alexandrine, what Hollinghurst calls 'a strict form, inescapable as time itself' (vi). Certainly, Hollinghurst treads a line between strict fidelity to the original and a looser sonic sense that foregrounds the restrained theatricality of Racine's original. In a recent translation into English that employs rhyming couplets, Geoffrey Alan Argent translates the last two lines of Atalide's speech as: 'And soon, my lord, *your* frightened eyes shall see / The bloody spectacle you'd planned for *me*.'[15] Hollinghurst's translation of this first line is faithful, almost literal. In the second line, agency moves from Atalide to Roxane. 'Je pourrai donner' (which translates literally as 'I [Atalide] will be able to give') becomes 'She'll [Roxane] let me stage'. In moving from 'donner' to 'stage' the theatricality of this moment is also highlighted. There is also an affective emphasis. In the original, Atalide suggests that Bajazet's eyes will be 'effrayés' ('frightened', as Argent more literally translates it). Hollinghurst's choice of the word 'sickened' makes Bajazet's potential response to Atalide's theatre of death much more visceral, corporeal and related to disease. It also compensates for Hollinghurst's decision to cut the word 'sanglant' (bloody) from the original. The self-conscious theatricality of Hollinghurst's word-choices is maintained when he translates Racine's French verb 'préparer' into the English 'to rehearse'.

This work of translation was nothing if not a historical project. But its occurrence in 1990 locates it in what Joshua Clover calls 'the long 1989', the year in which Francis Fukuyama famously declared 'the end of history'.[16] Clover locates the value of Fukuyama's assertion in the idea that '1989 witnessed the end of *historical thought*, that the public imagination of the West had abandoned a conception of ongoing historical process, of alternative arrangements of daily life'.[17]

If 1989 was the year in which the end of history was declared, it was also the year which saw the release of Denys Arcand's *Jesus of Montreal*, a film about efforts to revive a stale and stymied Passion play. In telling a story about frictions between the making of a playful, historically conscious piece of theatre and the petty political powers that both surround the play and bring it into being, Arcand's film also dramatized how theatre can provoke the eruption of history into collective orthodoxies about how time should work. So, for Clover, Fukuyama's declaration, which is coeval with the *Bajazet* of 1990, is 'a condition of consciousness arising in a new situation'.[18] It is a novelty of situation to which Hollinghurst's translation and Jarman's *Edward II* are strenuously resistant. Both focus on moments of historical transformation and are full – politically and linguistically – of a sense of historical process. The fact that, for Racine, writing plays was the prelude to a long tenure as Louis XIV's historiographer intertwines his work with the making of the history that Fukuyama had declared at an end. If the 'long 1989', was a moment when History was being denied, it was also a moment of historical development for gay politics and queer consciousness. Sedgwick's *Epistemology of the Closet*, which I discuss in the next section, was published that year, as was Judith Butler's *Gender Trouble*.

Both *Bajazet* and Jarman's *Edward II* make metaphorical connections between times: England's fourteenth-century internecine conflict as understood in 1593 becomes the ground for articulating the sexual-political conflicts of 1991; the internecine conflicts of the sultan's harem in the seventeenth century echo the international tensions of 1990. This means that while reflections on the historical process may be alive and kicking, the process itself is far from 'ongoing' or linear. Like the makers of popular music in the long 1989 as described by Clover – Nirvana,

KLF, Madonna – Jarman and Hollinghurst make work that often challenges Fukuyama's fantasy of history's end. For Clover, this happened through the agitated reworking of earlier musical styles (as in Nirvana's reworking of the styles of 1970s punk), through the use of sampling technology that amounted, in the work of the KLF, to a call for 'a time that is not in time, *a unity outside history*'), or through the tincturing of smooth fantasies of history's end with elements of excess and doubt that ultimately serve to collapse temporality and to end narrative (as in Madonna's 1989 song 'Like a Prayer').[19] All this contestation and collapse, combined with strange historical continuity, is very different to the unidirectional narrative on which Fukuyama insists, even as he declares history at an end.

Sedgwick's Racine

Strange historical continuity also marks Eve Kosofsky Sedgwick's reading of *Esther*. Sedgwick oscillates between Racine's text, which she translates herself, and what, in a less theatrical mode, she refers to, as 'the story of Esther'. In both cases, Sedgwick highlights Esther as speaking out and self-declaring with a view to saving herself and her people from genocidal annihilation. In either form, this narrative, for Sedgwick, 'seems a model for a certain simplified but highly potent imagining of coming out and its transformative potential'.[20] Reading the play as a model of gay coming-out creates, for Sedgwick, an agonizing 'balance of the holocaustal with the intimate'.[21] Using Racine's biblical play to reflect on pressures of late-twentieth-century, predominantly American, models of coming-out, enables Sedgwick to pick up on apocalyptic resonances that have much to do with what, elsewhere in *Epistemology of the Closet*, she refers to as genocidal fantasies around AIDS.[22] These resonances also make the step from personal, erotic revelation to transformative apocalyptic event very short indeed. Nowhere is this more evident than when Sedgwick writes: 'What? *you're* one of *those*? Huh? you're a *what*? This frightening thunder can also, however, be the sound of manna falling'.[23]

Splicing Racine with the Bible opens an imaginative space for Sedgwick, letting her access the apocalyptic fantasia of her historical moment. The power of this model of the Racinian-Biblical closet inheres in contrasts between what 'coming out', as Jewish, involves in the play and what coming out, as gay, might involve in a world Sedgwick recognizes. Sedgwick reminds us that no one suggests that Esther's Jewishness might be 'debateable' or 'porous' – a phase she might be going through.[24] The opposite is true in Sedgwick's scenario of gay 'coming out'. For her, there is a 'double-edged' and disorienting aspect to this process: it can produce other secrets, it makes one the victim, or potentially the perpetrator, of fantasies or acts of violence. Furthermore, 'the erotic identity of the person who receives the disclosure is apt also to be implicated in, hence perturbed by it'.[25] Even the certainties of surprise are, for Sedgwick, absent from the gay coming-out scenario, whereas they are rigidly operative in the Old Testament and Racine. '*Esther*,' Sedgwick writes, '*expects Assuerus to be altogether surprised by her self-disclosure; and he is*. Her confident sense of control over other people's knowledge about her is in contrast to the radical uncertainty closeted gay people are likely to feel about who is in control of information about their sexual identity.' [26]

There are temporal dimensions to all of these divergences. Any potential dismissal of Esther's Jewishness and any actual dismissal of a gay person's sense of their sexual being as a 'phase' would, or does, amount to a denigration of the now, the fantasist's fabrication of a different past and the opening up of a coercive future. For Sedgwick, coming-out can also give one access to a less than welcome – if, perhaps, Racinian – sense of the primal violence at the heart of one's familial or intimate relations. And in the final case of 'radical uncertainty', one without clear distinctions between structures of open and closed, or secret and surprised, there is a recalibration of the past, a recasting of assumptions about how one was known. Sedgwick starts off using *Esther* to open up temporal possibilities, but goes on to use it as a vividly clarifying site of temporal contrast.

In *Esther*, all disclosures radiate around *one* secret – Esther's Jewishness. Yet, as David G. Muller has recently noted, the play is unusual in Racine's *oeuvre* in that it shifts location. We go from Esther's private apartments in the first scene to Assuerus's throne room to Esther's gardens.[27] In *Bajazet*, we are confined to one secret space in the harem of the Sultan Amurat. It is referred to as 'a place we never glimpsed before' (*Bajazet* 85). This single place has multiple secrets which are variously assumed, suppressed, suspected, designed, missed. Above all, these secrets are maintained out of senses of devoted love or as the only forms of erotic pleasure – or the only possible access to power – available. Often or usually sexual, these secrets centre on what members of the play's convulsive trio might know of each other – and how that can be known.

Acomat assumes that both his 'favourite', Osmin and his sultan, Amurat have secrets. Having ordered the secret drowning of the slave charged, before the play begins, with killing Bajazet, Acomat also outlines the secret of Roxane's and Bajazet's liaison, itself begun, in his account, under the sign of deception. Acomat would appear to be 'onto' everyone's closets – until we get to Atalide. Unaware of her love for Bajazet, Acomat keeps secret his own possible love for her: he loves not Atalide but 'the blood from which she springs' and, through her, Bajazet (*Bajazet* 91). If Roxane and Atalide are, in different ways, hot for Bajazet, then so is Acomat. At the same time that she conceals from Roxane *her* love for Bajazet, Atalide is the secret courier of Roxane's own secret desire for him. Mirroring Acomat's queer desire, Roxane interweaves her own eros with that of another woman, Atalide. The latter's love is also perfectly consistent with her plan – 'mon artifice', as she puts it – that Bajazet gets made sultan. Bajazet conceals his love for Atalide – yet also wishes to use Roxane to gain access to the sultanate. And Roxane is onto this. Erotic pleasure, for both Bajazet and Atalide, seem to consist in walking on these knife-edges of revelation (*Bajazet* 108, 112). This is, as Bersani wrote of *Phaedra*, 'a community of sexual terror'.[28] Atalide encourages Bajazet to go ahead and marry Roxane but keeps secret from him her intention to kill herself once the marriage takes place. Bajazet claims disdain for Roxane and encourages Atalide in this belief. The letters in Act 4, one from Bajazet to Atalide asserting his love for her, and one from Amurat to Roxane demanding Bajazet's immediate death, serve to explode these closets. Roxane joins both letters together: 'I'll show him', she says, 'both his brother's ordinance / And this firm token of this treachery' (*Bajazet* 134). These letters have much in common with the thing-like subjects (mutes) and an object with deadly agency (a garotte), so menacingly invoked by Roxane from the start.

Sedgwick's reading of *Esther* is nothing if not a performance in itself. She uses Racine in the way that things, props, are used in theatre. The curtains and gears, the 'veil' (not 'vale') of tears of Kushner's verse, the letters read in Racine's, the garotte Roxane invokes with such menacing relish and the mutes on whom she relies are stage objects whose *use* is central to theatrical performance. In *Bajazet* the most explosive object is the letter that declares its hero's love, ends all secrets and opens the way to the deaths of all three protagonists. Such an object is endowed with the force of what Jane Bennett has termed 'vibrant matter'.[29] It has priority, agency and power that (like the agency and power of any human being) 'resists full translation', as Bennett puts it, but is nonetheless palpably there.[30] The things endowed with such onstage life can be read as *transitional* objects. Through their very imperfections and through their uncertain status as neither fully 'internal' (like a mother's breast), nor fully human (like letters, garottes or Roxane's 'mutes'), nor external (like 'reality'), transitional objects enable us to learn how to become human subjects – that is, in Barbara Johnson's words, to 'accept and tolerate frustration and reality'.[31] In the scenario of her essay, Sedgwick is *using* Racine. He becomes a transitional object – one whose ambivalent uses, and eventual abandonment – enable, through play, the redirection of psychic and social reality. Unphased by Racine's august cultural status and interweaving her reading with recollections of her own childhood, Sedgwick would exemplify Johnson's paradoxical sense, outlined in her work on Winnicott, of 'using people' as, '"trusting people," creating a sense of play and risk that does not depend on maintaining intactness and separation.[32] Such use is, of course, a precondition of translation.

For Winnicott, the step from considering the formative psychic work done by transitional objects to considering 'play ... artistic creativity ... obsessional rituals' – i.e. the raw materials of any theatre – is very short indeed.[33] But if a letter or a curtain can, in the performance of a playwright's work, be a transitional object, then in a critical sense that playwright's work – or a fantasy of that playwright – can also work as a transitional object. That the most powerful transitional objects in *Bajazet* are letters – written entities – would seem to underscore this. Theatre is full of transitional objects and also functions as a transitional object in itself. If the function of such objects is to enable us to accept and tolerate the frustrations of the real, then inevitably they, and our relations with them, are imbued with imperfection, loss and very primal levels of grief.

Theatre in time

Kushner's invocation of Racine with which I began this chapter feels so exuberantly theatrical because the temporal twisting which makes it such fun is theatre's greatest work. If, in the wider world, temporal reality is in part the product of utterance, then in theatre temporal reality is temporal utterance. When Racine ends *Bajazet*'s list of characters with the words: 'The Scene is at Constantinople, formerly called Byzantium, in the royal harem' (*Bajazet* 83), this is true – 'only' (and powerfully) because text and production find means of saying so. The audience then colludes in that fragile, and therefore powerful, artifice.

Not only does theatre makes time: it owes its very existence to the wish to access some truth about, and therefore to form, the past. Fundamentally a school play, Racine's *Esther* was written, according to C. H. Sisson, at the request of Madame de Maintenon, who asked 'for an instructive piece, with no love in it, which could be played by the girls of Saint Cyr.'[34] A different kind of instructive mission animates the Passion play at the heart of Arcand's *Jesus of Montreal*.

In the Preface to her *Grief Lessons*, translations of four plays by Euripides, Anne Carson asks: 'Why does tragedy exist? Because you are full of rage.' She goes on: 'Why are you full of rage? Because you are full of grief.'[35] Such ontological grieving underlies Racine's first play,

The Thebiad, a piece whose emotional archaeology consists, for Roland Barthes, of 'a theme inherited from the earliest folklore' (the hatred of one brother for another) and of yet older layers – blood and 'the Other's body'.[36] *Bajazet*'s affective archaeology is nearly identical. Theatre also – and this is superbly, extravagantly true of Racine – compresses and compacts time, making history's slow confusion and terror something that can be, on the one hand, processed and understood but left, at the same time, unpredictable and frayed.

Bajazet is exceptional among Racine's plays in that it deals with comparatively contemporary events: the 'real' Bajazet was killed about 1638 and the play was first performed in 1672. The practice of translation at the heart of, say, *Britannicus* or *Phaedra* underpins his translation of the reporting of a near-contemporary murder into classical tragedy. Racine addresses this explicitly in his Preface of 1676:

> I would not advise an author to take so recent an event as this as the subject of a tragedy if it had taken place in the country where he wished the tragedy itself to be performed, nor to choose heroes for the theatre who would have been known to most of the audience. Tragic personages must be regarded in a different light from that in which we ordinarily see those whom we have known ... The remoteness of the country to some extent makes good the excessive closeness of the events in time: for if I may say so, people scarcely distinguish between what is a thousand years and what a thousand leagues away from them. Thus it is that the Turkish people, for example, however modern they may be, have a dignity upon our stage. One sees them as ancients before their time. (*Bajazet* 81)

Hollinghurst's *Bajazet* is a further link in a chain of translations: literally (from Turkish and Arabic to French) and generically from both the official report on the murder of Bajazet written by the Count de Cézy, the French ambassador to Constantinople, and the more nebulous recollections of what Racine calls 'persons of quality who remember having heard him [Cézy] tell the story after his return to France' (*Bajazet* 80).

In *Bajazet*, time works in three ways. First, the play's events are unusually recent. Yet, second, their geographical remoteness makes them almost as good as temporally remote. Third, the near-contemporaneity of the play's events strangely produce a futurity. 'The details of Bajazet's death', Racine writes, '*do not yet appear* in any printed history' (*Bajazet* 80; my emphasis). To watch a production of this play, in Racine's terms, is to undergo an experience in the present that purports simultaneously to represent recent events whose geography makes them ancient but whose presentation onstage is *ahead* of known, 'printed', history.

A major dramatic drive in *Bajazet* is the wish to be married, a wish that both Atalide and Roxane have in relation to the same man. Yet the play invokes a world where the maintenance by the sultan of a favourite concubine (as opposed to entry into marriage) was the order of the day. Characteristically, Roxane has little time for an erotic orthodoxy that does not suit her. One of the play's most astonishing moments occurs when, in the course of making one of her (several) demands that Bajazet marries her, Roxane takes the time to cast an historical eye on how this status quo came into being. She invokes two instances, one where this inconvenient order of things was justified and one where it was overturned. The first instance involves the violent shaming of an (earlier) emperor called Bajazet. The second involves a subsequent empress whose name, Roxelane, is a rhetorically convenient near-homophone of Roxane's own and who serves equally well as an example of how to buck a prevailing social order. Hollinghurst's translation reads:

> Oh, I know that since the time of Bajazet
> Who bore the ravages of Tamburlaine
> And saw his queen behind the chariot
> Dragged chained through Asia by their conqueror,
> The sultans have been jealous of their honour
> And rarely deigned to take themselves a wife.
> But love cannot obey these fancied laws;
> I need not give you vulgar instances:
> You know that Suleiman – of your forebears,
> Who filled the world with fear of their success,
> The one who most advanced the Ottomans –
> This Suleiman set eyes on Roxelane.
> Despite his proud magnificence, this king
> Chose her to share his power and his bed –
> She who had no claims to be a sultaness
> Beyond slight charms perhaps and much deceit (*Bajazet* 100)

In the original, Roxane's speech reads:

> Oui, je sais que depuis qu'un de vos Empereurs,
> Bajazet d'un Barbare éprouvant les fureurs,
> Vit au Char du Vainqueur son Épouse enchaînée,
> Et par toute l'Asie à sa suite trâinée;
> De l'honneur Ottoman ses Successeurs jaloux

Ont daigné rarement prendre le nom d'Époux.
Mais l'amour ne suit point ces lois imaginaires.
Et sans vous rapporter des Exemples vulgaires,
Soliman (vous savez qu'entre tous vos Aïeux
Dont l'Univers a craint le bras victorieux,
Nul n'éleva si haut la grandeur Ottomane),
Ce Soliman jeta les yeux sur Roxelane.
Malgré tout son orgueil, ce Monarque si fier
À son Trône, à son Lit daigna l'associer,
Sans qu'elle eût d'autres droits au rang d'Impératrice
Qu'un peu d'attraits peut-être, et beaucoup d'artifice.[37]

There must be an audacious, almost comic, pleasure in watching actors playing Roxane and Bajazet, swathed in layer upon layer of toxic, life-or-death, sexually antagonistic secrecy, and trapped in a nightmare world where they await the remorseless return of the vengeful Amurat, coolly debate appropriate modes of action, mostly prompted by the contemplation of an historical accident of shared proper names. There once was another Bajazet who did x; there once was, if not another Roxane, then a Roxelane, who was permitted to do y. So the argument goes.

Hollinghurst's translation is, again, faithful and nuanced. 'Oui, je sais,' is gently modulated to 'Oh, I know'. The 'lois imaginaires' which love, in the original, in no way follows become 'fancied laws' which love 'cannot obey'. This passage also contains a (rare) instance of visible obtrusion. Hollinghurst turns the line 'Bajazet, d'un Barbare éprouvant les fureurs' into 'Bajazet / who bore the ravages of Tamburlaine' (*Bajazet* 100). Argent translates the phrase 'd'un Barbare' as: 'some barbarian'.[38] Through this change, Hollinghurst signals a powerful Marlovian connection by invoking the name of Marlowe's 1587 anti-hero and super-conqueror, 'thirsting with sovereignty, with love of arms'.[39] The addition highlights a factor utterly at odds with Roxane's purpose in this speech: Hollinghurst's change dramatizes her downplaying of the wild extent of the 'ravages' to which the earlier Bajazet (Bajazeth) was subjected. These included starvation, imprisonment in a portable cage and being used as Tamburlaine's human foot-stool. In Roxane's account this Bajazet simply witnesses his wife's humiliation. Invoking *Tamburlaine* explicitly makes him both witness and victim. In *Tamburlaine*, Bajazeth's way out of this is to brain himself against the cage in which he is imprisoned and, on seeing this, Zabina, his wife, does exactly the same. This also creates an ironic echo since, at the time of uttering these words, Roxane is mere hours away from joining her own Bajazet in a violent death. He is executed at her command and she, later, is killed on Amurat's secret order. The precedent Roxane uses to argue for marriage links it to spectacularly violent death in a way she seeks, unsuccessfully, to avoid. Paul Hammond has pointed out that 'in the spaces of *Bérénice* we see the proximity and the distance between the characters through their use of shared and not-quite-shared language.'[40] In this moment from *Bajazet* we see the space around and between isolated characters through Roxane's use of an example whose force, as Hollinghurst's Marlovian change emphasizes, she only partly understands. Naming Tamburlaine gives another nuance to the Elizabethan time which rhythmically structures Hollinghurst's translation and opens up another level on which time operates in theatre.

Marlowe, Shakespeare and theatrical possibility

For the Hollinghurst of the translator's introduction, the word 'Elizabethan' is almost equivalent to Shakespearean. But the metre of lines such as 'Perhaps you will recall the unfounded news / Which reached us here, that Amurat was dead' (*Bajazet* 89) echoes also the Marlowe of *Edward II*. Lines such as 'The Wild O'Neill, with swarms of Irish kerns, / Lives uncontrolled within the English pale' are as much of a metrical model for Hollinghurst's translation as the *Antony and Cleopatra* to whom he briefly compares his work as translator.[41]

There is another temporal dimension to this. Shakespeare's *Antony and Cleopatra* is the text with which, via Dryden's *All for Love* (1678), Hollinghurst most explicitly allied his translations of Racine. There are considerable similarities between Shakespeare's vast tragedy and Marlowe's *Tamburlaine*: preoccupations with global politics, a vast narrative canvas and some of the most gorgeous lyrical writing either playwright produced. Both texts also give a lot of time to description.

When, in *Antony and Cleopatra*, Enobarbus describes the passage down the Nile of Cleopatra's barge 'like a burnished throne', he is recalling a spectacle that has taken place in the play's past.[42] When Octavian fulminates against Antony giving Cleopatra 'the stablishment of Egypt' in the marketplace of Alexandria, he retells and reacts to events that have already taken place and that have been reported to him.[43] The descriptive speeches in *Antony and Cleopatra* are, then, nearly all events that have, in the play's action, actually occurred. It is only towards the play's end, envisaging the representational catastrophe that will await her if she is taken back in triumph to Rome, that Cleopatra herself moves the play's descriptive energies into the hypothetical, the future. Such a mode of description utterly dominates Marlowe's *Tamburlaine*. Across both parts, there are lengthy descriptions of territory to be conquered, of massed armies about to fight and of the sight of Tamburlaine himself about to be glimpsed. These are all cast in the mode not of what has happened or what has been reported but of what will, or may, happen. In Part II, for example, the King of Jerusalem promises Tamburlaine:

> That shortly heaven, filled with the meteors
> Of blood and fire thy tyrannies have made,
> Will pour down blood and fire on thy head.[44]

Jerusalem's speech is cast in subjunctive modes of threat and promise of what will, or might, be. To be in the audience at a performance of *Tamburlaine* is to witness a spectacle threaded through with descriptions of spectacles that will, or might, occur.

In this regard, *Bajazet* and *Tamburlaine* are remarkably similar. The first example of Hollinghurst's translation I discussed was one where Atalide threatened Bajazet with the staging of a 'bloody spectacle' in response to what she perceives as Bajazet preparing such a spectacle for her. Jerusalem's speech and Atalide's have in common a dependence on the subjunctive trigger 'that' ('que') which linguistically confers solidity on events that have yet to occur while at the same time indicating that those events 'dwell', as Emily Dickinson once put it, 'in possibility'.

To attend a performance of *Bajazet* is, similarly, to watch actors speak lines where their characters outline events that will or might happen. These events are regularly cast in terms of a spectacle, with characters working sometimes as participants, sometimes as directors and often as audience members. There are about twenty of these instances where the play's action consists in a character outlining the prospect of a spectacle to which they have sometimes hopeful, sometimes fearful, sometimes repugnant relations. This hope is sometimes attached to moments where power will be confirmed or re-established. They include Acomat's vision of his obedient, marshalled janissaries leading Bajazet 'to the sacred gate / Where the new sultan always first appears' (*Bajazet* 106) or of Roxane unfurling 'the holy prophet's flag / Before the awestruck people' (*Bajazet* 115).

The Sultan Amurat has, however, other plans for his younger brother, couched in very different terms of envisaged spectacle. 'You,' he writes to Roxane, 'if you have regard for your own life, / Will welcome me with his head in your hands' (*Bajazet* 129). Acomat's and Amurat's moments of envisaged spectacle are different versions, sacred and sadistic, of the same wish – that political power becomes established through the maintenance and creation of spectacles that by definition entail an audience: Bajazet escorted to that sacred gate, the unfurling of a flag, the proffering of a decapitated head. Another point of imagined spectacle is Bajazet's and Roxane's planned marriage. Atalide couches her aversive reaction to this in theatrical terms, as a negative audience reaction: 'Well, what?' she asks. 'Can I be witness to this scene?' (*Bajazet* 117). The speed with which an anticipated scene of marriage becomes one of execution is very striking. Roxane speaks of being 'Attentive to the details of his [Bajazet's] death' (*Bajazet* 134). Her first plan is to have Atalide executed in front of Bajazet. She invites him to 'to see her [Atalide's] death throes, strangled by my mutes' (*Bajazet* 143).

Later, Roxane's directorial ambitions change. In the first moment she is *metteur en scène* and bride. Later, she sees herself presiding over the union of her lover and rival in a death staged on her own terms:

> And far from separating you, I plan
> To bind you to him in eternal bonds:
> Soon you'll enjoy the lovely sight of him. (*Bajazet* 146)

Citing the Marlowe of *Tamburlaine* so explicitly, Hollinghurst stresses the importance of possibility that Jarman emphasized with the ending of his film of *Edward II* – the importance of what *can* happen, what the future *can* hold. In the book that accompanied his film's release, Jarman strikingly described the sequence of Edward's death as 'the murder seen as a premonition'.[45] The moments of planned or anticipated spectacle I have outlined in both *Tamburlaine* and *Bajazet* are, on one level, disciplined by the machinery of tragedy and the 'strict form' of Racine's verse. But these moments are also the propulsive engines of Marlowe's and Racine's tragedies. They move the plays along, giving them temporal energy.

This essay has documented a small turn in 1990 to a Racine whose very use is a resistant recognition of Fukuyama's hyperbole. And this is achieved through translation – Sedgwick and Hollinghurst translating Racine, who is himself a translator (of Tacitus, of Euripides, of diplomatic reports and court gossip). A future historian and the practitioner of an art he posits as the future of history, Racine translates across time in the most temporally concentrated and affectively trenchant form of the tragedy. His work is used (by Sedgwick, by Hollinghurst) to articulate differing senses of queer desire, to enable a contrastive sense of the 'present' of 1990 and, very theatrically, to open senses of time as possibility. This all amounts to a scenario that you could, in 1990, look at with grateful, quizzical pride – if your name were Jean Racine.

Acknowledgements

I am very grateful to Paul Hammond for reading an earlier version of this piece, to Steve Bottoms and to Joe Collier for their advice and encouragement, and to Roger Norum for talking to me about subjunctives. I dedicate this chapter, with love, to the memory of Trevor Cahill (1957–2014).

Notes

1   Pierre Corneille, *The Illusion: Freely Adapted by Tony Kushner* (New York: Theatre Communications Group Translations, 1994) 51.

2   The phrase is Jules Lemaître's and is quoted by Francis Wyndham in the Introduction to *Bajazet* in *Bérénice and Bajazet*, trans. Alan Hollinghurst (London: Faber, 2012) 77. Further references to Hollinghurst's translation are to this edition and are given in parentheses in the text.

3   Leo Bersani, *A Future for Astyanax: Character and Desire in Literature* (London: Boyars, 1978) 23.

4   Barbara Johnson, *Persons and Things* (Cambridge, MA: Harvard University Press, 2008) 105.

5   Roland Barthes, *On Racine*, trans. Richard Howard (Berkeley and Los Angeles: University of California Press, 1992) 103. For an account of the writing and making of *Edward II*, see Tony Peake, *Derek Jarman: A Biography* (London: Little, Brown, 1999) 466–71.

6   On this, see Leo Bersani, 'Is the Rectum a Grave?' in *AIDS: Cultural Analysis/ Cultural Activism*, ed. Douglas Crimp (Cambridge, MA: MIT Press, 1988) 197–222.

7   Barthes, *On Racine* 99–100.

8   Bersani, *A Future for Astyanax* 24.

9   Corneille, *The Illusion* 'Acknowledgements' page.

10 Elizabeth Freeman, 'Introduction', *GLQ* 13.2–3 (2007) 159–73: 160.

11 Ibid.

12 Lee Edelman, *No Future: Queer Theory and the Death Drive* (Durham, NC, and London: Duke University Press, 2004) 41–50.

13 These positions, and others, are outlined by various scholars in the field in 'Theorizing Queer Temporalities: A Roundtable Discussion', *GLQ* 13.2–3 (2007) 177–95.

14 Jean Racine, *Bajazet* in *Oeuvres Complètes I: Théâtre. Poésie*, ed. Georges Forestier (Paris: Gallimard, 1999) 2. 5. 766–8.

15 *The Complete Plays of Jean Racine Volume 2: Bajazet*, ed. and trans. Geoffrey Alan Argent (University Park, PA: Pennsylvania State University Press, 2011) 63.

16 Fukuyama discusses his employment of this phrase in his *The End of History and the Last Man* (London: Penguin, 1992) xi–xxiii.

17   Joshua Clover, *1989: Bob Dylan Didn't Have this to Sing About* (Berkeley and London: University of California Press, 2009) 2.

18   Ibid.

19   Ibid. 81, 70, 97–8.

20   Eve Kosofsky Sedgwick, *Epistemology of the Closet* (Berkeley: University of California Press, 1990) 75.

21   Ibid. 76.

22   Ibid. 127–30.

23   Ibid. 78.

24   Ibid. 79.

25   Ibid. 81.

26   Ibid. 79; original emphasis.

27   Muller makes this point in his essay 'Bajezet '37: Jacques Copeau's *Palais à Volonté* at the Comédie-Française', *Theatre Journal* 64 (2012) 1–24, 12.

28   Bersani, *A Future for Astyanax* 25.

29   Jane Bennett, *Vibrant Matter: A Political Ecology of Things* (Durham, NC and London: Duke University Press, 2010) 13.

30   Ibid. 122.

31   Johnson, *Persons and Things* 97.

32   Ibid. 105.

33   Donald Winnicott, *Playing and Reality* (London and New York: Routledge, 2005) 7.

34   Jean Racine, *Britannicus, Phaedra, Athaliah*, ed. and trans. C. H. Sisson (Oxford: Oxford University Press, 1987) xix.

35   *Grief Lessons: Four Plays by Euripides*, trans. Anne Carson (New York: New York Review of Books, 2006) 7.

36   Barthes, *On Racine* 64.

37   Racine, *Bajazet* in *Oeuvres Complètes I*, 2. 1. 455–70.

38   *The Complete Plays of Jean Racine Volume 2*, 51.

39   Christopher Marlowe, *Tamburlaine the Great, Part I* in *Tamburlaine, Parts I and II, Doctor Faustus, A- and B- Texts, The Jew of Malta, Edward II*, ed. David Bevington and Eric Rasmussen (Oxford: Oxford University Press, 1995) 2. 1. 20.

40   Paul Hammond, 'The Rhetoric of Space and Self in Racine's *Bérénice*', *Early Modern French Studies* 36.2 (2014) 141–55: 153.

41   Marlowe, *Edward II* in *Tamburlaine, Parts I and II, etc.*, 2. 2. 163–4.

42   William Shakespeare, *Antony and Cleopatra*, ed. Anita Loomba (New York: Norton Critical Editions, 2011) 2. 2. 197.

43   Ibid. 3. 6. 9.

44   Marlowe, *Tamburlaine Part II* in *Tamburlaine, Parts I and II, etc.*, 4. 1. 139–44.

45   Derek Jarman, *Queer Edward II* (London: BFI, 1991) 160.

11

'Who are you? What the fuck are you doing here?': queer debates and contemporary connections

Kaye Mitchell

Alan Hollinghurst's work is generally read – with good reason – in relation to Victorian and modernist forebears such as Henry James and Ronald Firbank. Thus Julie Rivkin writes of Hollinghurst's 'common ground' and 'conversation' with Henry James;[1] Denis Flannery identifies *The Line of Beauty* as part of a 'wave of recent fiction preoccupied with Henry James';[2] and Andrew Eastham argues that, although *The Line of Beauty* is set in the 1980s, 'its vision of the aristocracy, consumerism and the emerging culture of post-modernism is continuously informed by a deep involvement in nineteenth century Aestheticism'.[3] Georges Letissier notes, more generally, 'the retrogressive logic that informs Hollinghurst's fiction writing', and finds this in 'the characters' individual destinies', but also in an 'overarching concern with the past' evident in Hollinghurst's interest in architecture and antiques.[4]

This is a common suggestion: that Hollinghurst is a novelist who is peculiarly *not* of his own era in his influences and references, even though the majority of his novels take his own period as their main setting.[5] On the face of it, it is the 'homophile' fiction of the late nineteenth and early twentieth century that has been most influential on his writing, to the extent that Hollinghurst appears to have more in common with James and Forster than with contemporary peers; indeed, Joseph Bristow reads *The Swimming-Pool Library* as '[marking] the terminal point of a specific type of homophile writing that developed in England after 1885'.[6] Similarly there appears little that is obviously 'queer' about Hollinghurst's work, invoking as it does gay identities that pre-date Stonewall, never mind the activism and academic theorizing of the 1990s and since.

To read him as a 'contemporary' (i.e. late twentieth-, early twenty-first-century) novelist is, then, to read against the grain in some respects. Nevertheless, this chapter seeks to situate Hollinghurst's work within the contemporary contexts of late twentieth-/early twenty-first-century gay fiction by notable gay authors such as Edmund White, Colm Tóibín, David Leavitt and Michael Cunningham, and post-1990s queer theory, attending particularly to what has been called the 'antisocial thesis' in queer theory – a thesis most succinctly encapsulated in Leo Bersani's suggestion that homosexuality evinces 'a potentially revolutionary inaptitude – perhaps inherent in gay desire – for sociality as it is known'.[7] What, if anything, does Hollinghurst owe to the period in and of which he is writing? Is his writing immune to the political and theoretical developments of queer studies and queer theory in the late twentieth century?

I want to suggest that some of the qualities and concerns that lead Hollinghurst critics to associate his work with homophile writing of the late nineteenth and early twentieth century might equally be read as connecting him to the moment in which he is writing. The desire for, and yet 'impossibility of aesthetic detachment' which is, for Rivkin, 'the most Jamesian thing' about *The Line of Beauty* might be read differently as a meditation on the demands of sociality consequent upon the politicization of gay identities – demands to which Hollinghurst's protagonists respond with a telling ambivalence.[8] Similarly, Eastham's description of the aesthete 'living by irony, maintaining a posture of detachment and indifference, and thereby [protecting] his independence from use value, ethics and social life',[9] could equally be parsed as a description of Lee Edelman's *sinthom*osexual and his antisocial refusal of reproductive futurism. In the '*sinthom*osexual', Edelman combines the Lacanian '*sinthome*', 'which defines the specific formation of the subject's access to jouissance', and a conception of the homosexual as an 'abjected' figure, one who is 'opposed, in dominant fantasy, to life and futurity both'.[10] The attitude that allows Nick (in *The Line of Beauty*) to be part of the Feddens' world while still, he believes, exempting him from any more corrupting 'associations with Thatcherism' presents an idea of 'ironic detachment' as muting (or, more strongly, refusing) political responsibility.[11] Meanwhile, the 'mournful subjectivity of Hollinghurst's protagonist and his text' (again, *The Line of Beauty*) that Flannery connects to James might also be understood as speaking to the melancholic formations that Monica Pearl discerns in the literature of AIDS that emerges in the 1980s.[12] Daniel Hannah, then, asserts the impossibility of any separation of past and present in the elaboration of Hollinghurst's literary influences, by noting 'the changes that late-twentieth-century structures of reading have brought to the figure of Henry James' and claiming that 'new interests in discourses of sexuality, class and power' have 'allowed scholars to "see through" James in previously unexpected ways'.[13] This reading of

James by way of Hollinghurst suggests that, even though Hollinghurst is ostensibly a backwards-looking novelist (one more influenced by late nineteenth-century aestheticism than late twentieth century cultural and critical developments), the present crucially inflects and affects how he engages with the past.

Gay fiction, pessimism and compensation

Hollinghurst, as he himself is quick to point out, does not write only about 'gay life', and his work is also notably concerned with questions of class, race, history and politics, art and architecture, and classical music. Nevertheless, homosexuality remains, at least, a central theme in his fiction, and even in a novel like *The Stranger's Child*, which is less sexually explicit and less exclusively focused on gay relationships than his earlier fiction, Hollinghurst is still largely concerned with homosexuality as 'a *cultural* orientation': implying, in David M. Halperin's unpacking of it, 'a refined sensibility, a heightened aesthetic sense, a particular sensitivity to style and fashion, a non-standard relation to mainstream cultural objects', and so on.[14] In addition, Hollinghurst has undoubtedly benefited from the emergence of gay fiction as 'an identifiable and important literary category' in the 1970s and 1980s.[15] It has frequently been argued that this fiction has played a vital role in the constitution of gay identities and gay community. For example, Kenneth Plummer suggests that gay culture (including literature) works to 'make gay personhood tighter and ever more plausible'.[16] In *AIDS Literature and Gay Identity*, Pearl claims that, historically, 'gay literature reflected back gay culture to a gay reading public, often made up of individuals for whom gay fiction was the only aspect of community they experienced, especially while growing up'.[17]

If this seems like a wholly positive and emancipatory narrative of the rise and function of gay fiction, however, then Robert L. Caserio cautions that 'that public success ... has been pervaded by contradictions', and he proceeds to argue that, given 'persistent pessimism about homosexuality's achievement of public stature, forms or themes that divert the pessimism, or compensate for it, have helped shape contemporary gay genres'.[18] On this reading, Hollinghurst's apparent preoccupation with the past – and particularly with an era before the decriminalization of homosexuality – might be understood as a form of compensation at the level of theme. Nostalgia might be deployed as a diversion from the pessimistic present towards an apparently simpler past; there, homosexuality is 'underground' and thus 'unbelievably sexy' – in Charles Nantwich's words in *The Swimming-Pool Library* (247). Yet what is at work in Hollinghurst's writing is undeniably more complex than this. Caserio's reading of Hollinghurst finds in his writing 'two counterpoised intentions: to protect gay sex and gay lives from external aggression; and to subject gay sex and gay lives to internal criticism, an alternative form of aggression.'[19] In the remainder of the chapter, I will consider these questions of pessimism and internal criticism – as well as the questions of sociality, politics and community raised by much recent queer theory – by focusing on three common preoccupations of gay fiction of the last few decades: coming out, AIDS, and the family.

In highlighting the importance of literature for gay readerships, Pearl notes that 'coming out stories, narratives that chronicle the emergence of the individual into a gay identity, were crucial' because they 'were able to constitute for isolated individuals an imagined gay community'.[20] David Leavitt's *The Lost Language of Cranes* (1986) has at its centre Philip's painful coming-out to his parents – for his mother it is 'as if she had been thrown head-first into a distant, distasteful world about which she had little curiosity and toward which she felt a casual, unstated aversion.'[21] Colm Tóibín's *The Story of the Night* (1996) places the protagonist Richard's coming-out to his mother early in the story and although, as he tells her, he thinks that 'somewhere in her expression there was utter contempt', he later comes to believe that she approves of his homosexuality, because she thinks it means 'that I would not leave her.'[22] Richard's story is couched in terms of loneliness, disappointment, and what he experiences as a fundamental sense of separateness – 'at a certain age I began to see the world as separate from myself, I began to feel that I had nothing to do with anything around me.'[23] These feelings are not only due to his homosexuality – his indeterminate national identity also plays a part, as does his strange, isolated life with his mother following his father's death – but the novel nevertheless takes an excavatory approach to childhood which emphasizes the oddness of the queer child. Similarly, Michael Cunningham's *A Home at the End of the World* (1990) relates a scene in which the young Jonathan is caught playing with a doll by his father and experiences his 'first true humiliation. I recognized a deep inadequacy in myself, a foolishness.'[24] In Kathryn Bond Stockton's account of queer childhood, the child who 'already feels queer (different, odd, out-of-sync, and attracted to same-sex peers)' suffers 'an asynchronous self-relation. Certain linguistic markers for its queerness arrive only after it exits its childhood, after it is shown not to be straight.'[25] It is from that retrospective point of view that the novels of Leavitt, Tóibín, and Cunningham are narrated, with early scenes presented as precursors of their narrators' adult lives and indications (particularly in the case of Cunningham's characters) of a frustrated desire to belong.

Hollinghurst's fiction contains no coming-out scenes, shows little interest in the supposed causes or origins of homosexual feeling, and has little in the way of childhood reminiscence – excepting fond memories of schoolboy sexual indulgence. Nevertheless, if the coming-out scene is notably absent, Hollinghurst does often show us characters undergoing some kind of shift or transition: in awareness or in self-consciousness, in personality, in their relation to the world. Thus Will Beckwith in *The Swimming-Pool Library* becomes aware of the homophobic and colonialist histories of which he is the beneficiary; Alex in *The Spell* discovers the transitional euphoria and liberation of drugs and the gay club scene as he emerges from a period of mourning the demise of a serious relationship; Edward in *The Folding Star* is described by Alistair Stead as 'a passion-driven subject caught up in the project of transfiguring himself and others';[26] in *The Line of Beauty*, Nick Guest is forced to acknowledge his complicitous relationship with the Feddens and all they stand for, but also to realize his ultimate exclusion from their world, at least in part because of his homosexuality; in *The Stranger's Child* it is England itself that evolves, across the novel's five sections (which cover a period from 1913 to 2008), revealing shifts in attitudes to homosexuality and the unpredictable fluctuations of literary reputation. In each case, however, these are not triumphant moments of self-realization or assertion, or smooth transitions to some new way of being, but rather more conflicted and equivocal discoveries about the individual's relationship to the wider world and the responsibilities that such a relationship brings.

In addition, we find in Hollinghurst's fiction a fundamental ambivalence about assuming something as definite and concrete as a gay identity: Will romanticizes his schooldays, with their absence of 'cloying adult impurity' (*SPL* 141); Edward in *The Folding Star* fondly remembers a school relationship, since when everything has been 'in some way melancholy, frantic or foredoomed' (*FS* 200), and David Alderson reads Edward's pursuit of Luc as 'itself an attempt to repossess that moment prior to, if portending, his assumption of a sexual identity';[27] Nick, at the outset of *The Line of Beauty*, is not 'quite ready to accept' that any lover he might have now will be 'a gay lover – that compromised thing that he himself would then become' (*LB* 26). These examples do not amount to the painful self-loathing of Edmund White's explanation, in *A Boy's Own Story*, that 'what I wanted was to be loved by men and to love them back but not to be a homosexual', and his subsequent lament that 'there was no way to defend what I was. All I could fight for was my right to choose my exile, my destruction',[28] but arguably they evince both the pessimism at homosexuality's failure to achieve public stature that Caserio notes – such that being a 'gay lover' remains 'a compromised thing', despite the apparent advances in attitude – and a form of internal critique of gay male culture for its evasions and internalizations. What I have identified here as a fundamental ambivalence in Hollinghurst's attitude to homosexuality *as an identity* also, unwittingly or otherwise, echoes the queer theoretical perspective, elaborated by Lee Edelman, that 'queer can never define an identity; it can only ever disturb one'.[29] If *The Spell*, published in 1998, is, as Alderson asserts, 'the product of a moment in which being gay no longer feels so marginal or oppositional',[30] then it still retains a strong seam of critique – it is perhaps that that critique is directed inwards, at the selfishness or vapidity of various elements of the gay scene, rather than at the hostility of the so-called straight world beyond.

AIDS fiction and the 'attunement to loss'

In the novels of Hollinghurst's predecessors – such as Edmund White, Oscar Moore and Adam Mars-Jones – AIDS plays a crucial role; in the work of his contemporaries – such as Colm Tóibín and Michael Cunningham – it remains an intermittent shadow but not quite a defining preoccupation. *The Story of the Night* ends with Richard feeling once again 'singled out ... I felt that I had nothing in common with all of these people in the street', but this time because of his AIDS diagnosis; Tóibín's 1999 novel, *The Blackwater Lightship*, pivots around Declan's illness but tells the story through the relationships between three generations of women (his grandmother, mother, and sister); in *A Home at the End of the World* AIDS remains, euphemistically, 'the disease', as Jonathan muses:

> The last remaining event in our sensual histories – the fact that we had not exercised bodily precautions together. Now it was too late to protect ourselves from one another. There was no rational accounting, beyond the fact that even four years ago, when we'd met, the disease had still seemed the province of another kind of man. Of course we'd known about it. Of course we'd been scared. But no one we knew personally had gotten sick. We'd believed – with a certain effort of will – that it befell men whose blood was thinned by too many drugs, who had sex with a dozen people every night.[31]

That reference to 'another kind of man' bespeaks, perhaps, a process of disidentification from or disruption of homosexual identity that I have already noted in Hollinghurst's work and in Edelman's statements on queerness – but in Cunningham the ambivalence is more fleeting. As his former lover, Erich, begins a terminal decline, Jonathan begins to imagine himself sickening: 'something was wrong with me. I lacked some central ability to connect and I worried that it might be an early indicator of disease.'[32] This diagnosis is never confirmed, but the novel ends on a note simultaneously uplifting and elegiac; wading in a pond with Bobby and the dying Erich, Jonathan has a minor but significant epiphany:

> Something cracked. I had lived until then for the future, in a state of continuing expectation, and the process came suddenly to a stop while I stood nude with Bobby and Erich in a shallow platter of freezing water. ... I wouldn't say I was happy. I was nothing so simple as happy. I was merely present, perhaps for the first time in my adult life. The moment was unextraordinary. But I had the moment, I had it completely. It inhabited me. I realized that if I died soon I would have known this, a connection with my life, its errors and cockeyed successes. ... I would not die unfulfilled because I'd been here, right here and nowhere else.[33]

The Line of Beauty similarly has its protagonist, Nick, bear witness to the illness and sharp decline of his former lover, Wani Ouradi, while his own health remains an open question. At the end of the novel he is awaiting the results of a recent HIV test, and feeling 'unreachably alone' (*LB* 494):

> It came over him that the test result would be positive. The words that were said every day to others would be said to him .... He tried to rationalize the fear, but its pull was too strong and original. It was inside himself, but the world around him, the parked cars, the cruising taxi, the church spire among the trees, had also been changed. (*LB* 500)

And yet, like Jonathan in *A Home at the End of the World*, the immediacy of this threat brings him back to the marvel of the present, as Michèle Mendelssohn's chapter notes: 'It wasn't just this street corner but the fact of a street corner at all that seemed, in the light of the moment, so beautiful' (*LB* 501).

The year 1995 might be seen as 'a turning point in the AIDS crisis', according to Pearl, due to 'the advent of life-prolonging pharmaceuticals'. After this, AIDS becomes 'an aspect' of gay literature, 'rather than its main focus or drive or preoccupation'. She suggests that, 'by 1997 we are seeing a different kind of AIDS narrative',[34] in which the disease is no longer 'the central focus', but in which 'there is no way not to feature the devastations and the fundamental uncertainties that are harboured in the social psyche because of AIDS'.[35] This is perhaps what leads Alderson to describe *The Spell* as 'post-AIDS', because 'AIDS is invoked not as a future which colours our perspective on the past ... but as part of a superseded past in the form of Robin's memories of his former lover: the present is no longer so heavily clouded by this particular affliction'.[36] Nevertheless, there is a palpable grimness to Robin's memories of Simon's illness and death, coloured as those memories are by his guilt at the beginning of his affair with Justin:

> Robin watched him slip over a threshold, into the tapering perspectives of fatal illness, in which all but the mildest pleasures lay in the past. In a terrifying dream he was himself the dying man, a mere consciousness gazing out from the eyes of a paralysed body, unable to call on the friends who hurried past the open doorway, on their way to tennis and dinner and sex. (*S* 30)

Later those 'tapering perspectives of fatal illness' expand to take in Robin's own fears about ageing, exacerbated by his sexual jealousy of the terminally unfaithful Justin. He has 'a dread of life being different from now on, his powers steadily withdrawn, like cancelled memberships' (*S* 125–6), the metaphor itself a comment on the precarious forms of belonging and acceptance on offer within the gay community as it is represented here – another instance, then, of internal critique. Robin's critical reflections on the ageing male bodies he sees at the gym – 'the little fold of skin at the armpit, gooseflesh at the throat, the flattening of the buttocks, the slump of the chest' (*S* 180–1) – form part of a longer, more contentious tradition of the (inextricable) aestheticization and pathologization of the gay male body that extends at least as far back as Dorian Gray.

AIDS goes unmentioned in Hollinghurst's first novel, *The Swimming-Pool Library*, published in 1988 but set in the summer of 1983. Yet from the outset the novel hints at darker times to come, suggesting that the carefree hedonism of Will Beckwith's current life cannot continue unhindered. At the beginning of the novel we find Will 'riding high on sex and self-esteem ... but all the while with a faint flicker of calamity, like flames around a photograph, something seen out of the corner of the eye' (*SPL* 3). The aestheticization of danger here reveals a good deal about Will's vain self-absorption (and about the novel's own scopophilic propensities – a quality even more in evidence in *The Folding Star*), but the tone of endangerment is repeated just a page later, as Will feels 'the threat of some realisation about life, something obscurely disagreeable and perhaps deserved' (*SPL* 4). The emphasis on guilt/complicity here is telling (and tellingly reluctant – 'perhaps'), yet the nature of the 'threat' remains both obscure and diffuse for much of the novel. Certainly AIDS is hinted at, for example in references to the 'peculiar suggestiveness' of the modish scent 'Trouble for Men', which has 'permeated the gay world in a matter of weeks' (*SPL* 27); and undoubtedly Will comes to realize how much his own immensely privileged position (thanks largely to wealth inherited from his grandfather) links him to a history of homophobic persecution (his grandfather's witchhunt against gay men, including Nantwich, in the 1950s) and a longer history of colonial exploitation (evident in Nantwich's own diaries); but there are additional complicities and entanglements here, alongside a growing sense of the ineluctable interconnectedness of events and people, suggesting that Will cannot indefinitely continue his irresponsible individualism.

The 'threat', here, is targeting what Will represents again and again as a kind of 'innocence': seeing his first porn film he is impressed 'by the blatant innocence of it all' (*SPL* 52); he is delighted by his young nephew Rupert's 'cult of the gay, his innocent, optimistic absorption in the subject' (*SPL* 61); of the boys' boxing club in the East End, he comments, 'there was such an innocence to the place that they saw nothing suspicious in my presence there' (*SPL* 139); and, most strikingly, his elegiac description of the 'Swimming-Pool Library' of his schooldays (which is 'where at heart I want to be') includes the assertion that 'there was never, or rarely, any kissing – no cloying, adult impurity in the lubricious innocence of what we did' (*SPL* 141). Charles's diaries, meanwhile, extol the 'innocence' of the Nuba people as the primary source of his attraction to them, and laud the 'adoration and devotion' of his schooldays (*SPL* 108); indeed, he thinks that 'there will never again be a time of such freedom. It was the epitome of pleasure' (*SPL* 113). It is not only Will's awareness of his grandfather's and Nantwich's respective pasts that sullies this innocence, but also his beating by skinheads ('a universal violence had been disclosed to me, and I saw it everywhere' (*SPL* 176)), his connection to Arthur's more volatile, crime-ridden world, his friend James's arrest, and Nantwich's ultimate betrayal of him in the minor but significant act of concealing the photographs of the policeman who entrapped James. Again, this might be read as a form of internal critique, pointing up the tenuous loyalties and fleeting alliances within the gay milieu that Hollinghurst documents.

If this loss-of-innocence narrative speaks less directly to an engagement with or experience of AIDS, it nevertheless falls within a longer history of gay writing. It reflects what Pearl describes as 'a pre-existing link, not only between gay men and death, but between gay men and loss, disappointment, and grief'. She cites, as examples, Gore Vidal's *The City and the Pillar*, James Baldwin's *Giovanni's Room*, and Christopher

Isherwood's *A Single Man*, as well as more recent texts such as *A Boy's Own Story* and *The Lost Language of Cranes*.[37] While Caserio claims that 'homosexual desire, in contrast [to heterosexuality], stands at a distance from oppressive compulsions to reproduce, and is more attuned to loss and limitation',[38] Pearl draws finer distinctions between 'the specific psychoanalytic mechanisms of mourning and melancholia' in what she identifies, respectively, as 'gay AIDS fiction' and 'queer AIDS fiction'.[39] In neither instance, though, is the reading itself pessimistic: Pearl is quick to explain that, in associating queerness with an open-ended melancholia, she is not endorsing the view of 'the self-destructiveness or inherent masochism of a gay identity', because 'melancholia, while disabling in an individual, is productive in the texts'.[40] Caserio glosses Adam Mars-Jones's comments (in *Mae West is Dead* (1983)) about '"legitimate fears" of "isolation" and "dependence" in "a community which is constantly being reminded of its provisional status"', in order to argue that 'gay writing must express those fears of isolation and dependence if it is not to be overwhelmed by self-promoting misrepresentation and marketing'.[41]

By subtly but persistently expressing these fears of 'isolation' and 'dependence', and by highlighting the 'provisionality' of homosexual communities, Hollinghurst is much more in tune with his contemporaries than he first appears – part of a tradition of gay male writing 'attuned to loss and limitation'. Whether this is read as 'pessimism', or as some more productive form of 'critique', is another matter.

Family, society, relationality

As part of the trend of 'loss' within gay literature, pre-AIDS, Pearl includes coming-out narratives, which she reads as being *both* about 'the triumph of a gay identity over the disapproval of family, society, and friends' *and* 'about the yearning for and sacrifice of those entities'.[42] That dynamic of loss and yearning shows itself in what Pearl identifies as 'one of the strong themes' in 'early gay AIDS fiction' – a longing 'for family and home'.[43] Many of Hollinghurst's immediate predecessors and contemporaries thus express a desire for family and community. Writing in the introduction to the 1994 *Penguin Book of Gay Short Stories*, David Leavitt explained that:

> I flinched at the notion that coming out somehow meant that I would not only have to reimagine myself totally but to cut off my ties to my family, my heterosexual friends – indeed the totality of the world I'd grown up in. To do so, it seemed to me, was to risk doing myself real psychic violence. ... A new level of liberation needed to be achieved, I

decided then: one that would allow gay men and lesbians to celebrate their identities without having to move into a gulag.[44]

If this seems to be a definitively assimilationist impulse, then it nevertheless expresses itself in alternative formulations of 'family' in some of the fiction of the period, formulations that test our understanding of that institution and its meanings. In Cunningham's *A Home at the End of the World*, Jonathan ends up living in a platonic relationship with his friend Clare and his ex-lover Bobby; together, they form a kind of alternative family, to replace the families they have left behind them or lost. As Bobby explains:

> We took to calling ourselves the Hendersons. I don't remember how it started – it was part of a line tossed out by Clare or Jonathan, and it stuck. The Hendersons were a family with modest expectations and simple tastes. They liked having a few beers in a cheap little bar. When we went out together, the three of us, we called it 'a night with the Hendersons.' Clare came to be known as Mom, I was Junior, and Jonathan was Uncle Jonny.[45]

This dynamic is altered when Clare and Bobby begin a sexual relationship. When Bobby reveals this to Jonathan, he says, 'Now we're, like, really a family. ... The three of us. Man, don't you see how great it is? I mean, it's like, now all three of us are in love.'[46] But Clare comments, 'I guess this is the end of the Hendersons as we know them', and Jonathan feels 'angry and envious. I wanted Bobby. In another sense, I wanted Clare.'[47] If there is a marked disappointment in the transitory nature of this alternative family – part of a larger disappointment at what is elsewhere in the novel expressed as 'the gap between what we can imagine and what we in fact create' – the yearning for 'family' (in whatever form) remains undiminished.[48]

By contrast, we find in Hollinghurst's fiction a studied ambivalence about various forms of sociality and community, and relatively little interest in this recapturing or reconceptualizing of family. Indeed, Les Brookes opposes *The Swimming-Pool Library* to *The Lost Language of Cranes* and *A Home at the End of the World*, suggesting that Leavitt and Cunningham present their gay protagonists 'in relation to family, friends, and the heterosexual world, and as part of the wider social scene', while Hollinghurst's Will is characterized as a 'sexual [rebel], at odds with the world generally and romantically drawn to life on the margins'.[49] Brookes finds in *The Swimming-Pool Library* what he describes as 'the queer notion of homosexuality as dangerous, fluid, and marginal/central to mainstream culture' – a notably unassimilationist tendency.[50] However, this seems too reductive a distinction, given Cunningham's characters' sense of themselves as marginal *within* those traditional family arrangements, and their constitution of alternative family groupings; the unhappy family dynamics in Leavitt (notably the secret gay life of Philip's father, Owen) and in Tóibín's *The Blackwater Lightship*, for example; and Will's entrenchment within the moneyed upper-class establishment, via public school, Oxbridge and the minor aristocracy – such that he is not straightforwardly 'marginal'.

Of all Hollinghurst's novels, *The Spell* focuses most directly on the contemporary world and the gay scene; it is also the novel that comments most directly on the question of family, presenting us with an alternative configuration of family made up of ex-lovers and showing the peculiar alliances possible between a gay father and son. Indeed, Robin finds himself thinking of Justin, Alex and Danny as 'the kids' (*S* 51). However, these relationships are also marked by duplicity (particularly as far as Justin is concerned, because he is serially unfaithful to both Alex and Robin), awkwardness, and uncertain desire. The 'gay father and son' idea that largely plays out as tragedy and/or melodrama in *The Lost Language of Cranes* is presented more positively, but it is nevertheless a relationship tinged with regret:

> Danny's visits still left Robin with an aftertaste of disappointment, of adulterated sweetness; sometimes they had been anxious charades of the life they might have led together ... . The weekends, the half-vacations, were planned as treats, but for Robin were always reminders of his failure as a husband. The failure remained, however much he reinvented it as a triumph of instinct. (*S* 60)

Robin and Danny's relationship is presented as an uncomfortable mimicry of a heterosexual familial relationship – an 'anxious charade' of what might have been – its superficial success always tinged by the 'failure' of Robin's prior life of passing as a 'heterosexual' married man and thus by the melancholy of a loss that cannot quite be overcome.

In addition, *The Spell*'s descriptions of various examples of domestic architecture as (at best) aesthetically compromised or (at worst) dilapidated to the point of imminent ruin, serve to express a suspicion of the family structures that take root in such spaces. Architecture thus becomes a synecdoche for both the complex relations between past and present, and the crumbling of traditional configurations of family. This is evident in the description of Tony Bowerchalke's 'rogue Gothic' house, which Robin is working on, but it is there also in Alex's reaction to 'the air of stunned homeliness' at Robin's cottage, which gives him 'the sense of being an intruder in an ordered but not invulnerable world' (*S* 15–16). He thinks that it 'might still be possible, after all, to get back to the car and leave without being seen' (*S* 16) Even for Robin, whose home it is, the cottage can have unwelcome associations. When he returns to the countryside alone (during a trial separation from Justin), 'the house in its private hollow looked like an elaborate emblem of failure' (*S* 180).

Similarly, in *The Line of Beauty*, Nick's relationship with the Fedden family is frequently expressed via his admiration of their Notting Hill home and its furnishings. Early on in the novel we are told how each time he lets himself in he feels 'the still security of the house', noticing the 'confidential creak of oak' on the upper staircase and the sumptuousness of the surroundings (*LB* 5); but this is a house and a family in which he never quite belongs and from which, ultimately, he will be expelled. Though he is repeatedly affected by the house, it, like the family, remains impervious to him, and his presence in it is necessarily fleeting. When Gerald Fedden turns on him at the end, asking 'didn't it strike you as rather odd, a bit queer, attaching yourself to a family like this?' he parses it as 'an old homo trick. You can't have a real family, so you attach yourself to someone else's. And I suppose after a while you just couldn't bear it, you must have been very envious I think of everything we have ...' (*LB* 481). As if to underline Nick's otherness, his status as an interloper in a more fundamental sense, Gerald rephrases this as 'who are you? What the fuck are you doing here?' (*LB* 482).

In recent gay fiction, Pearl notes, 'marriage ... appears to be supplanting other issues as *the* issue', and she avers that, 'if the new AIDS novels are focused on survival, they suggest that the reward for surviving AIDS is marriage'.[51] As a result, however, 'those messy networks of filiation and friendship that gay people have had unique access to, for many dire and complicated and joyful reasons' are increasingly being forsaken.[52] These developments, though, are coincident with the emergence of what has come to be known as the 'antisocial thesis' in queer theory – a thesis that pits itself against the assimilationist tendencies of gay marriage, but which might also, in its refusal of more positive bonds of community and sociality, be seen as endangering some of the remaining 'messy networks of filiation and friendship' of which Pearl speaks.

In *Homos*, Leo Bersani calls for what he describes as a 'redefinition of sociality';[53] in 'Is the Rectum a Grave?' he had already criticized what he called 'the redemptive sex project', namely the tendency to present sex as 'less disturbing, less socially abrasive, less violent, more respectful of "personhood" than it has been in male-dominated, phallocentric culture'.[54] Instead, he advocated seeing sex as 'anticommunal, antiegalitarian, antinurturing, anti-loving'.[55] As Caserio explains, in a debate on the 'antisocial thesis', for Bersani, 'if there is anything "politically indispensable" in homosexuality, it is its "politically unacceptable" opposition to community'.[56] Lee Edelman, meanwhile, asserts – in his influential *No Future* – that 'queerness names the side of those *not* "fighting for the children," the side outside the consensus by which politics confirms the absolute value of reproductive futurism',[57] and he urges an embracing of negativity and a refusal of 'the insistence of hope itself as affirmation'.[58] Such acts (of negativity/refusal) do not constitute the 'pessimism' of which Caserio speaks in relation to gay fiction, but rather, as Edelman suggests, 'afford an access to the *jouissance* that at once defines and negates us'.[59] Edelman's figure of 'the *sinthom*osexual', significantly, 'has the privilege of refusing the responsibilities that come with collective life, the privilege, that is, of sexual license, political disengagement, and thus, most important, the privilege of remaining indifferent to the vulnerabilities of others' – but is thus likely to be 'denounced for affirming a jouissance indulgently fixed on the self'.[60]

How should Hollinghurst's work be plotted in relation to these queer rejections of the social and of futurity? The oft-quoted final line of *The Swimming-Pool Library* ('And going into the showers I saw a suntanned young lad in pale blue trunks that I rather liked the look of' (*SPL* 288)) notably presents a problem for any reading of Will's progression, suggesting a determined resistance to any newly acknowledged responsibilities, and a desire to prolong the hedonistic individualism that has characterized his life to date. The critical readings of this ending – and of the novel as a whole – have differed quite significantly. For Brookes, the novel's 'central concern ... is Will's discovery that he is not free of social and moral responsibility, as he has supposed, but deeply implicated in gay history' and, although his 'instincts ... are antirelational', he 'learns that the life of absolute freedom he aspires to is an illusion. Relationality, he discovers, is part of the human condition and therefore inescapable.'[61] However, I would suggest that the vision of 'relationality' the novel offers is one that vacillates between an ethical acknowledgement of necessary interconnectedness and a *sinthom*osexual-style rejection of sociality and futurity; it is this latter tendency, perhaps, that induces Alderson to read Will as more 'rake' than 'radical', more 'libertine' than 'libertarian'.[62] Hollinghurst never quite presents us with a view of sex as 'self-shattering' in the Bersani vein,[63] but in *The Swimming-Pool Library* in particular, he at least illustrates Bersani's point that, 'while it is indisputably true that sexuality is always being politicized, the ways in which *having sex* politicizes are highly problematical'.[64]

While revealing few obvious debts to recent queer theory, Hollinghurst's fiction nevertheless manages to touch on highly topical questions of politics and sociality, the instability of sexual identities, and the lure of negative affect. Furthermore, the very preoccupation with the past in his work that leads critics to read him in relation to Victorian and modernist influences also facilitates comparisons with contemporaries such as Cunningham (*The Hours*), Tóibín (*The Master*), Jamie O'Neill (*At Swim, Two Boys*), and even Sarah Waters (*Fingersmith*, etc.), and makes his work in tune with queer theoretical narratives of temporal lag, 'backwardness' and (past) shame,[65] contributing to a view of 'queer' as what Judith Halberstam calls 'the prehistory of gay, a history that must not be left behind in the rush to gay pride but must be excavated in all its contradiction, disorder, and eros'.[66] Hollinghurst is more of his time than we might imagine.

Notes

1   Julie Rivkin, 'Writing the Gay '80s with Henry James: David Leavitt's *A Place I've Never Been* and Alan Hollinghurst's *The Line of Beauty*', *Henry James Review* 26.3 (2005) 282–92: 289.

2   Denis Flannery, 'The Powers of Apostrophe and the Boundaries of Mourning: Henry James, Alan Hollinghurst, and Toby Litt', *Henry James Review* 26.3 (2005) 293–305: 294.

3   Andrew Eastham, 'Inoperative Ironies: Jamesian Aestheticism and Post-Modern Culture in Alan Hollinghurst's *The Line of Beauty*', *Textual Practice* 20.3 (2006) 509–27: 509.

4   Georges Letissier, 'Queer, Quaint and Camp: Alan Hollinghurst's Own Return to the English Tradition', *Etudes anglaises* 6.2 (2007) 198–211: 208.

5   The exception is *The Stranger's Child*, which focuses on various moments across the course of the twentieth century; *The Folding Star*, meanwhile, splits its focus between the present and the 1890s, while *The Swimming-Pool Library* includes excerpts from Charles Nantwich's diaries from earlier in the twentieth century, but is mainly set in 1983.

6   Joseph Bristow, *Effeminate England: Homoerotic Writings after 1885* (New York: Columbia University Press, 1995) 171, 172.

7   Leo Bersani, *Homos* (Cambridge, MA: Harvard University Press, 1995) 76. See also Robert L. Caserio, Lee Edelman, Judith Halberstam, José Esteban Muñoz and Tim Dean, 'The Antisocial Thesis in Queer Theory', *PMLA* 121.3 (2006) 819–28.

8   Rivkin, 'Writing the Gay '80s with Henry James' 289.

9   Eastham, 'Inoperative Ironies' 509–10.

10   Lee Edelman, 'Ever After: History, Negativity, and the Social', *South Atlantic Quarterly* 106.3 (2007) 469–76: 471–2.

11 Eastham, 'Inoperative Ironies' 513.
12 Flannery, 'The Powers of Apostrophe and the Boundaries of Mourning' 302.
13 Daniel K. Hannah, 'The Private Life, the Public Stage: Henry James in Recent Fiction', *Journal of Modern Literature* 30.3 (2007) 70–94: 93.
14 David M. Halperin, *How to be Gay* (Cambridge, MA: Belknap Press, 2012) 10.
15 Robert L. Caserio, 'Queer Fiction: The Ambiguous Emergence of a Genre' in *A Concise Companion to Contemporary British Fiction*, ed. James F. English (Oxford: Blackwell, 2006) 209–28: 209.
16 Kenneth Plummer, *Telling Sexual Stories* (London: Routledge, 1995) 87.
17 Monica Pearl, *AIDS Literature and Gay Identity* (London: Routledge, 2013) 7.
18 Caserio, 'Queer Fiction' 209, 219.
19 Ibid. 216.
20 Pearl, *AIDS Literature and Gay Identity* 7.
21 David Leavitt, *The Lost Language of Cranes* (New York: Bloomsbury, 2005 [1986]) 164.
22 Colm Tóibín, *The Story of the Night* (London: Picador, 1997 [1996]) 11, 32.
23 Ibid. 14.
24 Michael Cunningham, *A Home at the End of the World* (London: Penguin, 1990) 11.
25 Kathryn Bond Stockton, *The Queer Child* (Durham, NC: Duke University Press, 2009), 6.
26 Alistair Stead, 'Self-Translation and the Arts of Transposition in Allan [*sic*] Hollinghurst's *The Folding Star*' in *Translating Life: Studies in Transpositional Aesthetics*, eds Shirley Chew and Alistair Stead (Liverpool: Liverpool University Press, 1999) 361–85: 361.
27 David Alderson, 'Desire as Nostalgia: The Novels of Alan Hollinghurst' in *Territories of Desire in Queer Culture*, eds David Alderson and Linda Anderson (Manchester: Manchester University Press, 2000) 29–48: 40–1.
28 Edmund White, *A Boy's Own Story* (London: Picador, 1982) 169, 204.
29 Lee Edelman, *No Future: Queer Theory and the Death Drive* (Durham, NC: Duke University Press, 2004) 17.
30 Alderson, 'Desire as Nostalgia' 45.
31 Cunningham, *A Home at the End of the World* 174–5.
32 Ibid. 184.
33 Ibid. 342–3.
34 Pearl, *AIDS Literature and Gay Identity* 114.
35 Ibid. 116.
36 Alderson, 'Desire as Nostalgia' 45.
37 Pearl, *AIDS Literature and Gay Identity* 11.
38 Caserio, 'Queer Fiction' 211.
39 Pearl, *AIDS Literature and Gay Identity* 13, 20.
40 Ibid. 16.
41 Caserio, 'Queer Fiction' 214.
42 Ibid. 9.

43   Pearl, *AIDS Literature and Gay Identity* 143.

44   David Leavitt, 'Introduction' in *The Penguin Book of Gay Short Stories*, eds David Leavitt and Mark Mitchell (London: Penguin, 1994) xv–xxviii: xxii.

45   Cunningham, *A Home at the End of the World* 155–6.

46   Ibid. 177.

47   Ibid. 179.

48   Ibid. 336.

49   Les Brookes, *Gay Male Fiction since Stonewall: Ideology, Conflict, and Aesthetics* (New York: Routledge, 2009) 6.

50   Ibid. 26.

51   Ibid. 127.

52   Ibid. 142.

53   Bersani, *Homos* 7.

54   Leo Bersani, 'Is the Rectum a Grave?', *October* 43 (1987) 197–222: 215.

55   Ibid.

56   Caserio et al., 'The Antisocial Thesis in Queer Theory' 819.

57   Edelman, *No Future* 3.

58   Ibid. 4, 5.

59   Ibid. 5.

60   Edelman, 'Ever After' 475.

61   Brookes, *Gay Male Fiction since Stonewall* 138, 140.

62   Alderson, 'Desire as Nostalgia' 43.

63   Bersani, 'Is the Rectum a Grave?' 222.

64   Ibid. 206.

65   See, for example: Elizabeth Freeman, *Time Binds* (Durham, NC: Duke University Press, 2010); Heather Love, *Feeling Backward* (Cambridge, MA: Harvard University Press, 2007); *Gay Shame*, ed. David M. Halperin and Valerie Traub (Chicago: University of Chicago Press, 2009).

66   Judith Halberstam, 'Shame and White Gay Masculinity', *Social Text* 23.3–4 (2005) 219–33: 221.

12

What can I say?: secrets in fiction and biography

Hermione Lee interviews Alan Hollinghurst

This conversation between Hermione Lee and Alan Hollinghurst took place on 8 February 2012 at the Oxford Centre for Life-Writing at Wolfson College, Oxford. It was part of the Weinrebe Lectures, an annual lecture series at the Life-Writing Centre. Since the year's theme was the connections between fiction and auto/biography, a conversation between a novelist and a biographer seemed an appropriate format.

Hermione Lee: Alan Hollinghurst is one of our most daring, elegant, intelligent, and profound fiction writers. Your numbers here tonight attest to the following of readers there is for the Booker Prize-winning author of *The Swimming-Pool Library*, *The Spell*, *The Folding Star*, *The Line of Beauty*, and *The Stranger's Child*. He is an author who crosses the perilous bridge between high literary culture and popular storytelling with the greatest of ease and aplomb, who can be funny, ironical, touching, shocking, disturbing, and dark all on one page, who has never written a poor sentence or had a dull idea.

Could you start, Alan, by talking a bit about how you came to *The Stranger's Child*, why you decided to do this, what was it about this idea that grabbed you?

Alan Hollinghurst: The biographical element is only a part of it, I suppose. There are always many things that contribute to a book – but it's true that one of the things in this case was being foiled of the chance to write a biography myself. I'd always supposed that one day I would write a biography of the novelist Ronald Firbank, whom I'm very interested in. I had no particular claim or right to do this but I somehow assumed I would and I accumulated materials in a rather haphazard way. Then Richard Canning, whom I actually knew quite well, wrote to me and said, 'I'm intending to write a biography of Ronald Firbank.'

HL: [Laughs] And you thought, 'But he's mine!'

AH: And I felt he was mine, yes. I recognized this strongly possessive feeling about him and I said, 'Well, good luck. I'm sure you'll understand that, you know, I will have to keep my own discoveries to myself.' I behaved rather badly.

HL: You mean you said, 'I've got all kinds of things you might want to know but ...'

AH: Exactly. Then after a week or two I suddenly felt that it was an enormous relief and that I probably wasn't cut out to write biography. I don't have the patience for it. I'm not a scholar, and actually it was just a sign that what I ought to be doing was writing novels. But nonetheless the whole question of what's entailed in writing biography was in my mind. I knew that I wanted to write a novel which was about the First World War but that I very much didn't want to write a novel which actually described the First World War, which is just not the kind of thing I could do well. I think I tend normally to write about the social and intimate lives of, perhaps, slightly peculiar people. But the idea of something which would necessarily be deeply researched about life in the trenches and so on, I thought would probably end up being an inadequate simulacrum of all sorts of other things that have been written about that subject. So I wanted to avoid that. But I thought something about the impact of the war on a group of characters we'd met before the war started would be interesting, and this meshed with the biographical idea I suppose. And I also had the idea that one person who was killed in the war would be a poet – maybe twenty-five when he dies – and I was interested in writing about what happens to the memory, the name, of a poet who dies so young in heroic circumstances with everything still before them.

HL: It links in a way to some things that you have done in very different novels. So that in *The Folding Star*, there's a character who is a language teacher in Belgium who becomes very fascinated with the biographical secrets of the life of a symbolist painter and finds there's somebody – a curator – who's guarding the secrets who doesn't believe you should expose the secrets. In *The Swimming-Pool Library* Will Beckwith is writing, or trying to write, a biography, or never succeeds in writing a biography.

AH: Or trying not to write a biography.

HL: Or trying not to write a biography of someone, it turns out, whose life secrets actually do have a bearing on his own life. So this is clearly something that keeps on fascinating you in different ways.

AH: Yes, it is. Perhaps it's analogous to the process of writing a novel itself which is, in its way, unravelling the enigma of people. I'm very fascinated by the idea of the understanding that one comes to of earlier generations. And it's certainly something that I try to dramatize in *The Stranger's Child*, which covers nearly a century. We're inward with the lives of some people in 1913, then in 1926. Daphne (who is, I suppose, really the main character of the book) we then rejoin but from a completely different viewpoint much later in her life. The story, suddenly, is about the somebody quite different who happens to meet this seventy-year-old woman knowing nothing about her at all and then tries to piece together what's happened to her and what her connection is to this poet who has died. I think, perhaps because I've often had friends who are quite a lot older than myself, I'm fascinated by that, but it's only a more exaggerated form of the ignorance we have about people of our own age. It's amazing how little we know even about our close friends, I think. If we were to sit an exam on them, we wouldn't do very well: there's so much we don't know.

HL: Or have to write their obituary.

AH: Yes. Exactly.

HL: And there's an interesting parallel whereby each section of *The Stranger's Child* begins with the reader in that position too, of not having things explained and having to piece together who it is you're meeting, why are we here now, who these people are.

AH: Exactly. Yes.

HL: In *The Stranger's Child*, we have an awkward and edgy encounter between Daphne, the person who really was there, and Sebby, the extraordinarily diplomatic and polite interrogator who is clearly going to write a hopelessly compromised book under the thumb of the grieving mother, Louisa, who's been trying to call him up from the past. That's the first stage of his immortality – alongside a sentimental marble tomb of Cecil Valance in the family home which is a little like the tomb of Shelley in Univ.[1] You find that things are being made away with or burned. Then, gradually, as we come into the twenty-first century there is a biographer (who we'll come back to) who pieces this all together and unravels what's happened. So, were you thinking about the way in which biographical history has changed and developed? Were you using this story of Cecil Valance and his afterlife as a prototype or a metaphor for the way lives have been treated and written?

AH: I think I was, yes. There has, for instance, been a huge change in our notions of privacy, of what we can say about the private life. Someone who read a biography in the period when this book begins, in 1913, would not have expected to learn anything about the intimate life of the subject. Someone reading a biography at the time when it finishes, in 2008, would feel positively cheated if they weren't given every detail. I think that's an enormous change. I was just reading an essay by Mark Girouard about various fictions in Tennyson's biography and he has a wonderful phrase, saying around about the turn of the century behind what he calls the 'brassier' sounds of the era you can hear this constant sound of scratching and snipping and detect a faint smell of smoke on the air, which is all the widows and children of great Victorian figures doctoring, obliterating, burning the personal letters and documents of these figures.[2] Was it Princess Beatrice herself who edited Queen Victoria's – her mother's – diaries, copying out all the bits that she thought suitable and then burning the rest? The destruction of evidence, making things absolutely irrecoverable, was common practice.

HL: I think there are still people snipping away at their dearly departed's letters. But clearly the idea of censorship was much more ingrained in biography then?

AH: Ingrained, yes. And I was very interested obviously in the case of Rupert Brooke, though Cecil Valance's story is not exactly modelled on it. In that case, Eddie Marsh was commissioned by Rupert Brooke's mother to produce a memoir which she created an enormous amount of trouble about – in which almost the whole of Brooke's private life was erased and smoothed until he'd produced a portrait which was completely unrecognizable to anybody who'd actually known him. I mean Virginia Woolf wrote ...

HL: Outraged, about its sentimentality.

AH: Well, yes.

HL: You must always be asked this about this novel, but was the figure of Rupert Brooke the key – as a sentimentalized, mythologized First World War hero (though of course he wasn't killed in battle)? Or because of the way that his poetry becomes taken over and used in different ways by different generations of readers? So was Brooke the inspiration for you?

AH: I think it perhaps was, yes. I very much grew up with Brooke's poems myself and my mother loved them – still does love them – so from childhood I had couplets from 'Grantchester' and so on in my mind, and the long poem which Cecil writes in Daphne's autograph book is clearly a 'Grantchester'-type poem which is sentimental light verse really but after the war becomes a nostalgic vision of the world that they were fighting for and that, in a way, has been lost. Also the close custodianship – not only of the mother – but the close custodianship of Geoffrey Keynes who then edited Brooke's letters, that I think came out as late as 1968. But still, you know, very *trimmed*. And other details which complicated the picture of Rupert Brooke's sexual life really only appearing in the 1980s and '90s. So it's a very slow process of emergence of the intimate connections.

HL: And is he a useful figure to you for this because the biographical versions of Brooke – the way in which he has been written about – are inextricably bound up with a romanticized, sentimentalized version of him? In Cecil Valance – who obviously, is *not* Rupert Brooke – there's something of him in there. The *actual* Cecil Valance is rather unpleasant in lots of ways. He's not a very good poet and he's a bit of a bastard in lots of ways.

AH: Yes, I think that's right.

HL: And so that gets uncovered, doesn't it, as the book goes on – or it gets concealed and then uncovered.

AH: Yes. Well, he arrives to stay for the weekend with this more humble family – the Sawles – and they're all excited but rather anxious about him. They don't quite know what they are thinking about him because he's dazzling them, and they want to find him wonderful because he's the first friend that George has ever brought home. But the mother thinks, 'Well, perhaps he might make a nice husband for Daphne one day.' Though she doesn't really like him, or trust him, particularly. So I think there, one sees – I hope the reader sees – from early on, that Cecil's rather a mixed bag. But of course I was interested particularly here in something which is much more important than in Brooke's story, the fact that he's bisexual. And also of the ethics of the Cambridge world in which he and George live. They are both members of the Apostles, the secret Conversazione Society. Candour is a principle with them as it was with Cambridge figures like Lytton Strachey, who made a great point of talking with complete clarity about the private life, in a way which would never happen in suburban Stanmore where the Sawle family are living. So you've got different moral perspectives in play at the same time.

HL: Twentieth-century biography changed, in 1918, when Strachey published *Eminent Victorians* at the end of the war. It takes four statuesque, and somewhat mythologized figures: Florence Nightingale, Cardinal Manning, General Gordon, and Thomas Arnold, the headmaster of Rugby. And it explores them very piquantly and satirically, not for their public achievements but as neurotic case histories of repression and inner disturbance. That was a very shocking and enfranchising moment in the history of British biography. But it's as if, by using Strachey in the book – and you mention him and he's clearly a key figure – it's as if you're drawing a parallel between what happens to the history of biography and life-writing in Britain in the twentieth century and what happens to homosexual freedom or the increasing enfranchisement of gay people.

AH: Yes.

HL: So there's a strong parallel, isn't there, between these two subjects?

AH: There is a parallel, yes. The middle section of the book is set in the summer of 1967 and ends in the week before the passing of the Sexual Offences Bill, which decriminalized homosexuality in England. And that's obviously a very pivotal moment. And though nothing but the law perhaps changed overnight it initiated a period in which all sorts of things could be said that couldn't previously. It's remarkable that Michael Holroyd's great biography of Lytton Strachey was published just a few months after that. It seems uncannily to have been attuned to the coming changes in our society. And he writes wonderfully in his later introduction to the revised edition about that moment, about approaching these old Bloomsbury figures, who'd had candour as a watchword, and wondering if they were prepared to stand by it. Were they prepared to go public?

HL: One of them says to him, 'Am I going to go to prison if you publish this book?'

AH: Exactly. But most of them rose to the challenge. And I think I'm right in saying that this was the first biography to write in detail, unembarrassedly, with massive illustration from letters and so forth, about the private life of a gay writer.

HL: I think that's right. And he says in his retrospect on the writing of the book that he decided that the basic principle would be to write about homosexuality absolutely as a norm – to have no, as he called it, 'veils of decorum', a rather genteel phrase. That was the principle of the book. I don't think it could have happened before then.

AH: And it is a Strachey-esque principle, isn't it?

HL: Yes.

AH: And I think James Strachey, Lytton's younger brother, felt that Lytton wanted to prepare some much more organized defence of homosexuality at the time of his early death. Anyway, the events of 1967 brought my novel into the era in which I myself was growing up. When I was at Oxford I did my own graduate work in the mid-'70s about gay writers like Forster and so on who couldn't write openly about their homosexuality, and I remember very keenly the atmosphere of that period. There was the sense that things could at last be said, the sense of a new light in which things could be seen, and it led to a period of claiming figures for the gay cause, and perhaps at times a degree of wishful thinking.

HL: But it also presumably led to your own sense of yourself as having a duty to, or responsibility (as a novelist, as an imaginative writer) to write as openly and as candidly as you possibly could? So that if you take a history of gay fiction from Henry James and Proust, through Firbank and Forster and then to you and Edmund White, you are very much part of – you are a key player, actually – in a transformation that's taken about a century of writing.

AH: Yes, it seemed both a duty and an opportunity. It was a sort of catching up, too, of course, since comparable candour already existed in heterosexual writing – Updike and others had been writing with great candour about straight sex-lives. So, yes I wanted to avail myself of those new freedoms, too. And I think that first book, *The Swimming-Pool Library*, very much grew out of my thesis on gay writers, and what could and couldn't be said in different periods. I felt I was extraordinarily fortunate to have this fascinating subject to explore, which no one really had in England in literary fiction.

HL: We're talking in rather utopian and progressive terms. It's not clear from *The Stranger's Child* that the movement from censorship (decorums, hidden things, burned letters, secrets) through to a full narrative of someone's life which fills in all the gaps (and says, 'Ah! x *wasn't* the child of y. They were actually the illegitimate child' and so on) is necessarily a good thing. It doesn't necessarily show that biography has been constantly improving over the decades, does it?

AH: No, of course it doesn't, no.

HL: There's quite a lot of anxiety and gloom about the biographical project in this book. Not least in the figure of the central biographer, who's a rodent-like character – he pees in the back of other people's gardens to mark out his territory and he's seen peering into other people's windows and infiltrating himself into other people's houses. It's a very dubious picture of the biographer at work.

AH: [Laughing] It is. Obviously, there are great biographies and there are terrible ones – we've just been talking about some. Of course, we don't know in the end just how good Paul Bryant's biography is. He too avails himself of these new freedoms, perhaps rather overdoes it, one suspects.

My feeling is that biography, like writing a novel, is something which depends not only on proper scholarship and research but on the wisdom of the writer. You can have terrible novels and good ones, and the same is true of biographies. I think, as someone who has often been interested in rather minor figures, I'm aware of a particular sort of curse on them. The minor figure who is discovered by someone perhaps slightly cranky, who produces an inadequate book. I think for example of Ronald Firbank, who's a sort of major minor figure.

HL: Denton Welch springs to mind.

AH: Well, Denton Welch was an example very much in my mind, yes. I remember reviewing Michael De-la-Noy's biography which was published simultaneously with his edition of Denton Welch's journals – both very badly done.[3] And he was quoting constantly from the journals in the biography and I kept cross-checking. I think in at least eighty per cent of cases he had simply rewritten the quotations from the journal to fit the context in the Life. And it was, to me, very shocking ... I was rather naive perhaps. I remember commenting on this to a well-known Oxford biographer who said, 'Oh of course, I do that all the time!' I don't think I should say who that was.

But that was a bit of an eye-opener to me. And I was struck for the first time by the simple fact that a biography isn't only undertaken out of a desire to do justice to its subject but it's a significant stepping-stone in the career of its author.

HL: Yes. And you have that very brilliantly in this book. As it turns out, Cecil Valance's biography turns out to have been a first step in Paul Bryant's career and that's how we see him at the end. Having become a professional biographer who moves on from one to the next.

AH: Yes.

HL: You're very sharp in this book about the possibly scurrilous and base motives of the biographical project. And also about how difficult the whole thing is. It's a peculiar kind of game in which the biographer is trying to get people to tell him things which he may already think he knows, but he can't quite ask them. And then there's this thing which you describe brilliantly as 'a recurrent little knot of self-defeating resistance that perhaps all biographers of recent subjects had to confront and undo'. People wouldn't tell you things – and then they blamed you for not knowing them.

AH: Did that ring true to you?

HL: It rings very true. I think it's very funny and wry about the way in which there is only so far that the biographer can go – because of course people's memories (what they tell you) are often wonky or distorted.

AH: Yes. Well that is perhaps the central theme of the book, I suppose, to which the biographical one is, in a way, subservient. If memory (which of course is also the novelist's principal tool) is one of the main things that the writing of biography is dependent on, it's obviously an extremely fallible quantity. As I get older, I find I'm struck by this more and more. I think it's very hard to remember exactly more than a few words that someone said to me last week. So it's very hard to remember *anything* anybody said forty years ago. When someone writes a memoir with pages of verbatim conversation about something they did before the war you just know that they've made it all up. If you keep a journal, it's more likely to be accurate but a journal, too, is an exercise in selection, rearrangement, manipulation, often making the subject – the author of the diary – feel better about something. So the very materials that biography works with are liable to be partly inaccurate.

HL: So is it always a charade? In the last big scene with the biographer, Daphne says to herself, 'thing is, they all get it wrong. And they put it in as if it were gospel.' Does this book mean that one should never trust a biography again once one has read this novel?

AH: No, I really don't think so. I refer back to what I was saying just now. I think there are evidently untrustworthy biographers and I feel my book is more about how vague our grasp on things happening around us in the present is, much less in the past. What I was saying earlier on, how little we are sure of about the lives of others, indeed, after a while, about our own, because so much is effaced from them by the passage of time.

HL: You talk about your own life. I wanted to ask you one question which is perhaps more general about your work as a whole. To what extent are you putting yourself in the books? That sounds rather crude, but I'm interested in the way that style is important not just as a tool for you, but as a subject, actually, in a lot of your work.

In *The Line of Beauty*, Nick is writing a thesis on the late work of Henry James. He talks about his style, style that hides things and reveals things at the same time. *The Line of Beauty* is very much about style and spoils and possessions and objects. In several of the books there's a dominant style. There's the style of the Maeterlinck Symbolist artist, the vertigo of strangeness that you get from that in *The Folding Star*, and then there's a Firbankian high camp, in *The Swimming-Pool Library*. I'm not sure about *The Spell* – maybe there's a sort of *Vanity Fair* Thackeray-ish kind of comedy of manners there. In *The Stranger's Child* there's a very strong tone and legacy and feeling for Tennyson (who is in the title) and the Georgian poets, a kind of sweetness and melancholy and nostalgia that comes through in your own artefacts of these poems that Cecil wrote.

Do you think you use a kind of canopy of style to prevent self-disclosure? Or as a way, perhaps, of putting yourself into the novels? Putting your own obsessions and preoccupations into the novel without talking about yourself directly?

AH: Yes. I think I never do talk about myself directly. I certainly (in a narrative way, I mean) never write about my life, just changing the names and so on. But I think the books must be absolutely saturated with *me*. And I have a habit of giving my protagonists my own interests: writing a thesis on Henry James or being crazy about Wagner. The novel is a field of play for one's own enthusiasms.

HL: You can do what you like.

AH: You can do what you like. And it's nice to fill it up with things that you're interested in.

HL: But do you consciously say to yourself, 'I'm not going to give myself away. I'm going to put myself in but not give myself away'?

AH: I don't think of it as being an act of concealment like that because I'm invested in trying to imagine the lives of characters who often share something with me but are necessarily distinct from me. Paul Bryant, this 'rodent-like' biographer, was a difficult character to create in a way because he was someone from whom I was withholding a lot of these things that I enjoy. There's a scene where he goes to a piano recital. In *The Line of Beauty* I'd had a piano recital where young Nick – the main character – is the only person who's really enjoying it or getting anything out of it and he's surrounded by all these Tories who are bored and dying for a drink while he's very attuned to the music. So I decided I would do the reverse with this book: Paul Bryant is tone deaf. He's sitting in a room where everybody else is absolutely loving it and he hasn't got a clue what's going on. So that was a conscious withholding. I think the question of style is such a difficult one for any writer to answer about themselves and I think questions of analyses of style, or whatever, are things which are possible for a reader but not for the writer. To be too self-conscious about writing in a style would be terribly inhibiting.

HL: I suppose I meant more that you are a deeply literary writer. Your literary interests, your musical interests, your artistic interests and passions fill the books. They give the books a kind of tune.

AH: Mm, yes. Well I hope they have a tone, or something which is coherent. Again, I find it very difficult to say. And I'm aware, of course, of often crossing a corner of the territory of some great writer in the past and tipping my hat to them but getting on with my own business. The first part of this book very obviously takes place in Forster territory: before the Great War, London, the outermost suburbs of London, the Cambridge background and so on. I had to be a bit wary of that, in a way. When I started writing it I was writing pastiche Forster and I did want it to be by me and not by E. M. Forster.

HL: But it's a kind of tribute, *en passant.*

AH: It's a sort of tribute, yes. But the important thing was to preserve myself against pastiche and from just moving into somebody else's style.

HL: In *The Stranger's Child*, you have a quote from Forster's *The Longest Journey* and there's something of *Howards End* in the beginning. Forster's subject – particularly, I think, in those two books – is England and Englishness. Who's going to inherit England? Who are the real English? And where does England lie in people's minds? *The Stranger's Child* is a very English novel, it's about a history of England, too. It doesn't really go outside. Do you think of yourself as a very English novelist writing in an English tradition?

AH: I recognize that I am, but I'm not tingling with that feeling every time I sit down at my desk.

HL: So 'English'.

AH: I do feel profoundly attached to my native land, I have to say. One can sound a bit poncey talking about how books come into being ... there is an element of active construction in my novels, obviously, but in some strange way, before all that, they accumulate in my mind in various different strands. They come to me, they suggest themselves to me and I end up writing something which isn't by any means a wholly conscious strategic decision. It's just something which has come about. And that thing that comes about does tend to be very steeped in Englishness. But I'm not doing it out of a programme to analyse Englishness and so on.

HL: I'm sure that people in the audience would like to ask you a few questions.

Audience Member 1: My question is about Paul Bryant. I was a bit shocked when I read about his bit of trickery in Blackwell's. And then, at the end, we discover that perhaps he lost his job because of something slightly dishonest. Quite a bit of what he does in the book is written in the first person, so I wondered whether you introduced those two things to make us doubt him in some way?

AH: He's a bit of a kleptomaniac. I suppose there's a rather crude symbolic idea of him stealing these people's lives for his own gain, as it were. When you first see him, he's given this humiliating task by Corinna, Daphne's daughter, of having to empty out a trough full of manure and she immediately sets him to work – that, too, seemed to be a rather silly image of someone digging around in the dirt for this family but then getting his own back later on. Yes, I mean those were ways, certainly, I think of suggesting that he had issues.

AM1: Were you trying to position him as a bit of an unreliable narrator?

AH: Well, he's not really a narrator.

AM1: He is in places, isn't he?

AH: There are one or two tiny extracts from his own diary, which is another document waiting for somebody else to write the biography of Paul Bryant from, I daresay. Really, it was more a technical question. The fourth part of the book, when he's carrying out his investigations, interviewing the survivors of Cecil Valance, the structure of that section is really a series of interviews. I wanted to vary them formally and make each one different. So in one of them I simply used the device of the tape recorder not having worked so that he has to write down everything he can remember as soon as possible.

HL: I must say that one of the many moments in the book where I did laugh out loud (and laugh as a biographer) was while reading the scene in which you have him read the transcription of the tape and none of the questions have come out. But all the answers are there, transcribed like, 'Yes, he was, very ...'

AM2: You'll have to excuse me if my question is a bit convoluted because I'm writing on you at the moment.

AH: Oh no!

HL: It's a test.

AH: You're not writing my biography, are you?

AM2: [Laughs] No, no. So across the novels and certainly from the middle of *The Stranger's Child* there are themes of textuality, of creating histories, of outing previous gay men, and gay writers in particular. But in all the books there is also, I think, the eroticism of private spaces, private gardens, private swimming pools. How much do you think those things are in conflict with each other? Do you think they are? Is there an emphasis on privacy in tension with a wish to out, or to create, histories?

AH: Well, of course in the earlier parts of the book if two men want to get up to something they're going to have to do it in some more or less private way. They're doing something illicit, shocking probably, to their nearest and dearest. I know it is rather a theme in my books that gay men haven't got somewhere to go so that they're often making love in gardens and parks and woods and what have you, because they're not a sort of normal domestic unit. They don't have a space of their own. By the end of the book we're in a world where everything has changed so much. I mean one can't overestimate the enormous changes of the last quarter of a century: legal changes, changes in attitude, a great generational shift in the understanding of gay men and gay lives.

HL: In the first scene of *The Stranger's Child*, there's a parallel universe between the gay young men hiding out in the garden and the marital domestic family life that's going on inside the house. And then by the end everybody's in the same public space and there are people with civil partnerships and there are married men and there are married women so there's an open space at the end.

AM3: You've painted a picture of unreliable biographers and unreliable memories. What happens then when you move on and start thinking about autobiography? Does it actually become just as difficult as biography itself?

AH: I think much autobiography demonstrates not only a tendency to enhance and interpret the subject's life but the fallibility of memory itself. It's an inevitably fictional form.

HL: It's very interesting that when asked about autobiography you almost immediately start talking about writing about other people's lives.

AH: Deflecting as usual, yes. We perhaps shouldn't digress into the Jameses, but I've just read this fascinating book by Michael Anesko called *Monopolizing the Master*, which is about the James family's attempts to control its own biographical materials and the famous case, obviously, of Henry James supposedly editing his brother William's letters but heavily cutting them and rewriting them and enhancing the wording and so forth and then presenting these as historical documents. To be honest, I'm much more interested in all these things that go wrong.

HL: Yes, and of course I'm gripped by all that because of Henry James making this enormous bonfire in his garden towards the end of his life which included very many of the letters that Edith Wharton had written to him. As Edith Wharton's biographer, this is, as you can imagine, a very tantalizing thing to read about. Especially when his letters to her remain and some of them begin, as it were: 'Your letter with its dreadful news, so riveting and exciting I cannot wait to hear about this event.' And the letter's gone.

AH: All subjects should say quite clearly shouldn't they, 'Your news *about* so and so'? They should summarize.

HL: Or they shouldn't say in a letter, 'This is far too exciting to talk about in a letter, we must wait until we meet.'

AM4: I was just wondering about your 'real people'. For example, the biographer of Wilfred Owen, Jon Stallworthy, happens to be here on my left.[4] You have him come in as a walk-on role in the middle of *The Stranger's Child*. I was just wondering if you'd talk about how difficult it is to differentiate between fantasy and reality in your fictional characters and your real characters.

AH: I suppose the most prominent *real* character I've used was Mrs Thatcher in *The Line of Beauty*. She sort of had to appear and she makes a cameo appearance. I've actually never set eyes on Mrs Thatcher, but I feel as if I had because she was in our sitting rooms every day for many years.

HL: And you have a fine phrase when she comes into the room. You say, she walks 'with a gracious scuttle'.

AH: My general feeling is, for extended treatment, it's impossible. In *The Stranger's Child*, Jon Stallworthy is seen across a room at a slightly implausible conference about writing about war, which is happening in the early '80s. Paul Fussell, I pretend, is there as well, mixed up with other fictional writers. I think, to me, real people and fictional people do exist in quite different continua and I think I would find it very hard to put an extended treatment of a real person into a book.

HL: But you do like to do it, don't you, to introduce real people? They're offstage scenes but you quite enjoy it.

AH: There's something slightly electrifying about the possibility of that contact with some sort of significant, real person. And I love the idea that George and Daphne's mother had actually seen Tennyson when they were on the ferry going to their honeymoon on the Isle of Wight and that this was a wonderful, a real contact with this archetypal Victorian figure.

HL: By doing that you make the fiction more real? Isn't that a tactic?

AH: Well, I don't know. Possibly, yes. I mean, it could go wrong if you just kept on making it more authentic by putting in more and more people.

HL: It could go wrong, yes.

AM5: Quite by coincidence, I read your interview with Peter Terzian.[5] There was something that struck me there. You say at one point to him, 'I'm awed by the symphonic relevance of everything I am saying today.'

AH: [Chuckle]

AM5: Four or five pages later you say again, 'My books were going to form a sort of symphony'. Now, I think Hermione was in on that to some extent when talking about whether there was something underlying all your work. My question really is, do you have a certain desire or impulse to underline your work with some kind of unity? And does this connect in any sense with your being a poet?

AH: Again, it's a rather Jamesian idea, isn't it? Whether there is the figure in the carpet, whether there is the master idea to the whole *oeuvre*. Both those things were said with an awareness of their pretentiousness.

But I think it is a question which actually is something which one reads very little about: the sense that any writer has of what the accumulating shape of their own *oeuvre* is. I suppose there's Toby Litt whose books each begin with the next letter of the alphabet, so he sort of knows how far he's got.

HL: He'll have to stop, some time.

AH: He will, yes. Yes I don't know what happens when he gets there. *Zoo Story* or something. In my case, because I often tend to think by musical analogy, it was more a private thing to help me. I thought of my first four books as having formed a kind of symphony. I do think it sounds a pretentious thing to say but the first book was a sonata movement with two narrative voices, the second one was a long introspective slow movement, *The Spell* was a kind of scherzo, and *The Line of Beauty* went back to 1983, when the first book was set and developed it further.

HL: So you do. So the answer to the question is sort of 'yes'? I'm always leery, if I'm talking to a writer, about saying 'this connects to another book' or 'this is a little bit like something in an earlier book'.

AH: Yes.

HL: Because often writers bridle when you say that and they'll say: 'Are you trying to tell me all my books are the same? This is a completely different book and anyway I don't remember that book. I can't remember the names of any of the characters.' And that quite often happens. So it's very interesting to hear that you do actually think in terms of connections. It's not just your future biographers – of course, there are going to be many – who are going to try and create a whole shape out of what you do.

AH: I think they are perhaps slightly different things. I genuinely can't remember a lot about the books and I haven't read *The Swimming-Pool Library* for twenty years and sometimes people do ask me questions about it and I genuinely can't think what the hell they're talking about. But that is perhaps slightly different from this other sense I have of the general shape of the thing, and the question, starting this fifth book, of what (if the symphony was over) was I doing next?

HL: Do you know what's coming next?

AH: I can't say yet, no.

Notes

1 Edward Onslow Ford's sculpture in the Shelley Memorial at University College, Oxford.

2 Mark Girouard, 'The Myth of the Tennyson Disinheritance' in *Enthusiasms* (London: Frances Lincoln, 2011) 19–30: 19.

3 Alan Hollinghurst, 'Diminished Pictures', *Times Literary Supplement* 21 December 1984, 1479–80.

4 Jon Stallworthy's *Wilfred Owen* was published to great acclaim in 1974; a revised edition appeared in 2013. Stallworthy passed away on 19 November 2014.

5 Alan Hollinghurst, 'The Art of Fiction No. 214', *Paris Review* 199 (2011), www.theparisreview.org/interviews/6116/the-art-of-fiction-no-214-alan-hollinghurst (accessed 19 January 2016).

Index

Lightning Source UK Ltd.
Milton Keynes UK
UKHW022218090223
416780UK00010B/117